EXODUS TO INGATHERING
FIELD MANUAL

EXODUS TO INGATHERING
FIELD MANUAL

01 : 03.20 - 03.21

Only do not rebel against the LORD. And do not fear the people of the land,
for they are bread for us. Their protection is removed from them,
and the LORD is with us; do not fear them.
Numbers 14:9

ALLAN R. AGUIRRE

E2iS / CHAMELEON CHURCH RESOURCE SERIES
PLANET BLUE MEDIA
PARK CITY

Exodus to Ingathering Field Manual

Published by Planet Blue Media
2100 Park Ave., #684147, Park City, UT 84068
planetBlueMedia.com

For speaking engagements / business inquiries: info@chameleonChurch.com

Paperback: ISBN 978-0-9991300-5-6
The Amazing Journey from Exodus to Ingathering: ISBN 978-0-9991300-4-9

Cover Design: PBMInteractive

E2iS
E2i Series: E2iSeries.com
facebook l instagram l youtube: E2iSeries

Chameleon Church Resource Series
web l facebook l twitter l instagram l youtube: chameleonChurch

EXODUS TO INGATHERING
FIELD MANUAL

The thought of possibly having to write and publish a devotional of sorts first popped up in June. I was thinking maybe more of a "field manual," since a devotional conjured images of middle-agers of the opposite sex and Joyce Meyer inspirational desk calendars. I know... My only excuse is that I used to be a punk rocker, and I've been buying into the outdoor mountain life the last seven years – hence the "field manual."

The idea of creating and releasing a devotional persisted, so I downloaded *How to Write a Devotional* earlier this month, since I've never used or owned a devotional myself. I understand the value devotionals hold in a person's faith journey, so I've considered a companion piece for my book, *The Feasts Unlocked*, as it's been suggested multiple times and sounds like a good idea.

Being eager to begin work on my next book, *Incorruptible* (fka *Identity Crisis*), kept me from seriously looking "back" and considering the *Feast* devotional, so I started toying with the idea of maybe developing a devotional as a companion piece to go along with *Incorruptible*, but I wasn't completely sold on that idea, either. Now, a devotional companion for the book about men / husbands being the priests in their homes? That'll definitely be happening.

As my writing schedule approached and the setting up of a dedicated video / recording studio began, during one of our "to-dos & milestones" chats, the Mrs. strongly suggested a devotional in support of *Feasts* be produced ASAP. It was obviously the Father, because this time I could see it, and seeing it made it make sense.

Something my wife and I learned long ago is that unless there is agreement, prophetic words / utterances and basic Kingdom strategies cannot come to pass or they simply get lost in the "cyberspace" of the supernatural. When she brought up the devotional, my spirit not only bore witness, there was agreement and immediate vision for the task. Because of that, this is going to be more than just a doilies-and-warm-fuzzies-inspired devotional. Heh...

Allan R. Aguirre
October 2019
Park City, UT

THE PREMISE: EXAMPLES & INSTRUCTIONS

In regard to Israel's journey, their exodus from Egypt to their ingathering in the Promised Land, the Apostle Paul writes the following in 1 Corinthians 10:1-12:

> *Now these things happened to them **as an example**, but they were **written down for our instruction (warning)**, on whom the end of the ages has come.*
> *1 Corinthians 10:11 [Emphasis mine]*

The term "on whom the end of the ages has come" is also translated as:

- For us to whom the end of time has come
- Upon whom the ends of the world are come
- To us who are living in the "the last days"

Essentially, Paul is stating that what happened to the Children of Israel in the desert – as recorded in the books of Exodus, Leviticus, Numbers and Deuteronomy – were written down as a warning and for our instruction; "our" being the end-times New Testament church. The Message Bible puts verse 11 like this (emphasis mine):

> *These are all warning markers - danger! - in our history books, **written down so that we don't repeat their mistakes**. Our positions in the story are parallel - they at the beginning, we at the end - and we are just as capable of messing it up as they were.*

"Written down so that we don't repeat their mistakes."

Their "mistakes" cost them their lives, physically and spiritually. In fact, Paul says in verse five that with most of them, God was not pleased, and they never made it to their prophetic destiny – their prophetic inheritance: The Promised Land (Hebrews 3:7 - 4:1).

So what happened in the desert? What is Paul talking about? How do we heed these instructions? What *are* those instructions, and how do we avoid making the same mistakes? How do we enter our "Promised Land" – our prophetic destiny and inheritance? That's the amazing journey on which we're about to embark!

E2iS: EXODUS TO INGATHERING SERIES

Much of the correspondence we receive and the interaction that we have with our readers, online and offline, focuses on the practical hands-on "to do" aspects of Kingdom Lifestyle in light of God's appointed times – His *mo'edim* – and seasons. Thus, our goal with the publishing of this resource is to assist individuals, families and communities in experiencing and visualizing annually the life God intends for us to live with, in and for Him. To know the "instructions" that Paul says in 1 Corinthians 10:1 that he doesn't want us to be ignorant about. To understand instructions that he would have us "keep in mind," "to be sure of the fact" about, and not to "miss the significance of" as stated in various translations.

The *Exodus to Ingathering Series*, (*E2iS*: http://E2iSeries.com), is how we will meet that goal:

The Amazing Journey from Exodus to Ingathering
a 52-week resource:

- One part devotional
- One part journal, and
- One part calendar

Exodus to Ingathering Field Manual:

The annual deeper look and breakdown into each week's devotional and its tangible, real-world application that you're holding right now. The compass, if you will, with *The Amazing Journey* as your diary of sorts.

The Exodus Expedition:

The private, monthly subscription Facebook group that serves as the digital base camp for this expedition – this amazing journey. A safe place for you to gather with your fellow online travelers after being out in the field for

- Discussion
- Fellowship
- Regrouping
- Refreshing
- Strategizing
- Instruction

You have unlimited access to exclusive content:

- FB Live Chats
- Interactive Q&A Zoom Sessions
- Practical tips / lifestyle ideas
- Activities
- Teachings
- Additional digital resources, and more

You can access the *Exodus Expedition* from our Patreon page here: https://patreon.com/E2iS.

The Amazing Journey, the devotional, journal, calendar (DJC), is the resource you would use back at base camp, real and/or virtual, when you're alone or around the fire with close brethren; the ones with whom you have linked shields, the ones with whom you meditate on God's Word, worship, pray and supplicate with while fasting, pondering what He's speaking or showing you; those with whom you are sharing, encouraging, edifying, planning, strategizing and reflecting.

This *Field Manual*, on the other hand, is the resource you pull out when you're out in the actual field, keeping stock of:

- Supplies
- Provisions
- Ammunition

It's how we track our:

- Route / mapping
- Strategies
- Initiatives
- Progress
- Successes

FIELD MANUAL

Fundamentally and foundationally, Biblical precepts are designed to assist us as individuals, families and communities in experiencing and visualizing annually, monthly, weekly, daily, hourly the life God intends for us to live with, in and for Him.

Essentially, the act of keeping these Biblical precepts represents acknowledgements, agreements, alignments and assessments that we've made with Father God. This is crucial to understand for living an actual scriptural lifestyle. Again, successful obedience is how we align our lives and lifestyles with God for His specific Kingdom purposes "on earth as it is in heaven." Remember:

> *These things took place as examples for us, that we might not desire evil as they did.*
> *1 Corinthians 10:6*

Special thanks go to Cristina Aguirre and Elysa Hellermann for everything they do. Without their commitment, these resources would never see the light of day or make it into your hands.

We pray that this resource makes it easier and more fulfilling for you to acknowledge, agree, align and assess all that the Father has in store for you on this amazing journey from exodus to ingathering!

Allan R. Aguirre & The E2iS Staff

Comments, suggestions, and/or feature requests?
feedback@E2iSeries.com.

To get the most out of this resource, you'll want to join us over at:
http://E2iSeries.com/Expedition

TABLE OF CONTENTS

○ WEEK 01
FOR THE PLEASURE OF OUR KING (GENESIS 15:13-14, 16)

Then the Lord said to Abram, "Know for certain that your offspring will be sojourners in a land that is not theirs and will be servants there (Egypt), and they will be afflicted for four hundred years. But I will bring judgment on the nation that they serve, and afterward they shall come out with great possessions (the Exodus of Moses). And they shall come back here (Canaan, the Land of Promise) in the fourth generation, ***for the iniquity of the Amorites is not yet complete****."*
[Emphasis mine]

Do you ever get the feeling that you're serving someone else's agenda? That the season of your life isn't actually about you but about somebody or something else? That your needs, your "quieros" aren't being met? That you're... inconsequential? Unappreciated – irrelevant, even – and not just by your friends or loved ones, but maybe even by your pastor or by... God Himself...?

And this being overlooked – these feelings that are fostered within us: anger, resentment, bitterness, sadness... loneliness – how can any of this be from God or a part of His plan for our lives?

For Joseph, the boy with the coat of many colors, the "reward" for sharing a couple of prophetic dreams with his brothers, was to be thrown into a pit and then sold into slavery – to Ishmaelites no less! How was that a "part of God's plan"?

Think for a moment of the three principal players in the passage from Genesis above. And remember: this exercise – *these* exercises – are meant to be approached with and through your spiritual reasoning, not your carnal, physical, practical reasoning. These exercises are to be looked at with your spiritual eyes and to be listened to and heeded with spiritual ears, not your eyes and ears of flesh.

With that as our premise, think for a moment of the three principal players in the passage from Genesis above:

1. The offspring of Abram, the Hebrew people, Israel

They will be sojourners / foreigners in a strange land. It's because of this that Israel will be instructed to be merciful and kind to the sojourners in the land that they will eventually come to possess. Not only will they be strangers in a strange land, they'll end up "afflicted" slaves there – 400 years of Egyptian slavery, to be exact, is what Abram is told. This is to be Israel's prophetic destiny.

Then, and only then, will they be delivered "with great possessions," the wealth of Egypt (Ex. 3:21-22, 12:35-36). And it's a wealth they won't even be able to spend, because they'll spend 40 years in a desert dying off because of their fear, doubt and unbelief! *Then* they'll enter into their inheritance.

Tell me, what's so good about any of that?

2. Egypt, the nation that Israel will serve

Egypt is going to be blessed by Abram's descendant, Joseph. You know, that kid with the cool coat who was sold into slavery. This blessing stems from the prophetic promise that Abram was given about all the nations of the world being blessed by and through his line (Gn. 12:3).

Abram's descendants will ultimately move to Egypt with favor because of Joseph, but, as time goes by, the leadership of Egypt will forget Israel's favored status and enslave them, partially because of their sheer population numbers (another cause and effect of the blessing given to Abram (Gn. 12:2, 13:16, 15:5)).

Enslaving and afflicting Israel would bring judgment on Egypt through God's Levitical prophet Moses; judgment on Egypt *and* their gods (Ex. 12:12).

NOTE: Israel left Egypt 430 years after entering Egypt *to the very day!* (Ex. 12:40-41)

3. The Amorites

The Amorites were a mountain people that inhabited the land of Canaan and were the descendants of Canaan, the son of Ham and Noah's cursed grandson. They are historically credited for taking the small, then unimportant town of Babylon as their own, and raising it to minor independent city-state status and into the major power capital it is known for being today.

They worshiped the god Amurru who was married to the goddess Asherah, the 'queen of heaven,' who is referenced in Deuteronomy 12. Amurru could also be the fertility-god Ba'al.

Amos 2:9 describes the Amorites as a powerful people of great stature "like the height of the cedars." We would call them "giants." Deuteronomy 3:11 describes Og, the Amorite king, as the last "of the remnant of the Rephaim." Some of you may know the Rephaim as being descendants of the Nephilim of Genesis 6.

Israel would spend 430 years in Egypt, endure slavery and then wander an additional 40 years in the desert before being allowed to return to Canaan to claim and possess their Promised Land, their prophetic inheritance, because the iniquity of the Amorites had not yet matured. Prophetically, it would take the Amorites 470 years to run their sinful course before Israel, as instruments of God's wrath under Joshua's command, would be able to punish and exterminate them.

Do you ever get the feeling that you're serving someone else's agenda?

With our carnal mind and practical reasoning (i.e. the flesh), it's difficult to believe that our God would allow a 17-year-old to be beaten and sold into slavery by his brothers just because those brothers took offense to his prophetic dreams.

With our transformed spiritual mind, eyes to see and ears to hear (i.e. the Spirit), we are able to see the bigger picture. We see, as God saw, this act of Joseph's human rights being violated as the catalyst to saving the entire planet from a global famine.

Do we advocate or condone beatings and human trafficking? Of course not! Do people get beaten and sold into slavery? Unfortunately, yes.

In the practical (the flesh), it makes absolutely no sense to keep Israel away from their promised inheritance because an entirely different people group needs to mature in their evil godlessness. It makes no sense to enslave the people group of your choice (Israel) while you punk their oppressors over and over and over so that said Entity can flex their muscles.

> *"For my thoughts are not your thoughts, neither are your ways my ways," declares the LORD. As the heavens are higher than the earth, so are my ways higher than your ways and my thoughts than your thoughts."*
> *Isaiah 55:8-9 (NIV)*

Israel's slavery, liberation and then "systematic elimination" in the desert shows very little to no "love," "grace," "mercy" and the all-important "choice" and "free will" to those that are non-spiritual and forced to lean on their own understanding.

The constant hardening of Pharaoh's heart by God resulted in horrific plagues and ultimately the death of all the first born of Egypt's humans and animals. This is difficult to reconcile when there is very little-to-no historical, cultural and especially spiritual reference or understanding. Even then, many still decide not to comprehend or find it impossible to have "God's point of view" on the matter.

Israel and Egypt will have to interact – good, bad or indifferent – for 400 years, because a "not entirely human" people group (the Amorites) needs the time to mature in their demonic lives.

> *For those who live according to the flesh set their minds on the things of the flesh, but those who live according to the Spirit set their minds on the things of the Spirit.*
>
> *For to set the mind on the flesh is death, but to set the mind on the Spirit is life and peace. For the mind that is set on the flesh is hostile to God, for it does not submit to God's law; indeed, it cannot. Those who are in the flesh cannot please God.*
>
> *You, however, are not in the flesh but in the Spirit, if in fact the Spirit of God dwells in you.*
>
> *Romans 8:5-9a*

A large part of our disconnect with the biblical narrative is our inability to remember that we serve at the pleasure of our King – the Creator of heaven and earth; the Sovereign King of the Universe.

It's easier to just "read the Bible" through the filter of our practical reasoning and personal / religious reference experience than it is to "eat the scriptures;" the Word of God / Jesus (Jn 6:49-51, 53-58).

This is evident in how we process the absolute truths, instructions and character of God. And whether we *react* incorrectly or *respond* correctly to these absolutes is greatly affected by our choosing the carnal or the spiritual when making those determinations. How far we allow these truths to permeate and transform our lives and our identity has always been and will always be a matter of choice.

Welcome to the Amazing Journey from Exodus to Ingathering...

○ FIELD NOTES

DATE: / / TIME: : AM/PM PLACE:

○		A±
○		
○		
○		
○		
○		
○		
○		
○		
○		
○		
○		
○		
○		
○		
○		
○		
○		
○		
○		

ARMOR CHECK: Ephesians 6:10-18

Belt of Truth	S ☐	M ☐	T ☐	W ☐	T ☐	F ☐	S ☐
Breastplate of Righteousness	S ☐	M ☐	T ☐	W ☐	T ☐	F ☐	S ☐
Shoes / Gospel of Peace	S ☐	M ☐	T ☐	W ☐	T ☐	F ☐	S ☐
Shield of Faith	S ☐	M ☐	T ☐	W ☐	T ☐	F ☐	S ☐
Helmet of Salvation	S ☐	M ☐	T ☐	W ☐	T ☐	F ☐	S ☐
Sword of the Spirit / Word of God	S ☐	M ☐	T ☐	W ☐	T ☐	F ☐	S ☐

No weapon formed against you will prosper. This is the heritage of the servants of ADONAI.
Is. 54:17

○ WEEK 02
THE INHERITANCE OF SONSHIP
(JEREMIAH 7:22-26)

For in the day that I brought them (Israel) out of the land of Egypt, I did not speak to your fathers or command them concerning burnt offerings and sacrifices. But this command I gave them: 'Obey my voice, and I will be your God, and you shall be my people. And walk in all the way that I command you, that it may be well with you.' But they did not obey or incline their ear, but walked in their own counsels and the stubbornness of their evil hearts, and went backward and not forward. From the day that your fathers came out of the land of Egypt to this day, I have persistently sent all my servants the prophets to them, day after day. Yet they did not listen to me or incline their ear, but stiffened their neck. They did worse than their fathers."

Fake news has been around for centuries, but it wasn't a popular term until recently. A person's position in regard to a potentially-fake news item or belief in a false narrative has quickly become a contributing factor to the polarization of society, especially around political party lines. The same holds true within the church and the polarization that comes with denominational lines and constraints.

There was a lot of "fake news" surrounding Jesus. One such item was that He was originally from and born in Nazareth. He wasn't. This claim was incriminating and challenged Jesus' Messiahship. People have been creating false narratives out of the bible and they account for a massive portion of church history, especially in regard to Israel, Jews and Judaism.

A popular fake news item within mainstream Evangelical Protestantism is that the God of the Jews (Old Testament) was a heavy-handed and bloodthirsty deity that demanded the blood of bulls and goats. As we see in the passage above, that is hardly the case.

God didn't initially require "burnt offerings and sacrifices." He desired relationship:

"Obey my voice, and I will be your God, and you shall be my people. And walk in all the way that I command you, that it may be well with you."

That doesn't sound like an ogre to me. That sounds like a loving Father speaking to His children. And, like a loving Father whose children have chosen to rebel and go astray, He enacted discipline.

Jesus' parable of the prodigal son paints a beautiful example of this (Lk 15:11-32). The dishonoring, disrespectful, rebellious and disobedient acts and attitudes of the prodigal son didn't change his Father's heart toward him. However, those acts and attitudes did keep him lost and separated from his Father. If he hadn't returned and repented, those acts and attitudes would have killed him while he was lost and separated from his Father. The Father wasn't to blame for that. The petulant prodigal was to blame.

In fact, the entirety of Luke 15 is an example of the Father's heart toward His children:

- The parable of the lost sheep,
- The parable of the lost coin and
- The parable of the prodigal son.

Luke states that the listening audience consisted of tax collectors and sinners – the rabble – along with Pharisees and scribes who were grumbling about Jesus receiving and eating with such common folk; therefore, parables of compassion, mercy and grace.

After the parable of the shrewd manager (a parable that many overlook, don't comprehend and ignore), Luke states that the Pharisees – lovers of money – ridiculed Jesus, who in turn accused them of justifying themselves before men. Jesus rebuked them by stating that God ultimately knew their hearts and what they esteemed highly was an abomination in the Father's sight (Lk 16:14-15).

Another damaging "fake news" item prevalent in Christianity today is that Jesus opposed the Pharisees because they "followed the Law of Moses." Nothing could be further from the truth. The reality is that Israel's religious leaders perverted and side-stepped the Law, and that is why Jesus took issue with the Pharisees, Sadducees, scribes and Torah teachers. Jesus clearly states in Mark 7 that they made the scriptures, the "Law," null and void because of their religious traditions; traditions that actually caused men to break God's commandments, the "Law:"

"You have let go of the commands of God and are holding on to human traditions." And he continued, "You have a fine way of setting aside the commands of God in order to observe your own traditions!"
Jesus in Mark 7:8-9 (NIV)

Be sure to read Mark 7 for yourself.

Jesus is eating, drinking and associating with tax collectors and sinners in Luke 15 and sharing with them parables about compassion, mercy and grace to the disapproval and ridicule of the Pharisees.

Who is walking out "the Law" in this scenario? Well, Jesus is, of course! Remember: Jesus *is* this Living Word / the Scriptures / the Law (Hebrew: *"Torah"*) made flesh, and the parable of the prodigal son shows us the Father's "Heart of Torah" toward us:

*But while he was still a long way off, **his father saw him** and felt compassion, and ran and embraced him and kissed him.*

The prodigal's Father saw him coming from afar. His Father was anticipant and awaiting his son's return!

Now, take a look at the prodigal's heart toward himself and how it sometimes mirrors our own hearts with what he declares about himself:

*"I will get up and go to my father, and will say to him, 'Father, I have sinned against heaven, and in your sight; **I am no longer worthy to be called your son**; make me as one of your hired men.'"*

Is it possible for our sin, our situation, or our heart attitude to be stronger and more powerful than our actual identity in Him? In the parable of the lost sheep, when it was found, the man calls His neighbors to rejoice with Him. In like manner, the prodigal's father begins that celebration by reinforcing his son's true identity and his inheritance in his sonship:

- Bring out the best robe, and put it on him;
- Put a ring on his hand;
- Put sandals on his feet; and
- Bring the fattened calf, kill it, and let us eat and celebrate.

*...for **this son of mine** was dead and **has come to life again**; he was lost and has been found.' And they began to celebrate.*

Identity affirmation. Our Heavenly Father is constantly championing us to the naysayers and constantly affirming us to ourselves if we would only listen.

> *"But they did not obey or incline their ear, but walked in their own counsels and the stubbornness of their evil hearts, and went backward and not forward."*

We will touch on the rest of the parable regarding the older brother (the pharisaical heart of the religious spirit) some other time. It holds crucial understanding and warning for us all, even today.

But, for now, let us be thankful for God's heart for man; the Father's Heart of Torah for us all and the inheritance of sonship that comes with our rightful identity.

○ FIELD NOTES

DATE: / / TIME: : AM/PM PLACE:

○		A±
○		
○		
○		
○		
○		
○		
○		
○		
○		
○		
○		
○		
○		
○		
○		
○		
○		
○		
○		

ARMOR CHECK: Ephesians 6:10-18

Belt of Truth	S ☐ M ☐ T ☐ W ☐ T ☐ F ☐ S ☐
Breastplate of Righteousness	S ☐ M ☐ T ☐ W ☐ T ☐ F ☐ S ☐
Shoes / Gospel of Peace	S ☐ M ☐ T ☐ W ☐ T ☐ F ☐ S ☐
Shield of Faith	S ☐ M ☐ T ☐ W ☐ T ☐ F ☐ S ☐
Helmet of Salvation	S ☐ M ☐ T ☐ W ☐ T ☐ F ☐ S ☐
Sword of the Spirit / Word of God	S ☐ M ☐ T ☐ W ☐ T ☐ F ☐ S ☐

No weapon formed against you will prosper. This is the heritage of the servants of ADONAI.
Is. 54:17

○ WEEK 03

TRIUMPHAL ENTRY OR A CASE OF MISTAKEN IDENTITY

(MATTHEW 21:1-7)

Now when they drew near to Jerusalem and came to Bethphage, to the Mount of Olives, then Jesus sent two disciples, saying to them, "Go into the village in front of you, and immediately you will find a donkey tied, and a colt with her. Untie them and bring them to me. If anyone says anything to you, you shall say, 'The Lord needs them,' and he will send them at once." This took place to fulfill what was spoken by the prophet, saying, "Say to the daughter of Zion, 'Behold, your king is coming to you, humble, and mounted on a donkey, on a colt, the foal of a beast of burden.'" [Zch. 9:9] The disciples went and did as Jesus had directed them. They brought the donkey and the colt and put on them their cloaks, and he sat on them.

The streets of Jerusalem and the surrounding towns were teeming with people that had come to observe the first of the three yearly pilgrimage feasts: Passover and the week-long Feast of Unleavened Bread.

The streets were also filled with crowds that had heard that the prophet, Jesus of Nazareth, was on His way to Jerusalem. The same Jesus who, seven weeks ago during Purim, had raised his friend Lazarus from the dead.

As you can imagine, it was quite the scene when Jesus and the disciples arrived. Not only was the crowd anticipant of His entry into Jerusalem (where Jesus would surely announce His Messianic claim and reign), but the chief priests, Pharisees and Sanhedrin council members were also awaiting His arrival. Since the resurrection of Lazarus, they had already made plans to put Jesus to death due to their fear that the Romans would strip them of their positions and the nation, all on account of Jesus' supernatural and miraculous signs and wonders (Jn 11).

Most of the crowd spread their cloaks on the road, and others cut branches from the trees and spread them on the road.

And the crowds that went before him and that followed him were shouting, "Hosanna to the Son of David! Blessed is he who comes in the name of the Lord! Hosanna in the highest!" And when he entered Jerusalem, the whole city was stirred up, saying, "Who is this?" And the crowds said, "This is the prophet Jesus, from Nazareth of Galilee."
Matthew 21:8-11

What a triumphal entry into Jerusalem with manifestations and declarations such as

- Cloaks being spread on the road before Him;
- Shouts of "Son of David;"
- "Blessed is he who comes in the name of the Lord;"
- "Blessed is the King who comes in the name of the Lord;" (Lk 19:38)
- "Blessed is the coming kingdom of our father, David;" (Mk 11:10)
- "Hosanna in the highest;" and
- "The prophet, Jesus"

What could go wrong? It even says that, upon Jesus' entrance into Jerusalem, the whole city was stirred up.

Jesus' identity had been in question His entire public ministry. Although he had been born in Bethlehem, the prophetic birthplace of Messiah, everyone thought He was from Nazareth. In Matthew 16:13-16, Mark 8:27-30 and Luke 9:18-20, Jesus plainly asks His disciples, "Who do people say that I am?" John the Baptist, Elijah, Jeremiah and 'one of the prophets' were the common answers. Simon Peter answered that He was indeed the promised Messiah. Now, upon entering Jerusalem, His disciples and the pilgrimage crowds were all declaring the same.

It was the tenth day of the first month, the month of Abib, the day that the people are to select their Passover lamb. It was also the weekly Sabbath that year.

A form of "group think" was occurring as the initial crowd began to worship and praise Jesus as Messiah as He rode into Jerusalem from the Mount of Olives. The crowd was made up of His disciples and witnesses to the resurrection of Lazarus. Many in the crowds followed suit, as they would again four days later.

Then the Pharisees said to each other, "There's nothing we can do. Look, everyone has gone after him!"
John 12:19 (NLT)

John 12:20-36 continues with a prophetic declaration of His own death – to Gentiles, no less – and the third affirmation from the Voice from Heaven confirmed Jesus being the Passover Lamb that was slain before the foundations of the world (1 Pe. 1:18-20; Re 13.8).

Once the Passover lamb was selected, there were four days to inspect it to make sure no blemish was found, assuring that it was a worthy Passover offering.

After being inspected and tested as the Passover Lamb by the Pharisees, Herodians, Sadducees and scribes, and after making their final determination to murder Jesus, Jesus and the disciples prepare for the Passover.

MISTAKEN IDENTITY

After dinner with His friends, facilitating communion, washing their feet and singing a hymn, Jesus and the disciples went to the Mount of Olives to pray.

So as to be able to distinguish Jesus from the rest, Judas of Iscariot, being a thief and a massively-disgruntled disciple, brokers a deal to betray Jesus under cover of night by kissing Him on the cheek.

For as popular as He was and as accessible as He was – teaching in the temple, walking freely in the courtyard, a regular fixture in synagogues everywhere and having just been interrogated by every religious leader and their legal representation for the last few days – they needed someone to point Him out? Did they not know exactly who it was that threatened their precious religious order, who they wanted to kill?

The wife of Pontius Pilate, governor of the Roman province of Judea knew who Jesus was. Well, she knew not to bring Him any harm because of a dream.

King Herod knew who He was. Well, Herod had heard about some supernatural things that may or may not have happened and was only interested in witnessing a parlor trick himself.

The people knew who Jesus was. Well, they knew that He could feed people for free and that many miracles were attributed to Him. And there was that impressive entrance into the city the other day...

We don't know how much the notorious prisoner Barabbas knew or how many knew about him. What we do know is that the chief priests and the elders knew who he was, and they persuaded the crowds to pick Barabbas so that they could destroy Jesus.

The crowd. "Group Think."

Four days ago, multitudes of this same crowd were laying down their coats on the road in front of this man named Jesus as He rode into the city on a donkey colt.

Four days ago, multitudes of this same crowd were laying down palm branches on the road in front of this man as He rode into the city.

Four days ago, as this Prophet rode into the city on an ass, multitudes of this same crowd were declaring prophetic utterances like, "Son of David," "Blessed is he who comes in the name of the Lord," "Blessed is the *King* who comes in the name of the Lord," "Blessed is the coming kingdom of our father David" and "Hosanna in the highest!" What could go wrong? Who cared if the entire religious ruling authority wanted Him dead? The people didn't...

Oh, no... The people are now yelling, "Crucify Him! Crucify Him!" over and over...

> *So when Pilate saw that he was gaining nothing, but rather that a riot was beginning, he took water and washed his hands before the crowd, saying, "I am innocent of this man's blood; see to it yourselves." And all the people answered, "His blood be on us and on our children!"*
> *Matthew 27:24-25*

The streets of Jerusalem and the surrounding towns were teeming with people that were here to observe the first of the three yearly pilgrimage feasts: Passover and the week long Feast of Unleavened Bread.

The streets were also filled with crowds that had heard that the prophet, Jesus of Nazareth, was on His way into town. Seven weeks ago, during Purim, He raised his buddy Lazarus from the dead!

I wonder if we'll get to see him?!?

> *"He has blinded their eyes and hardened their hearts, so they can neither see with their eyes, nor understand with their hearts, nor turn — and I would heal them."*
> *John 12:40 (NIV) [Paraphrasing Isaiah 6:10]*

○ FIELD NOTES

DATE: / / TIME: : AM/PM PLACE:

○		A±
○		
○		
○		
○		
○		
○		
○		
○		
○		
○		
○		
○		
○		
○		
○		
○		
○		
○		
○		

ARMOR CHECK: Ephesians 6:10-18

Belt of Truth	S ☐	M ☐	T ☐	W ☐	T ☐	F ☐	S ☐
Breastplate of Righteousness	S ☐	M ☐	T ☐	W ☐	T ☐	F ☐	S ☐
Shoes / Gospel of Peace	S ☐	M ☐	T ☐	W ☐	T ☐	F ☐	S ☐
Shield of Faith	S ☐	M ☐	T ☐	W ☐	T ☐	F ☐	S ☐
Helmet of Salvation	S ☐	M ☐	T ☐	W ☐	T ☐	F ☐	S ☐
Sword of the Spirit / Word of God	S ☐	M ☐	T ☐	W ☐	T ☐	F ☐	S ☐

No weapon formed against you will prosper. This is the heritage of the servants of ADONAI.
Is. 54:17

○ WEEK 04
STRANGE FIRE
(LEVITICUS 9:16, 10:1-2)

He (Aaron) brought the burnt offering and offered it in the prescribed way (NIV).

Now Nadab and Abihu, the sons of Aaron, each took his censer and put fire in it and laid incense on it and offered unauthorized fire before the Lord, which he had not commanded them. And fire came out from before the Lord and consumed them, and they died before the Lord.

The term "strange fire" has steadily increased in popularity over time. I remember hearing it in the '80s and it being strictly "Charismatic lingo." A search on the Google yields a variety of blogs, podcasts, articles and assorted books from various authors on both sides of the aisle, cessationist and continuationist. Le sigh...

The term refers to the passage from Leviticus above and generally represents anything that would be done, used or said in the worship of God that is considered forbidden and/or unauthorized. This can range from however or whatever has not been deemed "lawful" or "in the prescribed way:" forms of prayer and/or worship, utensils and/or items, clothing, locations – even times and seasons. We find examples of these all throughout the scriptural narrative regarding Israel and how they were to be "set apart," holy unto the Lord, when they entered the Promised Land.

Our premise for the *Exodus to Ingathering Series* (E2iS) comes from the Apostle Paul and 1 Corinthians 10, where Paul is telling us to heed the warnings that were written down for our instruction regarding Israel and their time in the wilderness.

While in the desert, Israel was being taught the proper and acceptable way to live – how to interact with their fellow man and how to worship God in spirit and in truth (Mt. 22:36-40). They were also being warned against mixture, syncretism: the mixing of the holy and the profane (Dt. 12:1-4, 28-32).

While in the desert, Israel was being taught how to live, walk and worship "in the prescribed way," so that upon entering and living in the Promised Land, a land inhabited by what God described as "wicked nations" (Dt. 9), Israel wouldn't succumb to their godless influence and their demonic forms of lifestyle and pagan worship. Nevertheless, Israel would utterly fail in this regard, and this is largely the instruction, Paul says – the warnings that were written down for us of which we are not to be ignorant.

In like manner, the term "strange fire" is also used to describe the occult, paganism and the demonic in general. All the ways that Israel rebelled against God and Moses, both in the desert and after crossing the Jordan River into the Promised Land under Joshua's leadership, could be described as "strange fire."

A ROYAL PRIESTHOOD

The fundamental concept behind Christianity is to be transformed into the likeness of Jesus through the indwelling of the Holy Spirit. This is the power that gives us the power to distinguish and choose obedience over lawlessness, truth over falsehood, clean over unclean, righteousness over blasphemy, and the holy over the profane.

(Source: Aguirre, Allan R. "In Conclusion," in *This Thing Is Spiritual*, 162. Park City, Utah: Planet Blue Media, 2019. http://planetbluemedia.com)

Keeping to our premise that what Israel experienced in the desert wilderness took place as examples for us so "that we might not desire evil as they did," this mandate of walking and being "set apart" / holy unto the Lord was established from the very beginning of the exodus into God's ingathering:

> ***"I will take you to be my people, and I will be your God,*** *and you shall know that I am the LORD your God, who has brought you out from under the burdens of the Egyptians.*
>
> *Now therefore, if you will indeed obey my voice and keep my covenant,* ***you shall be my treasured possession*** *among all peoples, for all the earth is mine; and you shall be to me* ***a kingdom of priests and a holy nation****. These are the words that you shall speak to the people of Israel."*
>
> *Exodus 6:7, 19:5-6 [Emphasis mine]*

- To be His people
- His treasured possession
- A kingdom of priests
- A holy nation

Peter echoed this same mandate of being "set apart" ones:

> *But you are a chosen race, a royal priesthood, a holy nation, a people for his own possession, that you may proclaim the excellencies of him who called you out of darkness into his marvelous light.*
>
> *Once you were not a people, but now you are God's people; once you had not received mercy, but now you have received mercy.*
>
> *1 Peter 2:9-10*

The same promise, the same identity, the same prerequisite:

> *"...if you will indeed obey my voice and keep my covenant..."*

Jesus put it like this:

> *"If you love me, keep my commands."*
>
> *John 14:15 (NIV)*

The Apostle Paul encourages us not to be ignorant and evil like most of Israel was. They chose not to obey God's voice, not to keep His covenants and not to follow His commandments. They opted for the strange fire instead.

As believers in Jesus, we are on *this* side of Calvary; we are on *this* side of Pentecost. We live in the fulfillment of the Promised Messiah and the indwelling of Holy Spirit. Like Israel, we have eaten the same spiritual food and drank the same spiritual drink; for we drink from the spiritual rock that is Messiah – in the prescribed way.

NEHUSHTAN

In Numbers 21:4-9, we read the account of Israel becoming impatient in their exodus to ingathering, and they begin to speak against God and Moses, accusing them of bringing them out into the desert to die and complaining about the supernatural food with which God was feeding them – manna. This account in Numbers is what Paul is referencing in 1 Corinthians 10:9-10 about putting Messiah to the test and grumbling – actions that we still don't equate to being punishable by death, physical or spiritual.

The reason why this infraction was so severe was because of everything God had already done for and on behalf of Israel, both in Egypt and in the desert. He brought them out of 400 years of exile in Egypt to make them

His people, a holy nation – not to kill them! They were accusing Him of going against His very nature:

> *We must not put Christ (some manuscripts have "Lord": ADONAI – God) to the test, as some of them did and were destroyed by serpents...*
> *1 Corinthians 10:9*

So, Israel was punished yet again:

> *Then the LORD sent fiery serpents among the people, and they bit the people, so that many people of Israel died.*
> *Numbers 21:6*

Israel repents and asks Moses to pray on their behalf on account of their sin of speaking against God and Moses.

> *And the LORD said to Moses, "Make a fiery serpent and set it on a pole, and everyone who is bitten, when he sees it, shall live."*
>
> *So Moses made a bronze serpent and set it on a pole. And if a serpent bit anyone, he would look at the bronze serpent and live.*
> *Numbers 21:8-9*

This is why the medical community uses a snake wrapped around a pole for their logo. Hundreds of years later, this same bronze serpent is an article of worship in Jerusalem's Temple known as *Nehushtan.*

At the age of 25, Hezekiah began his reign as king of Judah, the southern kingdom of Israel. King Hezekiah worshipped God in Spirit and in Truth:

> *And he did what was right in the eyes of the LORD, according to all that David his father had done.*
>
> *He removed the high places and broke the pillars and cut down the Asherah. And he broke in pieces the bronze serpent that Moses had made, for until those days the people of Israel had made offerings to it (it was called Nehushtan).*
> *2 Kings 18:3-4*

Man took an artifact that God had ordained to be looked upon for healing in the desert, erected it in the Temple and began to make offerings to it: strange fire.

Assess yourself. Take an account. What strange fire are you burning as worship to your God?

> *Examine yourselves to see whether you are living in the faith. Test yourselves. Do you not realize that Jesus Christ is in you?— unless, indeed, you fail to meet the test!*
> *2 Corinthians 13:5 (NRS)*

○ FIELD NOTES

DATE: / / TIME: : AM/PM PLACE:

○		A±
○		
○		
○		
○		
○		
○		
○		
○		
○		
○		
○		
○		
○		
○		
○		
○		
○		
○		
○		

ARMOR CHECK: Ephesians 6:10-18

Belt of Truth	S ☐	M ☐	T ☐	W ☐	T ☐	F ☐	S ☐
Breastplate of Righteousness	S ☐	M ☐	T ☐	W ☐	T ☐	F ☐	S ☐
Shoes / Gospel of Peace	S ☐	M ☐	T ☐	W ☐	T ☐	F ☐	S ☐
Shield of Faith	S ☐	M ☐	T ☐	W ☐	T ☐	F ☐	S ☐
Helmet of Salvation	S ☐	M ☐	T ☐	W ☐	T ☐	F ☐	S ☐
Sword of the Spirit / Word of God	S ☐	M ☐	T ☐	W ☐	T ☐	F ☐	S ☐

No weapon formed against you will prosper. This is the heritage of the servants of ADONAI.
Is. 54:17

○ WEEK 05
CAN'T STAY HERE. CAN'T GO BACK. GOTTA MOVE FORWARD (2 KINGS 7:3-4)

Now there were four men who were lepers at the entrance to the gate. And they said to one another, "Why are we sitting here until we die? If we say, 'Let us enter the city,' the famine is in the city, and we shall die there. And if we sit here, we die also. So now come, let us go over to the camp of the Syrians. If they spare our lives we shall live, and if they kill us we shall but die."

Not everybody is a leader. Not everyone is an early adapter. Most people aren't entrepreneurs, and only "some" of us are apostles, prophets, teachers, evangelists and pastors (Eph. 4:11-12].

I didn't grow up with money, and when it came to my music career, I didn't have the luxury of "daddy" talking to his industry peers on my behalf and cashing in on a favor for my big break. We lived in Burbank, a media capital, but my dad didn't work in the industry. I was going to have to make my own "big breaks," and I was going to have to figure all that out without any of that money I didn't have.

Recording studio time, advertising know-how and budget, marketing, graphic design, concert bookings, radio promotions, legal representation... how was I going to secure any of those services without contacts and dollar bills? Easy. You learn how to do it for yourself. And that's what I did.

Need graphic design services for logos, flyers, magazine advertisements, merchandise and marketing materials? Become a graphic designer.

Can't get shows without a demo of your music? No problem: Figure out that there's an actual thing called a "spec deal," learn not only what it is but how to get one, and go! (A spec deal is the negotiation for free recording studio time from a recording studio on the speculation that your music is so good that some sort of profitable gain will occur from the recording made with the investment of the recording studio time that is needed to make said recording.)

Whew… confused yet?

Not enough people going to your shows? That's what marketing and promotions are for: advertise in all the right music magazines, get that new recording of that great new song of yours on the right radio stations, and have both the magazines and radio stations promote your new show. Check!

Don't forget that you'll first have to figure out the advertising business that incorporates the design and graphic skills you're developing as well as the new technical skills you didn't know about when it comes to the printing of printed matter. Add to that the radio promotions that you'll have to figure out that record companies pay a lot of people a lot of money to do, not including how to get your band a respectable time slot at the hottest club in Hollywood on Saturday night for all those people that are going to see your full-page ad in that music magazine that is going to remind them of your song that they heard on the radio while on the way to the beach earlier that day.

I won't mention the 10,000 other new acts migrating into Los Angeles every week with more skills, more connections, less scruples and more money than you have or the fact that we're all trying to do the exact same thing with all the exact same people.

And that's what I did. It took an unimaginable amount of excruciating hard work, long hours, luck and resources coupled with tenacity, singular focus of mind and determination. Anyone that has ever succeeded in anything will tell you the same.

I see these same attributes – hunger, tenacity, focus, ingenuity, entrepreneurship – championed and encouraged, even necessary… as traits of those "succeeding" and on the right side of things in the Proverbs and in the parables of Jesus.

I see in the biblical narrative what Noah had to undergo to meet his objective, the course Abraham literally walked to meet his calling and what Moses had to endure to fulfill his destiny. Joseph, Daniel, David, the Apostle Paul, the woman with the issue of blood and even Jesus Himself…

I don't see much in the way of succeeding in this thing called life if you're not aggressively going for it. How much more important is it, then, to be aggressive in our faith? I see in the biblical narrative a push toward instruction and encouragement – from either a biblical position, Jesus' point of view or even Paul's perspective – how because of and through the empowering of the

Holy Spirit, we can live our best possible life and be our best possible self in Him, for Him and through Him.

If you're not going for it, chances are you're compromising, or you're already compromised – your fire is going out or has gone out – you can't or you're not even trying to double what you've been given to steward, and your oil is running extremely low. I can't see it any other way. I don't want to see it any other way, and I've been looking at it hard for 40 years...

So, when I see four guys carrying their paraplegic friend through the streets and lowering him down into a room from a rooftop to get healing from Jesus? It makes sense to me. Aggressive proactivity and thinking outside the box to get what God has to offer? Count me in!

I don't see the mandate of "be set apart," "be perfect and holy" or "go and sin no more" as passive things. And, contrary to popular belief, I certainly can't see those commandments as suggestions or options that you can decide not to do and come out with the same results as those that do them aggressively and proactively. And neither did the four lepers.

Samaria was under siege, which brought about great famine. The famine was so great that the people had resorted to cannibalism (2 Ki. 6:26-31). They knew that this siege and famine was punishment from God, but instead of repenting and crying out to God, the king of Israel decided it was easier to go looking for the prophet of God and have him executed for bringing this trouble upon them. And this is what I'm talking about:

These people and their sin – their lack of obedience, their decision not to walk in the fear of the Lord and, as Proverbs puts it, their decision not to heed wisdom's cry in the street (Pr. 1:1-7, 20-33) – was the cause of their affliction and predicament. Proverbs says this sort of dilemma will befall them because they are simpletons – simpletons for not heeding the Word of the Lord and thus their inability to do otherwise. Instead of repenting (wisdom), Israel's king decided to go kill (foolishness) God's representative, Elisha the prophet. That makes a lot of sense. It does to a simpleton...

When they came for Elisha, he prophesied to the messenger that food was on its way (2 Ki. 7:1) and that the messenger would only see it but not eat of it, again, because of his foolishness and simple-mindedness that caused his unbelief. Are you seeing the pattern here?

> *Now there were four men with leprosy at the entrance of the city gate. They said to each other, "Why stay here until we die?*

If we say, 'We'll go into the city'— the famine is there, and we will die. And if we stay here, we will die. So let's go over to the camp of the Arameans and surrender. If they spare us, we live; if they kill us, then we die."
2 Kings 7:3-4 (NIV)

I like these guys. They've made a tactical decision not to sit around aimlessly and just die:

We can't sit here
We can't go back
We've gotta move forward

And they did!

Somehow, inaction, complaining and giving up have become the modus operandi of many in the church today, all under the guise of "God's will." No, it isn't. That's *your* will! How dare you attribute your lack of understanding, intelligence and action as God's will and character? Israel did that in the desert, and it got them killed. Don't do that!

I could sit here and list the various things I hear that come out of people's mouths – Christian mouths – that make me cringe every single time. Declarations and confessions that come from everywhere *but* the throne room of God! It would offend a majority of you if I listed them, so I won't.

Declarations and confessions about themselves or family members with which they identify, that identify them. *In Jesus*, no less! It's tragic. These declarations are not declarations or confessions of positivity, edification, success or winning. They come from another place, another kingdom, another realm. How do they not know this? How do they not understand that they continually speak and propagate curses over themselves? Have they never been told?

It doesn't help that accepting limitations and identifying with them is 100% acceptable and encouraged by the fallen world around them. Are you aware of what's happening out there? Who's influencing who?

These four lepers went forward against all odds and against all practical reasoning – all practical reasoning in the flesh. By doing so, they ended the siege and saved the city. You can read all about it in 2 Kings 7.

Christianity is all about allowing ourselves to be transformed into the likeness of Jesus. This involves us. It requires our involvement and cooperation;

it just doesn't happen all by itself.

> *Let us rejoice and exult and give him the glory, for the marriage of the Lamb has come, and his Bride has* ***made herself*** *ready; it was granted her to* ***clothe herself with fine linen****, bright and pure"— for the fine linen is the* ***righteous deeds*** *(acts) of the saints.*
> *Revelation 19:7-8 [Emphasis mine]*

Go. Make yourself ready. He's coming…

○ FIELD NOTES

DATE: / / TIME: : AM/PM PLACE:

○		A±
○		
○		
○		
○		
○		
○		
○		
○		
○		
○		
○		
○		
○		
○		
○		
○		
○		
○		
○		

ARMOR CHECK: Ephesians 6:10-18

Belt of Truth	S ☐ M ☐ T ☐ W ☐ T ☐ F ☐ S ☐
Breastplate of Righteousness	S ☐ M ☐ T ☐ W ☐ T ☐ F ☐ S ☐
Shoes / Gospel of Peace	S ☐ M ☐ T ☐ W ☐ T ☐ F ☐ S ☐
Shield of Faith	S ☐ M ☐ T ☐ W ☐ T ☐ F ☐ S ☐
Helmet of Salvation	S ☐ M ☐ T ☐ W ☐ T ☐ F ☐ S ☐
Sword of the Spirit / Word of God	S ☐ M ☐ T ☐ W ☐ T ☐ F ☐ S ☐

No weapon formed against you will prosper. This is the heritage of the servants of ADONAI.
Is. 54:17

○ WEEK 06
AT-ONE-MENT
(LEVITICUS 17:7)

So they shall no more sacrifice their sacrifices to goat demons, after whom they whore. This shall be a statute forever for them throughout their generations.

Yikes! I thought devotionals were supposed to be full of warm fuzzies?

I'm pretty sure I forewarned you that this wasn't going to be that sort of devotional. Heh.

Remember our premise: the Apostle Paul tells us not to be ignorant of the fact that Israel was also "saved" in the desert like you and I are. Nevertheless...

Nevertheless, with most of them God was not pleased, for they were overthrown in the wilderness. Now these things happened to them ***as an example****, but they were* ***written down for our instruction (warning)****, on whom the end of the ages has come.*
1 Corinthians 10:5, 11 [Emphasis mine]

Essentially, Paul is stating that what happened to the children of Israel in the desert – as recorded in the books of Exodus, Leviticus, Numbers and Deuteronomy – was written down as a warning and for our instruction; "our" being the end times, New Testament church – you and me. The Message Bible puts verse 11 like this (emphasis mine):

These are all warning markers - danger! - in our history books, ***written down so that we don't repeat their mistakes****. Our positions in the story are parallel - they at the beginning, we at the end - and we are just as capable of messing it up as they were.*

"Written down so that we don't repeat their mistakes"

Their "mistakes" cost them their lives, physically and spiritually. In fact, Paul says in verse five that with most of them God was not pleased... and they never made it to their prophetic destiny – their prophetic inheritance: the

Promised Land. And one of their mistakes was sacrificing to goat demons...

Israel had just spent 400 years in Egypt. During that time, they had acquired some habits, and an attitude, that were not in line with the nature of God or His ways.

I was 15 years old when I came to Jesus, and I had developed some pretty nasty habits and attitudes that were anything but godly. I had my share of "sacrifices to goat demons." This only increased when I backslid in my 20s. I share about those hard times in my book, *This Thing Is Spiritual*, and how doing so increased the demonic activity around me, just like Jesus said it would (Mt. 12:43-45):

> *"Anyone who isn't with me opposes me, and anyone who isn't working with me is actually working against me.*
>
> *When an evil spirit leaves a person, it goes into the desert, searching for rest. But when it finds none, it says, 'I will return to the person I came from.' So it returns and finds that its former home is all swept and in order. Then the spirit finds seven other spirits more evil than itself, and they all enter the person and live there. And so that person is worse off than before."*
>
> *Luke 11:23-26 (NLT)*

Here's what I'm saying – this is war, and the war is spiritual. What we do in the physical realm has cause and effect in the spiritual realm and, if that wasn't enough, the physical realm is a manifestation of what is happening in the spiritual realm! How's that for evening out the playing field?

(Here's the good news: the war has already been won!)

God is a good Father; He wouldn't leave us unarmed or ill-equipped. He has provided for us the best field manual and ammunition ever: His Living Word – the Sword of the Spirit – and the empowerment *of* that Holy Spirit. Hallelujah!

Here's the bad news: discipleship is almost unheard of among our ranks today. Now, that doesn't make it obsolete or mean that God has done away with a core principle just because *we* have. On the contrary, discipleship is needed now, at this very hour, more than ever. Discipleship is our spiritual boot camp, and the lack of it is painfully obvious. The good news? *The Amazing Journey from Exodus to Ingathering* – the entire *E2i Series*, to be honest – is basically an annual discipleship training course. (Shhhhh... don't tell anyone...)

Just like any engagement, there are rules, and our Commander-in-

Chief, the Commander of the Army of ADONAI (Jsh. 5:13-15), has provided us with those rules of engagement – His rules of engagement for this spiritual war – in His Word. This resource that you're holding was developed to assist you in learning and activating those very rules of engagement.

So, like I was saying, Israel had developed habits and attitudes while in Egypt that were contrary to the Spirit of God, just like you and I developed habits and attitudes that were contrary to the Spirit of God before coming to Jesus. Some of those habits were like Israel's sacrifices to goat demons. Let me explain:

> *Any Israelite who sacrifices an ox, a lamb or a goat in the camp or outside of it instead of bringing it to the entrance to the tent of meeting to present it as an offering to the LORD in front of the tabernacle of the LORD— that person shall be considered guilty of bloodshed; they have shed blood and must be cut off from their people.*
>
> *This is so the Israelites will bring to the LORD the sacrifices they are now making in the open fields. They must bring them to the priest, that is, to the LORD, at the entrance to the tent of meeting and sacrifice them as fellowship offerings.*
> *Leviticus 17:3-5 (NIV)*

Israel had a habit of sacrificing out in the open fields, a habit that they brought to the desert with them from Egypt. Chances are those acts of "worship," those sacrificial acts, were unsound and questionable. It's more than likely that there wasn't an authorized authority involved – an authorized leader, priest or in today's case, a "pastor." We can easily surmise this because of this new instruction, this new rule of engagement, designed to protect Israel – to protect Her from spiritual ignorance and/or the accidental or deliberate and conscious act of sacrificing to goat demons.

We learned two weeks ago about "strange fire," a sacrifice not made "in the prescribed way." Instead of making sacrifices on their own (that's the key here), in or outside of the camp, the new rule of engagement is for Israel to bring the animal that they wish to sacrifice to the entrance of the Tent of Meeting to be presented "to the Lord:"

> *This is so the Israelites will bring to the LORD the sacrifices they are now making in the open fields.*

Accountability.

God's "prescribed way" will always involve a designated earthly authority, otherwise known as a leader / leadership, and deter isolation:

> *They must bring them* ***to the priest****, that is, to the LORD, at* ***the entrance to the tent of meeting*** *and sacrifice them as* ***fellowship offerings****.*

Accountability. Earthly Authority. Publicly. Open / Community Fellowship.

Paul said we are not to be ignorant regarding Israel in the desert under Moses' leadership and how they were also saved like you and me. Yet, some of them were out in the fields making sacrifices to goat demons on their own and without sound scriptural leadership, "in Jesus."

Consider any possible ways you may still be out in the fields sacrificing to goat demons, alone, without Godly fellowship and/or sound scriptural earthly leadership, without Jesus…

○ FIELD NOTES

DATE: / / TIME: : AM/PM PLACE:

○		A±
○		
○		
○		
○		
○		
○		
○		
○		
○		
○		
○		
○		
○		
○		
○		
○		
○		
○		
○		

ARMOR CHECK: Ephesians 6:10-18

Belt of Truth	S ☐	M ☐	T ☐	W ☐	T ☐	F ☐	S ☐
Breastplate of Righteousness	S ☐	M ☐	T ☐	W ☐	T ☐	F ☐	S ☐
Shoes / Gospel of Peace	S ☐	M ☐	T ☐	W ☐	T ☐	F ☐	S ☐
Shield of Faith	S ☐	M ☐	T ☐	W ☐	T ☐	F ☐	S ☐
Helmet of Salvation	S ☐	M ☐	T ☐	W ☐	T ☐	F ☐	S ☐
Sword of the Spirit / Word of God	S ☐	M ☐	T ☐	W ☐	T ☐	F ☐	S ☐

No weapon formed against you will prosper. This is the heritage of the servants of ADONAI.
Is. 54:17

○ WEEK 07
GOD'S APPOINTED TIMES AND SEASONS (LEVITICUS 23)

The LORD said to Moses, "Speak to the Israelites and say to them: 'These are my appointed festivals, the appointed festivals of the LORD, which you are to proclaim as sacred assemblies.'" (NIV)

Instead of "appointed festivals," other translations say:

- Appointed times
- Designated times
- Appointed feasts
- The feasts of the Lord

But it never says, "Jewish holidays." Hmmm…

"Sacred assemblies" is also translated as:

- Holy convocations
- Holy meetings
- Holy occasions
- Holy assemblies
- Worship

Isn't it weird to think, teach and/or believe that Jesus came to do away with His Father's appointed times and holy occasions? Judge Judy says that if it doesn't make sense, it's usually a lie. I'm gonna go with Judge Judy on this one.

For the third and last time, we see Jesus, yet again, quoting Torah as His defense with the final challenge:

Again, the devil took him to a very high mountain and showed him all the kingdoms of the world and their glory. And he said to him, "All these I will give you, if you will fall down and worship me." Then Jesus said to him, "Be gone, Satan! For it is written, "'You shall worship the Lord your God and him only shall you serve.'"

Matthew 4:8-10 [Quoting Deuteronomy 6:13-14]

"Worship me," says Lucifer, a spiritual being. As Prince of this World, he had some level of authority to offer Jesus the kingdoms of this world, if He would only worship him.

This begs the question:

What then are the scriptural guidelines for worshiping in "truth?"

(Source: Aguirre, Allan R. "An Abundance of Obedience," In *This Thing Is Spiritual*, 8-9. Park City, Utah: Planet Blue Media, 2019. http://planetbluemedia.com)

I think it's a very good and legitimate question: what then *are* the scriptural guidelines for worshiping in "truth?"

Jesus says,

> *But the time is coming -- indeed, it's here now -- when the true worshippers will worship the Father spiritually and truly, for these are the kind of people the Father wants worshipping him. God is spirit; and worshippers must worship him spiritually and truly."*
> *John 4:23-24 (CJB)*

Where is He getting His information? What, then, *are* Jesus' guidelines for true and spiritual worship? I'm glad you asked.

First, we need to set up a biblical foundation so as not to leave any room for speculation or agenda. Let's start with Jesus' very own words, since He is, in fact, that very same Word made flesh. Jesus' own words can't cancel Himself or the Bible out, right? Right?

To clarify any misconceptions on where Jesus was getting His information, Jesus informs the religious leaders that His message wasn't actually His own original material:

> *So Jesus said to them, "Truly, truly, I say to you, the Son can do nothing of his own accord, but only what he sees the Father doing. For whatever the Father does, that the Son does likewise."*
> *John 5:19, 30*

> *I do nothing on my own authority, but speak just as the Father taught me.*
> *John 8:28b*

> *For I have not spoken on my own authority, but the Father who sent me has himself given me a commandment--what to say and what to speak.*
> *John 12:49*

Jesus did nothing and said nothing of His own accord. He only did what He saw the Father do, and He only said what the Father told Him to say. And, when it came to the scriptural guidelines for worshiping in truth, Jesus went to the source that the Father had established Himself through: Moses.

"For if you believed Moses, you would believe me; for he wrote of me. But if you do not believe his writings, how will you believe my words?"
John 5:46-47

Jesus fully defers to the authority of Moses here. Jesus clearly states that we cannot believe His words if we don't believe the writings of Moses. Jesus declares this, because He knows that God established Himself to His people through Moses and his writings, his instructions, his teachings: the Torah. This instruction came to Moses directly from the Father – every jot and tittle. That's how Jesus can make such a bold statement regarding Moses. And that's why He does. This is also why Paul warns us regarding the rebellion against Moses in the desert in our premise from 1 Corinthians 10.

Luke 16:19-31 is a parable about two men that die. The good man goes to Abraham's Bosom, while the bad man goes to Sheol-Hades. The bad man sees Abraham from far off – across the chasm that separates them – and asks if he can return to his family to warn them about the afterlife. The Abraham character in Jesus' parable has this to say:

"If they do not hear Moses and the Prophets, neither will they be convinced if someone should rise from the dead.'"
Luke 16:31

Once again, Jesus declares the importance of Moses and his role in the grand scheme of things.

I had to establish a biblical foundation – from Jesus – of the importance of Moses and his teaching since that's the source material Jesus is working with in regard to the scriptural guidelines for worshiping in truth. We find this information in the books of Moses: Exodus and Deuteronomy.

Jesus said to him, "Away from me, Satan! For it is written: 'Worship the Lord your God, and serve him only.'"
Matthew 4:10 (NIV)

Jesus is quoting Deuteronomy 6:13:

It is the LORD your God you shall fear. Him you shall serve and by his name you shall swear.

We see instructions for worship in the Ten Commandments (Ex. 20:3-4). The initial instruction above from Deuteronomy 6:13 is also repeated in

Exodus 34:14:

(for you shall worship no other god, for the LORD, whose name is Jealous, is a jealous God)

Exodus 34 is where we first find these scriptural guidelines on how to worship in truth. This is also where we find the guidelines on how *not* to worship in truth – false and pagan forms of worship. These are outlined in verses 12-17.

Verse 18 begins the "how tos" of worshiping in truth:

"You shall keep the Feast of Unleavened Bread. Seven days you shall eat unleavened bread, as I commanded you, at the time appointed in the month Abib, for in the month Abib you came out from Egypt."

The Feast of Unleavened Bread is a week-long celebration and the first of the three pilgrimage feasts (Ex. 34:23). Most of you probably know it as Passover. This week-long feast includes the observance of Passover, not eating of leavened bread for seven days and the Feast of Firstfruits, which is actually the resurrection of Jesus. The Feast of Un- leavened Bread is the first "how to" of worshiping in truth, contextually, of Exodus 34.

Next on the "how to" of worshiping in truth is the keeping of the Sabbath (Friday sunset to Saturday sunset) in verse 21:

"Six days you shall work, but on the seventh day you shall rest. In plowing time and in harvest you shall rest."

The keeping of God's Sabbath is also the Fourth Commandment of the Ten Commandments found in Exodus 20:8-11.

Back to Exodus 34 with verse 22:

"You shall observe the Feast of Weeks, the firstfruits of wheat harvest, and the Feast of Ingathering at the year's end."

The Feast of Weeks is also known as the Counting of the Omer. It's the 49-day count following the first weekly Sabbath after Passover during the Feast of Unleavened Bread leading us up to the 50th day, also known as Shavuot, "the firstfruits of the wheat harvest" / Pentecost, respectively. Shavuot / Pentecost is the second of the three pilgrimage feasts (Acts 2), and we see Paul in Acts interrupting his missionary travels to return to Jerusalem to keep this observance of worship in Acts 20:16. Again, my book, The Feasts Unlocked, goes into greater detail on all of this.

The third and final pilgrimage feast is the Feast of Ingathering, also known as Booths or The Feast of Tabernacles (which is also when Jesus was actually born).

These Feasts Days are sanctioned / approved forms of "Worshiping in

Truth," the "how tos," for all of God's people – regardless of race or era – by God Himself. Jesus, being this same Word / scriptural passages made flesh, would know this and that these were His Father's preliminary instructions on "worshiping in truth."

And the LORD said to Moses, "Write these words, for ***in accordance with these words I have made a covenant with you*** *and with Israel."*

So he was there with the LORD forty days and forty nights. He neither ate bread nor drank water. And he wrote on the tablets the words of the covenant [Torah], the Ten Commandments.

Exodus 34: 27-28 [Emphasis mine]

As much as this should be common sense, I feel like I should remind us that, as Christians, we acknowledge, recognize and observe the Ten Commandments as foundational orthodoxies of the faith. The contextual instructions of Exodus 34, leading up to verses 27 and 28, must also be recognized as such.

(Source: Aguirre, Allan R. "An Abundance of Obedience," In *This Thing Is Spiritual*, 14-16. Park City, Utah: Planet Blue Media, 2019. http://planetbluemedia.com)

> *But the time is coming and is already here, when by the power of God's Spirit people will worship the Father as he really is, offering him the true worship that he wants.*
> *John 4:23 (GNT)*

So, I asked the Father,

"How do I begin to worship you as You really are by offering You the true worship that You want, because the time is here; the power of God's Spirit is here?" And He said, "Start with My appointed festivals which you are to proclaim as sacred assemblies:"

- The Feast of Unleavened Bread
  - Passover
  - Feast of Firstfruits
- My Sabbath
- The Feast of Weeks
  - Shavuot
  - Pentecost
- The Feast of Ingathering

So, I did.

For more information on how to observe the Feasts of God and worship in Truth, see my book *The Feasts Unlocked* at http://planetbluemedia.com.

○ FIELD NOTES

DATE: / / TIME: : AM/PM PLACE:

○		A±
○		
○		
○		
○		
○		
○		
○		
○		
○		
○		
○		
○		
○		
○		
○		
○		
○		
○		
○		

ARMOR CHECK: Ephesians 6:10-18

Belt of Truth	S☐ M☐ T☐ W☐ T☐ F☐ S☐
Breastplate of Righteousness	S☐ M☐ T☐ W☐ T☐ F☐ S☐
Shoes / Gospel of Peace	S☐ M☐ T☐ W☐ T☐ F☐ S☐
Shield of Faith	S☐ M☐ T☐ W☐ T☐ F☐ S☐
Helmet of Salvation	S☐ M☐ T☐ W☐ T☐ F☐ S☐
Sword of the Spirit / Word of God	S☐ M☐ T☐ W☐ T☐ F☐ S☐

No weapon formed against you will prosper. This is the heritage of the servants of ADONAI.
Is. 54:17

○ WEEK 08
THE DIMENSIONAL REALM OF PRACTICALITY (ROMANS 8:5)

For those who live according to the flesh set their minds on the things of the flesh, but those who live according to the Spirit set their minds on the things of the Spirit.

Outside of the red letters of Jesus, Romans 8, could stand as the foundation of our theology and doctrine. It addresses

- Charismatica;
- Obeying God's commandments (Torah: the "Law" of Moses) as Gentiles in Light of Jesus' Messianic fulfillment;
- Obedience to God's commandments as the outcome of our walking spiritually verses carnally;
- Immortality;
- Physical and spiritual life and death;
- Sonship and inheritance through the Spirit of adoption;
- Suffering;
- Our supernatural role in the scheme of things;
- Our future hope;
- Praying in the Spirit / speaking in tongues and its role and place in our daily life;
- Predestination;
- Our calling, transformation, justification and glorification;

and on and on and on. It would require an entire book to explain what I mean, and entire books have been written, so...

I want to briefly look at the dilemma that arises from our natural tendency to process and react *in* and then resort *to* our physical / carnal mindsets – the flesh – and what I call the dimensional realm of practicality vs processing – walking and responding in the Spirit.

At the top of Mark 6, we find Jesus back in His hometown of Nazareth with his disciples. When the Sabbath arrived, Jesus went and taught in the synagogue:

[...] and many who heard him were amazed. "Where did

this man get these things?" they asked. "What's this wisdom that has been given him? What are these remarkable miracles he is performing?

Isn't this the carpenter? Isn't this Mary's son and the brother of James, Joseph, Judas and Simon? Aren't his sisters here with us?" And they took offense at him.

Mark 6:2b-3

I want to propose that a convergence of dimensional realms occurred that day in the synagogue of Nazareth. Jesus' townspeople could not grasp the fact that this common, everyday man – a carpenter's son, a man they knew from childhood – was a wise miracle worker. And because of that, they were offended by Him. I say "a convergence of dimensional realms," because the "realm" or "dimension" that His townspeople functioned from couldn't comprehend or accept that it was their Jesus that was teaching them with wisdom, power and authority.

The reason for this is quite simple, but even still, I find it amazing how something this "simple" causes so many to walk not only outside of the mandates, mysteries and precepts of God, but how something so simple causes so many to be so offended by Him.

Again, it's an issue with identity: Jesus' perceived identity and the townspeople's lack thereof. Remember when Jesus asked His disciples, "Who do the people say that I am?" in Mt. 16:13-20, Mk 8:27-30 and in Lk 9:18-20, and after revealing to them that He was indeed the promised Messiah, He told them not to tell anyone? Offending people wasn't a surprise to Jesus. He knew that He offended people with His words and actions.

When John the Baptist was in prison and he sent his disciples to ask Jesus if He was truly the Messiah, Jesus ended His list of criteria with

"And blessed is the one who is not offended by me."

Matthew 11:6

This is a crucial point to understand.

Your dimensional realm of understanding and comprehension *cannot* be based on the practical. That realm, that dimension of practicality that we all function from, completely contradicts and opposes "...on earth as it is in heaven." This is why the townspeople couldn't and didn't believe. This is why man has historically struggled with the basic concept of intimacy, obedience and stewardship toward Father God. His dimensional realm isn't our "natural" dimensional realm, and until we make it our natural and live "outside" of our known "realm of practicality," we will continually miss Him.

> *"For my thoughts are not your thoughts, neither are your ways my ways," declares the LORD. "As the heavens are higher than the earth, so are my ways higher than your ways and my thoughts than your thoughts."*
> *Isaiah 55:8-9 (NIV)*

And because of this, many of us choose not to believe. We choose to doubt, and we choose to be offended by the things of God. (By "believe" I don't mean "believing" for salvation, unless, of course, it applies. By this I mean there is so much more for which to believe of Him *after* salvation).

This is the same fear, doubt and unbelief that we have been seeing as the cause of Israel's demise in the desert. Jesus would have known this.

Jesus was incapable of doing any miracles in Nazareth that day, and it says that He was amazed at their lack of faith. Take this simple concept of functioning from a "realm of practicality" as the biggest hindrance in our lives. When we choose to function from a dimensional realm of practicality (fear, doubt, unbelief) – the flesh – we not only miss Him, we render Him powerless in our situation.

Here's a more direct scenario regarding what I'm talking about. Right after revealing Himself to the disciples, Jesus began to tell them of how they were going to go to Jerusalem where Jesus was going to be abused by the elders, the chief priests and the scribes and ultimately be killed by them. Peter took Jesus aside and started to rebuke Him; whereas, Jesus rebuked Peter in return:

> *But Yeshua (Jesus) turned his back on Kefa (Peter), saying, "Get behind me, Satan! You are an obstacle in my path, because **your thinking is from a human perspective, not from God's perspective!**"*
> *Matthew 16:23 (CJB) [Emphasis mine]*

Peter wasn't thinking with God's thoughts or from God's perspective. Peter was thinking from a human perspective with human thoughts. He was functioning from his dimensional realm of practicality – the flesh – and the things *of* the flesh and not according to the Spirit or on the things *of* the Spirit. Jesus called thinking from your dimensional realm – the flesh – demonic: "Get behind me, Satan!"

You might be asking yourself, "How is it possible for us, as mere mortals, to make that leap from thinking from a dimensional realm of practicality – our human perspective, the flesh – to thinking from and with God's dimensional realm of the supernatural, the Spirit?"

Isn't that what your salvation was for – to be saved from your mortal self and your mortal demise? Wasn't the same required by everyone we read about in the Old Testament? Wasn't that the entire purpose for Jesus? Isn't that what He taught all throughout the gospels?

> *Do not be conformed to this world, but* ***be transformed by the renewal of your mind****, that by testing you may discern what is the will of God, what is good and acceptable and perfect.*
> *Romans 12:2 [Emphasis mine]*

That's the purpose behind all of this, isn't it? To be transformed into the image and likeness of Jesus? Yes, it is.

Paul says the power not to conform to the world is accomplished by the renewing and transformation of our minds, *after* we present our bodies as living sacrifices – *holy* living sacrifices – which is our *spiritual worship*. Remember studying about spiritual worship last week? See how all of this contextually connects?

Israel made the choice not to live and walk in the Spirit – in this spiritual and contextual connecting of God's Word. They instead made the choice to walk in their flesh and to process everything that was happening to them with and in their dimensional realm of practicality.

You *cannot* live and walk in the dimensional realm of your practical comprehension and understanding. That realm, that "flesh," that carnal mind that we all function from, completely contradicts and opposes God's Kingdom Lifestyle – our spiritual lives "...on earth as it is in heaven."

> *For to set the mind on the flesh is death, but to set the mind on the Spirit is life and peace. For the mind that is set on* ***the flesh is hostile to God, for it does not submit to God's law****; indeed, it cannot. Those who are in the flesh cannot please God.*
> *Romans 8:6-8 [Emphasis mine]*

The common thread is that success in living for God (in the earth realm, spiritually and not carnally in the flesh) and the mechanics of that spiritual lifestyle (the transforming and renewal of our minds by presenting our bodies as holy, living sacrifices) is all connected to our obedience. The common thread is obedience to God's commandments – His Word, the Torah – as you'll continue to see. We have 43 more weeks to see if that's true or not, both for Israel in the desert and for ourselves in the here and now. It's called the inheritance of sonship...

> *For all who are led by the Spirit of God are sons of God. For you did not receive the spirit of slavery to fall back into fear, but you have received the Spirit of adoption as sons, by whom we cry, "Abba! Father!"*
>
> *Romans 8:14-15*

○ FIELD NOTES

DATE: / / TIME: : AM/PM PLACE:

○		A±
○		
○		
○		
○		
○		
○		
○		
○		
○		
○		
○		
○		
○		
○		
○		
○		
○		
○		
○		

ARMOR CHECK: Ephesians 6:10-18

Belt of Truth	S ☐ M ☐ T ☐ W ☐ T ☐ F ☐ S ☐
Breastplate of Righteousness	S ☐ M ☐ T ☐ W ☐ T ☐ F ☐ S ☐
Shoes / Gospel of Peace	S ☐ M ☐ T ☐ W ☐ T ☐ F ☐ S ☐
Shield of Faith	S ☐ M ☐ T ☐ W ☐ T ☐ F ☐ S ☐
Helmet of Salvation	S ☐ M ☐ T ☐ W ☐ T ☐ F ☐ S ☐
Sword of the Spirit / Word of God	S ☐ M ☐ T ☐ W ☐ T ☐ F ☐ S ☐

No weapon formed against you will prosper. This is the heritage of the servants of ADONAI.
Is. 54:17

○ WEEK 09
PLUMB LINES & MEASURING RODS (AMOS 7:8)

And the Lord said to me, "Amos, what do you see?" And I said, "A plumb line." Then the Lord said, "Behold, I am setting a plumb line in the midst of my people Israel; [...]"

The prophet Amos lived during the forty-year reign of King Jeroboam II, who was king over the northern ten tribes of Israel. Under Jeroboam II, enemies were subdued and conquered, and the fractured relationship with the southern kingdom of Judah was mended, affording the northern kingdom of Israel one of its most prosperous periods.

Many in the north became wealthy and lived luxurious lifestyles that were introduced and influenced by the Phoenicians. Commandments regarding the poor, the practice of justice and lovingkindness were ignored and replaced with this newfound luxurious influence, turning this prosperous era into an age of corruption.

Along with this moral decay was Israel's increasing idolatry:

- Altars in the high places were built to serve the gods of Canaan: the Baals and Ashtarte
- The golden calves built by the first Jeroboam to keep Israel from worshipping in Jerusalem (1 Kings 12:25-33) were worshiped more than ever before, and
- The teachings of the Torah, the holy commandments, were viewed with contempt

Time and time again, prophets were sent by God to warn Israel of the curses foretold by Moses that would befall them. They and the land would be doomed should they stop doing His commandments (Torah), fall into idolatry and not repent.

The prophets went unheeded, and Israel did what was right in their own eyes; going their own way. Sound familiar?

Amos was one of those prophets sent by God.

God established His plumb line – His alignment, His Word – way back in the desert with Moses. He warned Israel what would happen if they didn't toe that line in the same way He warns us through the epistles of the New Testament.

As we have previously discussed, Israel didn't heed that warning *in* the desert or even *after* the desert. So, here we are, more than twelve generations later, and God is still warning Israel to obey. Remember, we are exactly like Israel.

> *"For three transgressions of Judah, and for four, I will not revoke the punishment, because they have rejected the law of the LORD, and have not kept his statutes, but their lies have led them astray, those after which their fathers walked."*
> *Amos 2:4*

To the ten tribes of Israel in the north that would eventually be scattered throughout the globe and assimilated by the gentile nations, He prophesied:

> *"For three transgressions of Israel, and for four, I will not revoke the punishment, because they sell the righteous for silver, and the needy for a pair of sandals-- those who trample the head of the poor into the dust of the earth and turn aside the way of the afflicted; a man and his father go in to the same girl, so that my holy name is profaned; [...]"*
> *Amos 2:6-7*

And it only gets worse. Feel free to continue reading in Amos.

Israel's divided kingdom had a total of 42 kings and one queen. All 19 kings of Israel were evil. Eight out of the 19 kings of Judah were good. This was determined by who kept God's commandments (Torah, the "law") and who didn't. Those that didn't keep God's commandments, statutes and rulings failed to worship God in the manner He determined and prescribed as "truth." Furthermore, they killed God's prophets and served other gods and worshiped them. They introduced false worship and idols into the temple, and they kept the high places – everything they had been warned not to do. The result was that both the people and the land suffered from the godlessness of their leaders, and all turned away from serving the One True God that had delivered them from Egypt.

This is called syncretism; the mixture of the holy and the profane, and we hold to the position that this is highly frowned upon by God (Deut. 12:1-4, 28-32) and strictly forbidden. Yet, Israel's faith, our faith, is riddled with it.

(Source: Aguirre, Allan R. "The Abstinence from Paganism," In *This Thing Is Spiritual*, 33. Park City, Utah: Planet Blue Media, 2019. http://planetbluemedia.com)

Remember our premise – in 1 Corinthians 10, the Apostle Paul is warning us against doing what Israel did in the desert: disobeying God's commandments (Torah, the "law"), His statutes and rulings, and not worshiping God in the manner He determined and prescribed as "truth." He warned us in the desert so that we would be obedient upon entering His Promised Land. God's establishing of a plumb line for Israel once again, hundreds of years later, speaks to His mercy and lovingkindness.

> *Hear this word that the LORD has spoken against you, O people of Israel, against the whole family that I brought up out of the land of Egypt: "You only have I known of all the families of the earth; therefore I will punish you for all your iniquities.*
>
> *Is a trumpet blown in a city, and the people are not afraid? Does disaster come to a city, unless the LORD has done it? For the Lord GOD does nothing without revealing his secret to his servants the prophets. The lion has roared; who will not fear? The Lord GOD has spoken; who can but prophesy?"*
>
> *Amos 3:1-2, 6-8*

He also reminds us of our identity in Him: "You only have I known of all the families of the earth…"

A plumb line has been set in our midst. Alignment.

Maintaining that plumb line of the absolutes found in His Word in our lives and aligning ourselves to and with that measuring rod is crucial in enduring, navigating and accomplishing this amazing journey to our being ingathered by Him.

Now, just in case we're not seeing the correlation with Amos and our premise from 1 Corinthians 10, Paul writes in verse 5, as read in the Complete Jewish Bible translation:

> *Yet with the majority of them God was not pleased, so their bodies were strewn across the desert.*

The prophecy in Amos 8:3 against the northern kingdom of the ten tribes of Israel that would become the gentile nations prophesied by Jacob / Israel in Egypt over Ephraim in Genesis 48:19 states:

"The songs of the temple shall become wailings in that day," declares the Lord GOD. "So many dead bodies!" "They are thrown everywhere!" "Silence!"

A plumb line has been established. Alignment.

Establishing an absolute: "measuring what is right and upright according to His Word" so that we can know whether it's "plumb" or not.

(Source: Hal Sacks. October 2014. YouTube)

God establishes His plumb lines throughout our lives as markers, measuring rods. These markers / measuring rods are established to keep us on course and lead us into repentance, when necessary, by realigning us with His absolutes and the characteristics of His Spirit:

- Obedience to His commandments
- Remembering the poor
- The practice of justice and lovingkindness

Amos said it like this:

"Seek me and live;

Seek good, and not evil, that you may live; and so the LORD, the God of hosts, will be with you, as you have said.

Hate evil, and love good, and establish justice in the gate; it may be that the LORD, the God of hosts, will be gracious to the remnant of Joseph."

Amos 5:14-15

...because G-d has chosen them as His people, He demands of them higher standards, and, like a loving father punishes his erring son just because he loves him, so G-d would punish them for their sins.

(Source: Mindel, Nissan. "The Prophet Amos," *Chabad.org: https://www.chabad.org/library/article_cdo/aid/112277/jewish/The-Prophet-Amos.htm*)

Because God has also chosen us, Gentiles, as His people (Eph. 2) through His Spirit of adoption, He also demands the same higher standard from us as He does His native Israel. And, like a loving Father, He punishes his children, regardless, because He loves them.

Thankfully, He has set plumb lines and measuring rods in our lives with which we can align ourselves to seek Him and live, to seek good and not evil, to hate evil and to love good and to establish justice within our gates.

The shed blood of Messiah, of Jesus, and our receiving of that sacrifice on our behalf brought us into this Hebraic family of God through adoption as Paul constantly wrote about.

The power of Holy Spirit gives us the wherewithal to make those remeasurements and realignments to those established plumb lines and measuring rods we find in the absolutes of God's Word.

Make a list of those realignments and remeasurements when they come up. Record them as "provisioning ideas" to assist you in moving ever forward – further up and further in – on your amazing journey from exodus to the ingathering of the Bride for the Marriage Supper of the Lamb. Hallelujah!

○ FIELD NOTES

DATE: / / TIME: : AM/PM PLACE:

○		A±
○		
○		
○		
○		
○		
○		
○		
○		
○		
○		
○		
○		
○		
○		
○		
○		
○		
○		
○		

ARMOR CHECK: Ephesians 6:10-18

Belt of Truth	S ☐	M ☐	T ☐	W ☐	T ☐	F ☐	S ☐
Breastplate of Righteousness	S ☐	M ☐	T ☐	W ☐	T ☐	F ☐	S ☐
Shoes / Gospel of Peace	S ☐	M ☐	T ☐	W ☐	T ☐	F ☐	S ☐
Shield of Faith	S ☐	M ☐	T ☐	W ☐	T ☐	F ☐	S ☐
Helmet of Salvation	S ☐	M ☐	T ☐	W ☐	T ☐	F ☐	S ☐
Sword of the Spirit / Word of God	S ☐	M ☐	T ☐	W ☐	T ☐	F ☐	S ☐

No weapon formed against you will prosper. This is the heritage of the servants of ADONAI.
Is. 54:17

○ WEEK 10
I WHO SPEAK TO YOU AM HE
(JOHN 4:25-26)

The woman said to him, "I know that Messiah is coming (he who is called Christ). When he comes, he will tell us all things." Jesus said to her, "I who speak to you am he."

The Pharisees had heard that Jesus was baptizing more people than John. This put Jesus even more on their radar and at the top of their list.

After the week-long Feast of Unleavened Bread, to avoid a confrontation with the Pharisees, Jesus departs Jerusalem for the Galilee, a trek that had Him crossing through Samaria.

Around noon, and weary from His journey, Jesus stops at Jacob's well for a drink in the Samaritan town of Sychar while the disciples go into town.

While He sat there resting at the well,

A woman from Samaria came to draw water. Jesus said to her, "Give me a drink." (For his disciples had gone away into the city to buy food.) The Samaritan woman said to him, "How is it that you, a Jew, ask for a drink from me, a woman of Samaria?" (For Jews have no dealings with Samaritans.)
John 4:7-9

Thus begins one of the most engaging conversations found in the Gospels.

A main premise for my book, *This Thing Is Spiritual*, is found in this conversation between a Gentile Samaritan woman and our Jewish Messiah. Their conversation includes the following:

- Living water
- Genealogy
- Eternal Life
- Mundane chores
- Marriage and Divorce
- Sexual immorality

- The prophetic
- Theology and Doctrine
- Worship
- Salvation comes from the Jews
- True Worshipers
- Spiritual and true worship
- What the Father seeks
- God is Spirit
- Messianic prophesy, and
- And that Jesus is indeed the Promised Messiah of the world.

Wow...

Just then, states John's narrative, the disciples came back and "marveled" and were "greatly surprised," "astonished," "shocked" and "amazed" to find Jesus talking with a woman, (some suggest "that *kind* of a woman") but they didn't say anything.

Commentaries suggest that the disciples were surprised to find Jesus talking in public with a woman because

1. It was contrary to a direct rabbinical precept to do so,
2. Rabbis considered it a scandalous act for a man of distinction, and
3. Tradition forbade it.

Gill's Exposition of the Entire Bible states:

[...] according to the Jewish canons, it was not judged decent, right, and proper, nor indeed lawful, to enter into a conversation, or hold any long discourse with a woman. Their rule is this,

"do not multiply discourse with a woman, with his wife they say, much less with his neighbour's wife: hence the wise men say, at whatsoever time a man multiplies discourse with a woman, he is the cause of evil to himself, and ceases from the words of the law, and at last shall go down into hell (a)."

And especially this was thought to be very unseemly in any public place, as in an inn, or in the street: hence that direction (b),

"let not a man talk with a woman in the streets, even with his wife; and there is no need to say with another man's wife."

And particularly it was thought very unbecoming a religious man, a doctor, or scholar, or a disciple of a wise man so to do. This is one of the six things which are a reproach to a scholar, "to talk with a woman in the street" (c). And it is even said (d),

"let him not talk with a woman in the street, though she is his wife, or his

sister, or his daughter."
(a) Pirke Abot, c. 1. sect. 5. Abot R, Nathan, c. 7. fol. 3. 3. & Derech Eretz, fol. 17. 3. (b) Bemidbar Rabba, sect 10. fol. 200. 2. (c) T. Bab. Beracot, fol. 43. 2. (d) Maimon. Hilch. Dayot, c. 5. sect. 7.

Either way, it is suggested that the disciples

had such respect and reverence for him that they did not dare to ask him the reason of his conduct, or even to appear to reprove him.

(Source: *Barnes' Notes on the Bible*)

For whatever reason, I love the fact that my Jesus didn't necessarily always play by the rules. When you realize that there are three women of questionable or even ill repute in His family line, this conversation, and the fact that He revealed who He was to her, isn't all that surprising. He's a regular guy having a regular convo around the water cooler, and He's telling this woman all about herself, and that's going to change the entire dynamic of that village. I'm all for that.

In fact, there is more "outside the lines" found in the scriptural narrative than many people want to admit or are comfortable with – for example the fact that there are three questionable women in the bloodline of Messiah. We should be more offended by the fact that we have a religious spirit than by what the Spirit of God actually says and does. Do we really think that our "human sensibilities" will actually sway the heart and mind of the King of the Universe?!?

Even more astonishing than the fact that he was publicly speaking to her is the fact that He revealed Himself to her. Many believe this was the first and only time that He directly and openly declared to a human who He was – and to a gentile female, no less!

"And blessed is the one who is not offended by me."
Jesus in Matthew 11:6

This Samaritan woman leaves Jesus with His disciples and her water pot at the well to tell everyone in town about the man that told her everything that she has ever done.

If you have ever been around the spiritual gifts of prophecy, discernment, words of knowledge, words of wisdom, etc., then you know how quickening this is to your spirit. This Samaritan woman has just had her mail read by Messiah!

While she is back in town letting all the townsfolk know that the literal

Messiah is at their well, the usual game of flesh vs spirit ping pong between Jesus and His disciples commences:

The disciples, functioning from their dimensional realm of practicality, try to get Jesus to eat.

Jesus, anticipant of what was about to happen, retorts in the spiritual.

The disciples counter even deeper in the physical, and Jesus begins to, once again, speak to them in agricultural metaphors – "feast speak" (Jn 4:31-38).

I love the way Michael Rood puts what happens next:

{Jn 4:35:1} The Hebrew agricultural term afil refers to immature grain, the stalks and leaves of which are "dark" (Exodus 9:32), while barley grain that has reached the stage of aviv is both "light in color" and "ready for the harvest." Yeshua, looking back over the shoulders of his disciples coming from the city, saw thousands of Samaritans walking toward him with their white jalabeas blowing in the breeze. With excitement pounding in his heart and with a lump in his throat, he knew that the time of the harvest of the gentiles was now at hand and not in the distant future.

(Source: Rood, Michael John "Passover through Shavuot 4027," In *The Chronological Gospels*, 85. Fort Mill, SC: Aviv Moon Publishing, 2012)

> *Many Samaritans from that town believed in him because of the woman's testimony, "He told me all that I ever did." So when the Samaritans came to him, they asked him to stay with them, and he stayed there two days. And many more believed because of his word.*
> *John 4:39-41*

Isn't that amazing? What an incredible evangelistic model that Jesus functioned in and taught His disciples to also follow and teach to *their* disciples: back up the spoken word of the Gospel of Peace with supernatural signs and wonders. I am so grateful that this is the same model I was brought up with after coming to Jesus 40 years ago.

Staying with these Samaritans in their town for two days is significant, especially considering that Jesus is going to instruct the original twelve in the coming months not to go among the Gentiles or enter any town of the Samaritans when He sends them out. Sounds like another nugget to unpack…

I think the goal of every teacher or pastor should be to want to hear the words spoken by the people of Sychar that day – the day that Jesus invaded the life and town of a Samaritan woman:

They said to the woman, "We no longer believe just because of what you said; now ***we have heard for ourselves****, and* ***we know that this man really is the Savior*** *of the world."*
John 4:42 (NIV) [Emphasis mine]

To hear for yourself and to know that He is indeed the Savior – that's my goal for you, dear and precious reader…

○ FIELD NOTES

DATE: / / TIME: : AM/PM PLACE:

○		A±
○		
○		
○		
○		
○		
○		
○		
○		
○		
○		
○		
○		
○		
○		
○		
○		
○		
○		
○		

ARMOR CHECK: Ephesians 6:10-18

Belt of Truth	S ☐ M ☐ T ☐ W ☐ T ☐ F ☐ S ☐
Breastplate of Righteousness	S ☐ M ☐ T ☐ W ☐ T ☐ F ☐ S ☐
Shoes / Gospel of Peace	S ☐ M ☐ T ☐ W ☐ T ☐ F ☐ S ☐
Shield of Faith	S ☐ M ☐ T ☐ W ☐ T ☐ F ☐ S ☐
Helmet of Salvation	S ☐ M ☐ T ☐ W ☐ T ☐ F ☐ S ☐
Sword of the Spirit / Word of God	S ☐ M ☐ T ☐ W ☐ T ☐ F ☐ S ☐

No weapon formed against you will prosper. This is the heritage of the servants of ADONAI.
Is. 54:17

○ WEEK 11
SHAVUOT (WEEKS) / PENTECOST
(LEVITICUS 23:17, 20-21)

"You shall bring from your dwelling places two loaves of bread to be waved. They shall be of fine flour, and they shall be baked with leaven, as firstfruits to the LORD. And the priest shall wave the bread of the firstfruits as a wave offering before the LORD. They shall be holy to the LORD for the priest. And you shall make proclamation on the same day. You shall hold a holy convocation (a High Sabbath). You shall not do any ordinary work. It is a statute forever in all your dwelling places throughout your generations."

SHAVUOT

"In Exodus 19, we see that Moses and all of Israel have assembled before the Living God, per His instructions, at the base of Mount Sinai. This is when and where God established His instructions in written form for those that would call upon His name – His instructions for mankind, for those that make the voluntary decision to serve Him – His covenant instructions for those who call themselves "believers."

"This was the reason they had traveled those difficult and endless 40-some-odd days from Egypt to Sinai.

So Moses came and called the elders of the people and set before them all these words that the LORD had commanded him. All the people answered together and said, "All that the LORD has spoken we will do." And Moses reported the words of the people to the LORD.

When Moses told the words of the people to the LORD, the LORD said to Moses, "Go to the people and consecrate them today and tomorrow, and let them wash their garments and be ready for the third day. For on the third day the LORD will come down on Mount Sinai in the sight of all the people."
Exodus 19:7-8, 9b-11

"Three days later, there was a blast from a shofar summoning Israel to Mount Sinai where there was smoke, fire and earthquakes while the shofar's blast grew louder and louder. When God finally spoke, it sounded like thunder. He gave them the Ten Commandments while everyone listened to His thunderous voice in fear.

> *Now when all the people saw the thunder and the flashes of lightning and the sound of the shofar and the mountain smoking, the people were afraid and trembled, and they stood far off and said to Moses, "You speak to us, and we will listen; but do not let God speak to us, lest we die."*
> *Exodus 20:18-19*

"That long-standing identity of fear as a people was now keeping them from the very reason God delivered them from Egypt: covenant relationship.

> *"...**if you will indeed obey my voice and keep my covenant**, you shall be my treasured possession among all peoples, you shall be to me a kingdom of priests and a holy nation."*
> *Exodus 19:5-6 [Emphasis mine]*

"Instead of desiring that personal relationship with ADONAI – the relationship He also desired for them – a relationship that required / requires "obeying His voice" and "keeping His covenants," they balked out of fear and opted for Moses to be their mediator:

> *"You speak to us, and we will listen; but do not let God speak to us, lest we die."*

"This gripping and debilitating fear, their identity, was keeping Israel from wanting to hear His voice, "...lest we die," and it would continue to stand in the way of their relational obedience to God. In addition, this same fear and stubbornness would cause them to reject His prophets as well and, consequently, Messiah.

"Moses drew near to the thick darkness where God was manifest as He set out the parameters of the Covenant and His promises of their eventual and successful possession of the land of Canaan.

"In Exodus 24, Moses tells Israel everything ADONAI spoke, including His rules, and to that the entire assembly responded with a resounding, *"Na'aseh v'nishma"* – "All these words and rulings that ADONAI has spoken '*we will do and we will hear / understand.*'" Then Moses wrote down all that ADONAI had spoken. An altar was built, and twelve pillars representing the twelve tribes were erected. Burnt offerings and peace offerings were made.

"The Covenant was confirmed. Moses went back up into the mountain for 40 days and nights while God gave him the rest of Torah, the commandments, for their instruction.

PENTECOST

"Acts 2 tells us that it was the "day of Pentecost." Strong's #G4005 *"penthkosthv"*:

Pentecost = "the fiftieth day"

1. the second of the three great Jewish feasts, celebrated at Jerusalem yearly, the seventh week after the Passover, in grateful recognition of the completed harvest

"Even the Greek speaks of Shavuot.

"It was the 50th day of the Omer count, Shavuot, and 120 disciples were waiting in Jerusalem in an upper room as Jesus had instructed them 10 days earlier (Lk. 24:49; Ac 1:4). Being the second of the three pilgrimage feasts meant that all firstborn males were in Jerusalem celebrating the completed wheat harvest and the giving of Torah on Mount Sinai. Then, the whirlwind of the Holy Spirit came. With the advent of Pentecost, Shavuot now prophetically pointed to Mount Zion, not just Mount Sinai.

"Read Hebrews 12:18-29 for an amazing perspective on the merger of these two events.

"Because of the fulfillment of Messiah at Passover (death), the Feast of Unleavened Bread (burial) and the Feast of Firstfruits (resurrection), and because of the indwelling of the Holy Spirit at Pentecost, the Covenant made at Sinai, Shavuot, is attainable (Zion)! Torah was given, and the covenant to keep those instructions occurred at Sinai: Shavuot. Messiah rose from the dead, the power of Holy Spirit – the fire of Sinai – fell as covenant fire on those in the upper room to keep those instructions for Zion's sake: Pentecost (Ac 2:1-4).

"So while all of Jerusalem was reaffirming their covenant with Torah during the second of the three pilgrimage festivals, God was indwelling Israel with His Spirit and repositioning Torah to its original place: the invisible intentions of the heart (Mt. 5).

Just as the resurrection of Yeshua represents the Firstfruits of those who have died (1 Cor. 15:20) and fulfills the prophetic ritual of the waving of the omer on the festival of First Fruits, so the giving of the Holy Spirit to the church fulfills the wave offering of the wheat loaves on the day of Shavuot.

(Source: John J. Parsons, "Shavuot - Revelation and the Fruit of the Spirit," In *Hebrew for Christians,* http://www.hebrew4christians.com/Holidays/Spring_Holidays/Shavuot/shavuot.html)

"The 50th day of the Omer count is a High Shabbat of rejoicing. You are to bring a freewill firstfruits offering and also offer, as a firstfruits wave offering, two loaves of baked leavened bread made of flour.

"We see how God betrothed Himself to Israel through the giving of Torah as His marriage contract. Israel failed to consummate the wedding ceremony at Sinai, but a final way for covenant was made in Messiah. We see that Jesus is the Bridegroom, and believers are betrothed to Him. Jesus is man's final hope for that consummation – the consummation of "I will take (marry) you (the bride) to be my people (my wife), and I (the Bridegroom) will be your God (your Husband).

"We see this in Exodus 6:7, and we see it again in Revelation 21:3:

> *I will take you to be my people, and I will be your God, and you shall know that I am the LORD your God, who has brought you out from under the burdens of the Egyptians.*

> *And I heard a loud voice from the throne saying, "Behold, the dwelling place of God is with man. He will dwell with them, and they will be his people, and God himself will be with them as their God.*

"This is the gospel!

"This is God's "Master Plan:" the Wedding Feast of the Passover Lamb that was slain before the foundations of the earth.

"Our future, as seen in John's Revelation, started all the way back in Egypt!

"For more about being His people and His being our God, see also: Gen. 17:7-8; Exod. 29:45; Lev. 11:45; 25:38; 26:12; Num. 15:41; Psa. 81:10; Jer. 7:23; 11:4; 30:22; 31:1, 33; 32:38; Ezek. 11:20; 14:11; 34:31; 37:23, 27; Zech. 8:8; 2 Cor. 6:16 (quotes Lev. 26:12; Exod. 6:7; Jer. 31:32; 32:38; Ezek. 37:27); Heb. 8:10 (is a requote of Jer. 31:30-33); Rev. 21:7;

"Thus, with Shavuot / Pentecost, we conclude the Passover season with the counting of the Omer linking the two pilgrimage feasts together."

(Taken from "Shavuot (Weeks) / Pentecost," In *The Feasts Unlocked.* Park City, Utah: Planet Blue Media, 2018. http://planetbluemedia.com)

○ FIELD NOTES

DATE: / / TIME: : AM/PM PLACE:

○		A±
○		
○		
○		
○		
○		
○		
○		
○		
○		
○		
○		
○		
○		
○		
○		
○		
○		
○		
○		

ARMOR CHECK: Ephesians 6:10-18

Belt of Truth	S ☐ M ☐ T ☐ W ☐ T ☐ F ☐ S ☐
Breastplate of Righteousness	S ☐ M ☐ T ☐ W ☐ T ☐ F ☐ S ☐
Shoes / Gospel of Peace	S ☐ M ☐ T ☐ W ☐ T ☐ F ☐ S ☐
Shield of Faith	S ☐ M ☐ T ☐ W ☐ T ☐ F ☐ S ☐
Helmet of Salvation	S ☐ M ☐ T ☐ W ☐ T ☐ F ☐ S ☐
Sword of the Spirit / Word of God	S ☐ M ☐ T ☐ W ☐ T ☐ F ☐ S ☐

No weapon formed against you will prosper. This is the heritage of the servants of ADONAI.
Is. 54:17

○ WEEK 12
THE CHAMELEON-LIKE ABILITY (MATTHEW 14:15-18)

Now when it was evening, the disciples came to him and said, "This is a desolate place, and the day is now over; send the crowds away to go into the villages and buy food for themselves." But Jesus said, "They need not go away; you give them something to eat." They said to him, "We have only five loaves here and two fish." And he said, "Bring them here to me."

Jesus summoned the Twelve and started sending them out in pairs, giving them authority over demons, evil and unclean spirits and to cure diseases. He instructed them to take nothing for their journeys except a staff – no bread, no bag and no money in their belts. They were to wear sandals but not to take an extra tunic. They were also to stay in the same guest home for the duration of their stay in that particular town.

When they returned to report to Jesus all that they had done and taught, there were so many people coming and going in and out of their small fishing town of Capernaum that they couldn't even take time out to eat. Jesus suggested that they go away together to a secluded place where they could rest.

Now many saw them going and recognized them, and they ran there on foot from all the towns and got there ahead of them.

When he went ashore he saw a great crowd, and he had compassion on them, because they were like sheep without a shepherd. And he began to teach them many things.
Mark 6:33-34

Matthew says that Jesus also healed their sick. Luke states that Jesus took the disciples to Bethsaida, and upon seeing the crowd, He welcomed them and spoke about Kingdom. John says the people followed because they "saw the signs He was doing on the sick and diseased." People are attracted to miracles, signs and wonders. Take note of that. (Also, take note that John 6:4 states that it was almost Passover. That can't be the case, especially when chapter seven starts with Jesus going to Jerusalem for the Feast of Tabernacles 18 days later.

Passover to Tabernacles are 7.5-months apart – not 18 days apart. Jesus would also be in Jerusalem for the Feast, not the Galilee. This single verse doesn't coincide with the chronological time frame established by all four gospels.)

Where were we? Oh yeah, the disciples… They had an agenda that day – rest and relaxation with their beloved Rabbi – and rightly so. I use the word "agenda," because the plan was for them to go to "...a place where we can be alone and rest awhile," not "let's minister to a crowd of people."

A major convergence between the dimensions of heaven and earth was about to take place. Something was about to happen that would quicken the need for the disciples to step outside their own "dimensional realm of practicality." Let's take a look.

The hour was late. Matthew, Mark and Luke have the disciples coming to Jesus and telling Him the obvious: they're in a desolate place, it's late, people are hungry, send them away to neighboring towns for food and lodging, and Jesus answers them, "You give them something to eat." John's account has Jesus going up to Philip and asking him:

> *"Where are we to buy bread, so that these people may eat?"*
>
> *He said this to test him, for he himself knew what he would do. Philip answered him, "Two hundred denarii would not buy enough bread for each of them to get a little."*
> *John 6:5b-7*

Two hundred denarii was roughly eight months' wages.

"You feed them…"

Some of you are thinking, "How else were they supposed to respond?" The disciples' response was practical. Instead, let's put ourselves in this scenario with what we "know" to be true, and we'll see that even though we know, oftentimes we still choose to function from our dimensional realm of practicality – our flesh.

We "know" that when Jesus speaks, it will be done. It will come to pass. What differentiates us from all other religions and belief systems is that we serve a risen Savior and a God that isn't a man that he would lie – a Good Father to that Savior that gives us bread when we ask and not a rock; fish and not a snake.

Every Christian would agree to this. Yet the majority of us respond in the very same way the disciples did when told to feed the multitude. Jesus speaks, and we look at how many zeros we have – or don't have – in our bank accounts. We determine that what Jesus is asking of us isn't practical, or we decide it's not really Him speaking at all – both responses go hand in hand. Others of us are offended by what He may be asking... and we all know that, practically speaking, God would never ask or require of us anything impractical or anything that would offend... (That was sarcasm…)

Here's a basic rundown of how it usually works:

1. Jesus speaks: This is a good start. It means that He's your shepherd, and you're His sheep, and you know His voice. An important first step.
2. We usually begin the practical process of disqualification: no money; lack of skills and giftings; is it really You, Lord, etc.
3. He speaks again: He asks us what we do have. What are our resources? Again, it's crucial for you to be in a place to hear that question. It's almost more important than step one, because 80% of us can't hear Him this second time.
4. Our response: We'll always be able to come up with a resource if we really look.
5. He then asks us for this resource: He takes it from us, blesses it, consecrates it and then gives it back to us and tells us to do what He originally told us to do in the first place!
6. The lesson: Once we will to do His will, He provides the resources necessary to accomplish His will.

Here's the above example from Mark 6:37-44 (NIV)

1. But he answered, "You give them something to eat."
2. They said to him, "That would take more than half a year's wages! Are we to go and spend that much on bread and give it to them to eat?"
3. "How many loaves do you have?" he asked. "Go and see."
4. When they found out, they said, "Five — and two fish."
5. Then Jesus directed them to have all the people sit down in groups on the green grass. So they sat down in groups of hundreds and fifties. Taking the five loaves and the two fish and looking up to heaven, he gave thanks (blessed it) and broke the loaves. Then he gave them to his disciples to distribute to the

people. He also divided the two fish among them all.

6. They all ate and were satisfied, and the disciples picked up twelve basketfuls of broken pieces of bread and fish. The number of the men who had eaten was five thousand.

So, what just happened here?

Obviously, a huge convergence of dimensional realms – an example of the power of heaven here on earth – just occurred.

The disciples had just recently received authority and power over evil and unclean spirits and all manner of sickness. They had just come back from driving out "..many demons" and anointing "..many sick people with oil and healing them." Essentially, Jesus was asking these men early on in their relationship to function *in* and *from* a deeper level of understanding of scriptural teaching.

For the sake of argument, to some extent, these men would have known and might have possibly been raised on the Teachings of Moses (*Tora*h), the Prophets (*Nevi'im*) and the Old Testament (*Tanakh*) in general. Now, Jesus was challenging them to actually function in the same dimensional realm that He Himself functioned from simply because they should have known that it was in their power to do so. I make this potentially-bold statement for the following two reasons:

They would have known what scripture stated about them as Hebrews, and their Rabbi was already functioning from that realm and dimensional plane. As Israeli men, they would have known about the promises, covenants, blessings and favor over their lives as taught in scripture. Of course, reading and believing these things is another thing entirely and the same holds true for us today. We often find ourselves lost in our own identity crisis:

- Who and what the scriptures *say* I am
- Who I *think* and *believe* I am

The second reason is the rabbi / disciple relationship. Rabbis handpick their disciples. They choose disciples in whom they feel they can successfully duplicate themselves. The goal of a rabbi is to raise up disciples that will surpass them. That's the sign of a good rabbi. They knew this. They also knew that what Rabbi does, they can do too.

With these two things in mind, they surely would have known or heard of Deuteronomy 8 and the promises and stipulations of blessings upon entering the Promised Land and of God's favor over them as a people. Let's take a quick look at Deuteronomy 8:18:

You shall remember the LORD your God, for it is he who gives you power to get wealth, that he may confirm his covenant that he swore to your fathers, as it is this day.

The Hebrew word for "power" in this verse is *"koach"* (Strongs #H03581): a small reptile, a kind of lizard, chameleon.

The Hebrew word for "get" or "make" is *"`asah"* (Strongs #H06213): to act, act with effect, to create, to create from nothing.

This word *`asah* is also used in Genesis 1:26:

And God said, Let us make (`asah*) man in our image...*

Deuteronomy 8:18 is then basically saying "...you are to remember ADONAI your God, because it is He who is giving you the power (*"koach,"* the chameleon-like ability) to make (*"`asah"*, create out of nothing, to work with the substance of creation) wealth..."

Chameleons have the ability to adapt to any situation, any environment, any economy, any climate and to create the necessary resources that are conducive to their own success. This is why Isaac is able to go to the land of famine, increase in flocks, herds, etc., and reap 100-fold from that famine-infested land (Gn. 26).

Because of his covenant relationship and his understanding of *who* and *what* he was, Isaac was able to create the necessary resources conducive to his own success. A deeper look into the line of Abraham (Gn. 24) reveals an example of how this "chameleon-like ability" of spiritual authority, blessing and power is transferable.

The chameleon-like ability to work with the substance of creation – to make something out of nothing – is powerful. It also can't be manipulated. This spiritual authority requires one to be functioning deeply in three basic areas of personal relationship with Father God through the blood covenant of Jesus via an interactive relationship with the Holy Spirit:

- Extreme intimacy
- Extreme obedience
- Extreme stewardship

We must be confident in our identity as far as *knowing* who we are: a royal priesthood; a people with a spiritual kingly and priestly anointing. And then we must *believe* this is who we are: joint heirs with Messiah; functioning as sons and daughters of our Father, the living King of the Universe. This is how we'll walk in the spiritual authority expected and desired of us by our Father.

The disciples were being taught this, and today's lesson used five loaves of leavened bread (another clue that it wasn't Passover) and two small fish. I love the mundane simplicity that He tends to use to teach us.

Jesus was challenging the disciples into deeper realms of "on earth as it is in heaven." At some point, while they were breaking up pieces of bread and fish, it had to kick in: "this is really happening…!" They were working with the *`asah*, the substance of creation!

Jesus was provoking and testing His disciples as the Gospel of John says, because He knew what He was going to do. He also knew that they were going to have to pick up the pace, as they soon would see, because Jesus would be leaving them soon.

We also need to understand that Jesus is provoking and testing us, His disciples, because of what we prophetically know He's about to do. He also knows that we're going to have to pick up the pace, as we're hopefully seeing, because Jesus will be returning soon.

Welcome to Chameleon Church…

○ FIELD NOTES

DATE: / / **TIME:** : AM/PM **PLACE:**

		A±
○		
○		
○		
○		
○		
○		
○		
○		
○		
○		
○		
○		
○		
○		
○		
○		
○		
○		
○		
○		

ARMOR CHECK: Ephesians 6:10-18

Belt of Truth	S ☐	M ☐	T ☐	W ☐	T ☐	F ☐	S ☐
Breastplate of Righteousness	S ☐	M ☐	T ☐	W ☐	T ☐	F ☐	S ☐
Shoes / Gospel of Peace	S ☐	M ☐	T ☐	W ☐	T ☐	F ☐	S ☐
Shield of Faith	S ☐	M ☐	T ☐	W ☐	T ☐	F ☐	S ☐
Helmet of Salvation	S ☐	M ☐	T ☐	W ☐	T ☐	F ☐	S ☐
Sword of the Spirit / Word of God	S ☐	M ☐	T ☐	W ☐	T ☐	F ☐	S ☐

No weapon formed against you will prosper. This is the heritage of the servants of ADONAI.
Is. 54:17

○ WEEK 13
THE GIANTS SHALL BE YOUR BREAD (NUMBERS 14:9)

"Only do not rebel against the LORD. And do not fear the people of the land, for they are bread for us. Their protection is removed from them, and the LORD is with us; do not fear them."

Numbers 13 and 14 are both exhilarating and tragic at the same time (see also Dt. 1:19-45). Exhilarating because they're about to walk into a 400-year-old prophecy! Tragic because, well... these two chapters deal so much with what we've been studying:

- Prophetic destiny
- The inheritance of Sonship
- New wine and our accommodating of God's new thing
- Identity – always identity
- Going forward and the trust that it takes
- Our realm of practicality that constantly battles with God's spiritual reality, and so on...

In Numbers 13, God instructs Moses to send 12 men, 12 spies representing the 12 tribes of Israel, into the land of Canaan. This is Israel's prophetic inheritance, the land of which Abraham walked the borders. Their mission?

- See if the land is good or bad, rich or poor.
- Are the people strong or weak, few or many?
- Do the people live in cities, camps or strongholds?
- Does the land have trees? If so, bring back fruit samples, etc.

Their expedition would last 40 days and cover a vast amount of the terrain and territory.

They went up into the Negeb and came to Hebron. Ahiman, Sheshai, and Talmai, the descendants of Anak, were there. (Hebron was built seven years before Zoan in Egypt.) And they came to the Valley of Eshcol and cut down from there a branch with a single cluster of grapes, and they carried it on a pole between two

of them;
Numbers 13:22-23a

Remember discussing the iniquity of the Amorites on Week 01? We discussed how the Amorites were a powerful people of great stature "like the height of the cedars." Giants; a remnant of the Rephaim and descendants of the Nephilim of Genesis 6. Well, the descendants of Anak, forefather of the Anakim, were also very tall descendants of the Nephilim, and they occupied the land. The spies returned after 40 days with the following report:

> *"We came to the land to which you sent us. It flows with milk and honey, and this is its fruit. However, the people who dwell in the land are strong, and the cities are fortified and very large. And besides, we saw the descendants of Anak there. The Amalekites dwell in the land of the Negeb."*
> *Numbers 13:27-29*

The news of Nephilim in the land was troublesome to a people that complained about everything and were already convinced that God only wanted to kill them out there in the desert. Thus, they began their usual clamoring and dissension.

Two of the 12 spies – Joshua, Moses' assistant, and Caleb, leader of the Tribe of Judah – tried calming the people down and encouraged them that they could overthrow the inhabitants and possess and conquer the land. Unfortunately, the other ten spies put fear, doubt and unbelief in the hearts of the people; causing them to "think rationally" and to process the report "practically" and to "lean on their own understanding:"

> *Then the men who had gone up with him said, "We are not able to go up against the people, for they are stronger than we are." So they brought to the people of Israel a bad report of the land that they had spied out, saying, "The land, through which we have gone to spy it out, is a land that devours its inhabitants, and all the people that we saw in it are of great height. And there we saw the Nephilim (the sons of Anak, who come from the Nephilim), and we seemed to ourselves like grasshoppers, and so we seemed to them."*
> *Numbers 13:31-33*

So, the people rebelled. Again. They yelled out in dismay and cried themselves to sleep that night. They grumbled more than usual against Moses and Aaron, saying, "Dying in Egypt (translation: separated from God) or in this desert by now would have been better than this." "Why is God bringing us to die in battle in this land? Our wives and children will become prey. Wouldn't it be best to go back to Egypt now?" and began the dialog to choose a leader that would lead them back to Egypt.

Read that paragraph again. This is such an important piece to the failure or success of your amazing journey from exodus to ingathering that I want to make sure I've explained the severity of what Israel is doing.

The people rebelled. How did they rebel?

- They threw a temper tantrum, yelling in a panic and crying themselves to sleep.
- They grumbled / complained to the leadership and verbally assaulted them.
- They professed / confessed that death in bondage (Egypt) was better than God's plan for their lives – the Promised Land.
- They professed / confessed that death in general was better than God's plan for their lives – prophetic destiny.
- They believed in their heart that God's plan was too difficult and futile to accomplish.
- They believed that God brought them to this point to die by the hands of the Nephilim in battle.
- They truly believed that they were going to die and that their families would become prey to the enemy.
- These ideas in their hearts and minds – this practical, rational and emotional thought process – led them to conclude that going back into bondage – Egypt, separation from God – was the best course of action and began making plans to go back.

Moses and Aaron fell on their faces before the Living God on behalf of these people. Israel, individually and corporately, could not understand or see that they were sinning. Joshua and Caleb tore their clothes,

> *and said to all the congregation of the people of Israel, "The land, which we passed through to spy it out, is an exceedingly good land. If the Lord delights in us, he will bring us into this land and give it to us, a land that flows with milk and honey.* ***Only do not rebel against the Lord. And do not fear the people of the land****, for they are bread for us. Their protection is removed from them, and the Lord is with us; do not fear them." Then all the congregation said to stone them with stones. But the glory of the Lord appeared*

at the tent of meeting to all the people of Israel.

And the Lord said to Moses, "How long will this people despise me? And how long will they not believe in me, in spite of all the signs that I have done among them? I will strike them with the pestilence and disinherit them, and I will make of you a nation greater and mightier than they."

Numbers 14:7-12 [Emphasis mine]

Wow. Joshua and Caleb are attempting to talk down people who are besides themselves. Is it possible that the entire assembly has allowed themselves to fall into a demonic, spiritual terror?

I say this because of what happens: Joshua and Caleb's declaration of truth and sound reasoning is completely lost on the people. They are not of sound mind. They're terrified, and their reaction is to stone them. Kill them. So great was their propensity for sin, their hearts so far removed from what God was doing, that He appeared before them to stop them from sinning further by murdering God's elect.

Meditate on this for a moment...

"How long will this people despise me?

How long will they not believe in me, in spite of all the signs that I have done among them?"

God is asking you. God is asking us. Right now... the same questions. How long?

The sin of the people was so great that God was going to disinherit them. *Disinherit them!*

Oh, Father... mercy, Father... mercy...

God was going to disinherit Israel and start over with Moses and his offspring alone.

How could the fear, doubt and unbelief of Israel in the face of this demonic strain of humanity upon the earth, the Nephilim, be such a great sin in the eyes of God?! The answer is right there. Difficult as it may be for some, it's there all the same:

"How long will this *people despise me*? How long will they *not believe in me*, **in spite of** *all the signs* that *I have done among them*?"

Here's the key: our understanding and acceptance of what is evil in His sight **isn't the same**, evidently, as *God's* knowledge of what is acceptable and evil in His sight.

The perception of what we deem evil and the reality of what He knows to be evil live in two opposite extremes:

- Ours: the temporal
    - the carnal
    - the flesh
- His: the Absolute
    - the Spiritual
    - Truth

This is when and why all that New Testament teaching about picking up the cross daily, putting on the Mind of Christ, voluntarily being a living sacrifice, walking in the Spirit instead of the flesh, keeping God's commandments, drawing near to God, resisting the devil, etc., etc., etc., is supposed to kick in. Le sigh...

Israel was on the wrong side of what God was doing on their behalf. So many of us today are on the wrong side of what God is desiring and trying to do – in our lives, in our families, in our churches, in our marriages, at our jobs, in our businesses, in our nations, prophetically on our behalf. We. Are. Not. Cooperating. We'd rather react with our practical reasoning and lean on our own understanding. Just. Like. Israel.

BUT THE EGYPTIANS WILL HEAR OF IT

Numbers 14:13-19 is one of the most amazing prayers of intercession out there. Go read it right now and come back...

Moses is preoccupied with God's reputation. Oh, if we would be preoccupied with His reputation! Moses even quotes *back* to God His own words about Himself! It's truly an amazing prayer of intercession on behalf of a rebellious people.

Verse 20 (NIV):

> *The LORD replied, "I have forgiven them, as you asked."*

And God relents!!!

Just sit there for a second, and let the waves of His Spirit of Forgiveness, His Spirit *that is for you*, roll over you.

God relented but not without consequence, just like the Good Father that He is. God swore the following against Himself: anyone that had seen God's glory and the miraculous signs that He did – in Egypt and in the wilderness – that had put Him to the test, that despised Him, and that did not obey His voice would *not* see the land.

That which Israel said in God's hearing about themselves and their children, He would do to them:

- Anyone twenty years old and up, their dead bodies would fall in the wilderness for grumbling against Him.
- Their children would enter into the land after suffering for their faithlessness for 40 years, "until the last of your dead bodies lies in the wilderness," a year for each day they were spying out the land.

The ten spies that gave a bad report about the land died "by plague before the Lord."

Only Joshua and Caleb would live to enter the land (Nu. 14:20-38).

Remember our premise from 1 Corinthians 10? This is exactly what Paul was writing to us about, *warning* us about. Everything we just read was written down as an example and a warning for us, the end-time church.

Please. Re-read this weekly entry. Understand – *eat* Numbers 13 and 14. Brand this information into your heart and mind. Don't do what Israel did. It caused them *not* to inherit their prophetic destiny. *Do* what Moses, Aaron, Joshua and Caleb did instead.

We don't want our actions, our words or the attitudes of our hearts and minds to cause us to be disinherited… *I* don't want my actions, my words or the attitudes of my heart and mind to cause me to be disinherited…

The idea behind this amazing journey from exodus to ingathering is to arrive at the *west* banks of the Jordan River whole and intact. We want to hear:

"Well done, good and faithful servant. Enter into the joy of your Lord."

○ FIELD NOTES

DATE: / / TIME: : AM/PM PLACE:

○		A±
○		
○		
○		
○		
○		
○		
○		
○		
○		
○		
○		
○		
○		
○		
○		
○		
○		
○		
○		

ARMOR CHECK: Ephesians 6:10-18

Belt of Truth	S ☐ M ☐ T ☐ W ☐ T ☐ F ☐ S ☐
Breastplate of Righteousness	S ☐ M ☐ T ☐ W ☐ T ☐ F ☐ S ☐
Shoes / Gospel of Peace	S ☐ M ☐ T ☐ W ☐ T ☐ F ☐ S ☐
Shield of Faith	S ☐ M ☐ T ☐ W ☐ T ☐ F ☐ S ☐
Helmet of Salvation	S ☐ M ☐ T ☐ W ☐ T ☐ F ☐ S ☐
Sword of the Spirit / Word of God	S ☐ M ☐ T ☐ W ☐ T ☐ F ☐ S ☐

No weapon formed against you will prosper. This is the heritage of the servants of ADONAI.
Is. 54:17

○ WEEK 14
THE REBELLION OF KORAH (NUMBERS 16:3)

They assembled themselves together against Moses and against Aaron and said to them, "You have gone too far! For all in the congregation are holy, every one of them, and the LORD is among them. Why then do you exalt yourselves above the assembly of the LORD?"

Last week we looked at both the exhilarating and tragic account of the 12 spies who were sent to assess the land of Canaan and the horrible curse that Israel brought upon themselves with their rebellious fear, doubt and unbelief.

We are studying through these various "prefigurative historical events," these lessons and warning examples, because the Apostle Paul taught that they were written down for our instruction. We're traveling the same desert journey that Israel embarked on — from exodus to ingathering — in order to determine

- What Israel did right,
- What Israel did wrong,
- What Father God required of them, and
- How Israel responded corporately and individually.

Again, our purpose and desire is to learn from their experiences and apply the same while avoiding the many pitfalls that befell so many in the desert.

Not long after the spies returned with the news that the Nephilim inhabited their prophetic destiny, out of that frustration and fear arose a Levite named Korah.

Korah was a well-liked and established Levitical leader. We know this, because he was able to assemble a faction of three additional cohorts – the brothers Dathan and Abiram and a man named On from the Tribe of Reuben. Together, scripture says, they "took men." It was a well-organized faction.

And they rose up before Moses, with a number of the people of Israel, 250 chiefs of the congregation, chosen from the assembly, well-known men.
Numbers 16:2

Here we go again:

They assembled themselves together against Moses and against Aaron and said to them, "You have gone too far! For all in the congregation are holy, every one of them, and the Lord is among them. Why then do you exalt yourselves above the assembly of the Lord?" When Moses heard it, he fell on his face [...] Numbers 16:3-4

Once again, the authority of the leadership of Moses is being challenged. This time, it comes in the form of an organized rebellion – mutiny. This isn't another mob deal exercising their "right," yet again to "group think." This is serious.

I referenced the rebellion of Korah in a lyric back in 1989, in a song about Los Angeles gang life called "Lights Out:"

I understand the need for man to clan together. But in your haste, remember Korah.

It's a subject matter that I've studied and taught for quite a while, because again, just like the lessons we can greatly benefit from regarding the 12 spies, we can also benefit greatly – if not more so – from learning the lesson here regarding this rebellion led by a Levite that is convinced he's doing the right thing, the godly thing, on behalf of the people...

The first thing we need to note is the initial charge of "you have gone too far!"

We're not entirely sure what they might be referring to, but contextually, Moses had a man executed in the previous chapter, Numbers 15:32-36, for breaking the Sabbath. This, and the instruction following regarding the wearing of tassels, did impact the entire community.

The second thing we need to understand is what was said next. This is key:

"...the entire community is holy, every last one of them, and the LORD is with them."

Another translation puts it this way:

"All the members of the community belong to the Lord, and the Lord is with all of us."

This organized insurgency by at least 254 well-known congregational leaders, "leaders of the people," fully believed that the entire community – every person, the "all-inclusive" assembly of Israel, across the board – were *holy*.

"Every last one of them," says the Common English Bible. Sound familiar?

And, "the Lord is *with* them / *among* them - "all of us," states the Good News Translation.

Inclusion, equality, commonality – in essence, "spiritual socialism." The people's leaders have deemed them, one and all, equally holy, and ADONAI is with and among them all – "every last one of them."

The next thing they say is an accusation in the form of a question:

"Why, then, Moses, do you set yourself above the Lord's community?"

They are accusing the ruling authority of God on earth, Moses, of setting *himself* up above God's community, as they see it. It's passive-aggressive actually, because it's based on *their* concept that "*everyone* is holy" and that God is *with* and *in* "everyone," and therefore, Moses is out of line for being "over" all of them.

They see it as a socialist community and that all are holy and equal in and with God. I mean, it's hard to believe how this angle still rings true today. Let's see how this popular rhetoric, even back then, stands true.

When Moses hears this, he falls on his face yet again. Moses invites them to a challenge to determine *exactly* what is what. Let's let *God* determine the three items in question:

1. Who, in all actuality, is the authority over Israel?
2. Who, in all actuality, is "holy?"
3. Who, in all actuality, is God "with" and "among?"

> *[...] and he [Moses] said to Korah and all his company, "In the morning the LORD will show who is his, and who is holy, and will bring him near to him. The one whom he chooses he will bring near to him.*
>
> *Do this: take censers, Korah and all his company; put fire in them and put incense on them before the LORD tomorrow, and the man whom the LORD chooses shall be the holy one. You have gone too far, sons of Levi!"*
> *Numbers 16:5-7*

It's on. God is going to settle this.

> *And Moses said to Korah, "Hear now, you sons of Levi: is it too small a thing for you that the God of Israel has separated you from the congregation of Israel, to bring you near to himself,*

to do service in the tabernacle of the LORD and to stand before the congregation to minister to them, and that he has brought you near him, and all your brothers the sons of Levi with you? And would you seek the priesthood also?

Therefore it is against the LORD that you and all your company have gathered together. What is Aaron that you grumble against him?"

Numbers 16:8-11

Take note of what Moses says: "...is it too small a thing for you..."

Whoa... it's not just 250 congregational leaders, it's 250 Levitical priests! This is a full-on coup d'etat! Not only are they coming against Moses as leader, they're also coming against the Aaronic Priesthood! How insane is that?!?

But again, these men actually believed that they were

- Working on behalf of the good of the people, and
- Doing God's will.

They were absolutely convinced of this.

After rebuking Korah and the Levites, Moses called for the brothers, Dathan and Abiram. They refused to go see Moses:

"We will not come up. ***Is it a small thing that you*** *have brought us up out of a land flowing with milk and honey, to kill us in the wilderness, that you must also make yourself a prince over us?*

Moreover, you have not brought us into a land flowing with milk and honey, nor given us inheritance of fields and vineyards. Will you put out the eyes of these men? We will not come up."

Numbers 16:12b-14 [Emphasis mine]

Things have escalated into full-blown insubordination. They even mock Moses with their tone:

"Is it a small thing that you..."

They even stick to the false narrative, the "fake news" that's circulating around the camp, "...you have brought us up out of a land flowing with milk and honey (*they're talking about Egypt!*), to kill us in the wilderness..."

They've bought into the propaganda hook, line and sinker! They even take a page from our present-day playbook by using the term used by God

Himself to describe the Promised Land (Ex. 3:8) to describe the 100% opposite – the "antichrist" version of the narrative, if you will – to describe Egypt as "a land flowing with milk and honey!!"

Oh man, I need a breather here...

Ok. Whew... where were we? Unlike typical Moses, who is constantly falling on his face to intercede for these people, he becomes very angry. He uncharacteristically tells God *not* to respect their offering and clarifies that he has not taken a single thing from them nor harmed them in any way. He is free of any wrongdoing against Israel.

The next day, Moses and Aaron, along with all the men, with their censers full of fire and incense, stood at the entrance to the tent of meeting.

Korah assembled all of Israel against them at the entrance, and the glory of ADONAI appeared to them all. Numbers 16:20:

> *And the LORD spoke to Moses and to Aaron, saying, "Separate yourselves from among this congregation, that I may consume them in a moment."*

Respectfully, I'm going to say that this clarified *exactly* what was what:

1. Who, in all actuality, was the authority over Israel?
2. Who, in all actuality, was "holy?"
3. Who, in all actuality, was God "with" and "among?"

> *But Moses and Aaron fell facedown and cried out, "O God, the God who gives breath to all living things, will you be angry with the entire assembly when only one man sins?"*
> *Numbers 16:22 (NIV)*

I find it absolutely amazing that, once again, Moses and Aaron, *Levites themselves*, would put themselves between the anger of the Most High God and the rebellious and petulant child known as the people of Israel.

Moses is instructed to tell the congregation of Israel to get away from the tents of Korah, Dathan and Abiram. Moses gets up, goes to the brothers and tells the people of Israel, "Please..." Yes, he says "please." Moses tells them to move away from the tents of Dathan and Abiram. He calls them "wicked men" and instructs the people not to touch anything of theirs so as not to be associated with their sins.

I can imagine the terrifying confusion, the debilitating disbelief, these men are feeling right about now. How could this be? How could *they* be the ones on the wrong side of this thing?!

So Israel moved away from Korah, Dathan and Abiram. Dathan and Abiram even came outside of their tents and stood in the doorways with their wives and children… their little ones… This isn't going to be good. I can't bear to watch!

> *And Moses said, "Hereby you shall know that the LORD has sent me to do all these works, and that it has not been of my own accord.*
>
> *If these men die as all men die, or if they are visited by the fate of all mankind, then the LORD has not sent me. But if the LORD creates something new, and the ground opens its mouth and swallows them up with all that belongs to them, and they go down alive into Sheol, then you shall know that these men have despised the LORD."*
>
> *And as soon as he had finished speaking all these words, the ground under them split apart. And the earth opened its mouth and swallowed them up, with their households and all the people who belonged to Korah and all their goods.*
>
> *So they and all that belonged to them went down alive into Sheol, and the earth closed over them, and they perished from the midst of the assembly.*
>
> *Numbers 16:28-33*

Nothing like this has happened before or since. Fire also came out from God and consumed the 250 rogue Levitical priests…

You have to have the discernment to be able to distinguish between a Korah and a Moses. This is why Paul lists factionalism as such an evil sin in his epistles. When in doubt, be quiet, fast and pray.

Do you have any idea how often a spirit of Korah, of factionalism, rises up in a normal church congregation? Every time there's a negative comment made about a leader; when a disrespectful email is sent to a pastor; when, as Paul says, old women get together and grumble and gossip about things; when you complain that the pastor and his wife aren't doing things to your specifications or standards… any thought, word or deed that is not honoring or respectful towards leadership is a demonic spirit of Korah at work.

Don't be a Korah. Be a Joshua, a Caleb, an Aaron, a Moses. Be like David who didn't insult God's elect. Be like Jesus…

○ FIELD NOTES

DATE: / / TIME: : AM/PM PLACE:

		A±
○		
○		
○		
○		
○		
○		
○		
○		
○		
○		
○		
○		
○		
○		
○		
○		
○		
○		
○		
○		

ARMOR CHECK: Ephesians 6:10-18

Belt of Truth	S ☐ M ☐ T ☐ W ☐ T ☐ F ☐ S ☐
Breastplate of Righteousness	S ☐ M ☐ T ☐ W ☐ T ☐ F ☐ S ☐
Shoes / Gospel of Peace	S ☐ M ☐ T ☐ W ☐ T ☐ F ☐ S ☐
Shield of Faith	S ☐ M ☐ T ☐ W ☐ T ☐ F ☐ S ☐
Helmet of Salvation	S ☐ M ☐ T ☐ W ☐ T ☐ F ☐ S ☐
Sword of the Spirit / Word of God	S ☐ M ☐ T ☐ W ☐ T ☐ F ☐ S ☐

No weapon formed against you will prosper. This is the heritage of the servants of ADONAI.
Is. 54:17

WEEK 15
PATCHWORK & WINESKINS
(MARK 2:21-22)

"No one sews a piece of unshrunk cloth on an old garment. If he does, the patch tears away from it, the new from the old, and a worse tear is made. And no one puts new wine into old wineskins. If he does, the wine will burst the skins—and the wine is destroyed, and so are the skins. But new wine is for fresh wineskins."

I've been wearing black Czechoslovakian infantry boots, otherwise known as "monkey boots," since 1983. Popular with the English Mods of the mid to late 60s, monkeys were also a hit with skinheads and punks, alongside a trusty pair of oxblood Doc Martens, until the dissolution of Czechoslovakia in January 1993. It would be almost ten years before monkey boots would come back into production and circulation.

You're probably wondering, "Why this tidbit of niche alternative fashion history?" Well, you see, my experience in losing my favorite foot attire for almost a decade would cause me to begin to purchase at least two of everything in regard to my favorite clothing items, including boots.

You can say I've always had a thing for clothes, and coming to the understanding of how clothing makes a statement about you – good, bad, or indifferent – would forever alter my dress code professionally, socially and casually. Regardless of whether or not you agree, what you wear and how you wear it greatly affects your trajectory in life.

I know a woman who was interviewing for a professional job. She arrived early to her destination and decided to grab a cup of coffee in the coffee shop of the building at which she was interviewing. While in line and waiting for her order she engaged in small talk with three people who were also in line for coffee. After more than five minutes, they asked my friend if she worked in the building, and she explained that she was there to interview for a position with one of the firms there. Not only were these three people from the same company, they were the people with whom she was there to interview.

"Don't bother coming up for the interview," they told her as they excused themselves.

How my friend presented herself and looked socially to this hiring team lost her the interview. It's a harsh lesson to learn but a lesson all the same.

If you're not the kind that is conscious of what they wear – style, fashion sense, trends, etc. – it might be difficult to connect life and clothing.

Clothing (trousers, dresses, etc.) can also be used as an analogy for life, and life causes tears, rips, holes and frays in that clothing. What we use to patch up those unsightly blemishes – things like sex, drugs, rock and roll, money, anger, success, religion and poverty (yes, even religion and poverty) – may speak even more loudly about us than the actual clothes themselves.

Clothing has always been a part of man's identity. Jesus said that the religious leaders of His day loved to wear the longest robes and the longest tassels as an arrogant sign of their self-gratifying spiritual superiority (Mt. 23:1-7; Mk 12:38-39). Contrast that with the rich clothing supplied to the prodigal son by his father to reestablish his rightful identity (Lk 15: 11-24). Like I said, clothing is a powerful statement about yourself – good, bad or indifferent – and the Bible has quite a lot to say about it.

In Exodus, we see the instructions from God to Moses in regard to the priestly garments; holy, supernatural clothing:

God, being a methodical God, is very specific when giving out instructions, and in this case, it was absolutely crucial that every detail was followed precisely as He had communicated it to Moses. So crucial, in fact, that the Priestly garments alone, prophetic clothing actually, were "holy garments for glory and beauty" (Ex. 28:2); clothing that would not only consecrate Moses' brother Aaron, the High Priest, and his sons for God's priesthood, but also keep them alive while ministering in the Holy Place before ADONAI! There was no room for error when it came to understanding and communicating these designs, let alone in the construction of these designs!!

(Source: Aguirre, Allan R. "Bezalel, Son of Light," In *This Thing Is Spiritual*, 62. Park City, Utah: Planet Blue Media, 2019. http://planetbluemedia.com)

In Leviticus 16:4, we are told that these priestly garments are sacred:

> *He [Aaron] is to put on the sacred linen tunic, with linen undergarments next to his body; he is to tie the linen sash around him and put on the linen turban. These are sacred garments; so he*

must bathe himself with water before he puts them on.
(NIV)

The priestly garments were so holy and powerful in their anointing that any and all priestly duties that required them to go outside to the outer court and/or among the people meant that the garments had to be removed first:

> *Once the priests enter the holy precincts, they are not to go into the outer court until they leave behind the garments in which they minister, for these are holy. They are to put on other clothes before they go near the places that are for the people.*
> *Ezekiel 42:14 (NIV)*

This is a good example of the common and uncommon, the holy and the profane. There are even instructions regarding the wearing of clothing as object lessons with deeper spiritual significance. Consider the following and Paul's instruction regarding head coverings for women in 1 Corinthians 11:10 "because of the angels."

> *A woman shall not wear a man's garment, nor shall a man put on a woman's cloak, for whoever does these things is an abomination to the Lord your God. You shall not wear cloth of wool and linen mixed together.*
> *Deuteronomy 22:5, 11*

One of my favorites passages about clothing is found in 1 Samuel 2:18-19:

> *Samuel was ministering before the Lord, a boy clothed with a linen ephod. And his mother used to make for him a little robe and take it to him each year when she went up with her husband to offer the yearly sacrifice.*

I find it fascinating that as a boy, Samuel was wearing a linen ephod, one of the most powerful pieces of the priestly garments, and I think it's adorable that his mother would make and bring him "a little robe" once a year.

Jesus said,

> *"No one puts a piece of unshrunk cloth on an old garment, for the patch tears away from the garment, and a worse tear is made."*
> *Matthew 9:16*

"No one sews a patch of unshrunk cloth on an old garment. Otherwise, the new piece will pull away from the old, making the tear worse."
Mark 2:21 (NIV)

"No one tears a piece from a new garment and puts it on an old garment. If he does, he will tear the new, and the piece from the new will not match the old."
Luke 5:36

Nobody uses the new, unmatched or unshrunk to repair the old.

Jesus repeats the same parable using wineskins:

"Neither is new wine put into old wineskins. If it is, the skins burst and the wine is spilled and the skins are destroyed. But new wine is put into fresh wineskins, and so both are preserved."
Matthew 9:17

"And no one pours new wine into old wineskins. Otherwise, the wine will burst the skins, and both the wine and the wineskins will be ruined. No, they pour new wine into new wineskins."
Mark 2:22 (NIV)

"And no one puts new wine into old wineskins. If he does, the new wine will burst the skins and it will be spilled, and the skins will be destroyed. But new wine must be put into fresh wineskins. And no one after drinking old wine desires new, for he says, 'The old is good.'"
Luke 5:37-39

Emptied wineskins would dry and harden. Before reusing them for the fermentation process of pressure and expansion, they would have to be renewed and softened. The wineskin would be soaked in water and then rubbed with oil. When it was soft and pliable again, it could handle the pressure of the fermentation, the maturing process of the new wine.

Renewing the wineskin, patching up the old garment – the process of being put into position of handling the pressure of the process of the new.

If you don't go through that process, you can't use the wineskin again. It could handle last season's wine, but it can't handle the next season's wine.

(Dutch Sheets. Sept 3, 2019. King of Kings Worship Center)

We don't want to fall out of production and circulation, like those monkey boots, because we've allowed ourselves to turn into hard and dry wineskins or a tattered and torn piece of clothing.

A religious spirit does everything it can to militate and avoid everything and anything to do with renewal, maturity. We need to constantly be pliable, softened and renewed in and by the Spirt of God, in order to be a vessel worthy of His new wine season, a new garment of His Identity.

○ FIELD NOTES

DATE: / / TIME: : AM/PM PLACE:

○		A±
○		
○		
○		
○		
○		
○		
○		
○		
○		
○		
○		
○		
○		
○		
○		
○		
○		
○		
○		

ARMOR CHECK: Ephesians 6:10-18

Belt of Truth	S ☐ M ☐ T ☐ W ☐ T ☐ F ☐ S ☐
Breastplate of Righteousness	S ☐ M ☐ T ☐ W ☐ T ☐ F ☐ S ☐
Shoes / Gospel of Peace	S ☐ M ☐ T ☐ W ☐ T ☐ F ☐ S ☐
Shield of Faith	S ☐ M ☐ T ☐ W ☐ T ☐ F ☐ S ☐
Helmet of Salvation	S ☐ M ☐ T ☐ W ☐ T ☐ F ☐ S ☐
Sword of the Spirit / Word of God	S ☐ M ☐ T ☐ W ☐ T ☐ F ☐ S ☐

No weapon formed against you will prosper. This is the heritage of the servants of ADONAI.
Is. 54:17

○ WEEK 16
BE JEALOUS WITH MY JEALOUSY (NUMBERS 25:10-13)

And the LORD said to Moses, "Phinehas the son of Eleazar, son of Aaron the priest, has turned back my wrath from the people of Israel, in that he was jealous with my jealousy among them, so that I did not consume the people of Israel in my jealousy. Therefore say, 'Behold, I give to him my covenant of peace, and it shall be to him and to his descendants after him the covenant of a perpetual priesthood, because he was jealous for his God and made atonement for the people of Israel.'"

After the last two weeks and the examples of how we are *not* to be like Israel by doing what they just did in regards to the report of the spies and the rebellion of Korah, I thought it would be a good idea to look at an example of *how* to be like Israel in the midst of pagan worship and disobedience.

But first, a lot has happened since Korah's rebellion. For example; the day after Korah and his friends were swallowed up by the earth and the 250 Levites were literally torched by God, all of Israel came up against Moses (yet again!) and accused him of killing God's people the day before – those people being Korah, Dathan, Abiram, their entire families and the 250 rogue Levites. Did Israel not see that it was God that killed those people that they are calling "God's people?!?" Le sigh... proof that when you're drunk on the proverbial Kool-Aid, you just can't see straight no matter what is going on. And yes, this does indeed apply to today!

Needless to say, a horrific plague came upon the people, and 14,700 lay dead by the time Aaron finished the atoning sacrifice for their sin (Nu. 16:41-50). I know. It's almost impossible to believe. And it was a horrific sight and sound to behold...

To make it very clear, yet again, who God had put in charge, all the chiefs of the tribes – including Moses' brother, Aaron, for the tribe of Levi – were to bring their staffs to the tent of meeting, and the staff that sprouted would be the man whom God would choose to be His tribal representative among the tribes:

> *On the next day Moses went into the tent of the testimony, and behold, the staff of Aaron for the house of Levi had sprouted and put forth buds and produced blossoms, and it bore ripe almonds.*
>
> *And the LORD said to Moses, "Put back the staff of Aaron before the testimony, to be kept as a sign for the rebels, that you may make an end of their grumblings against me, lest they die."*
> *Numbers 17:8, 10*

In chapter 20 of Numbers, Miriam, the sister of Moses, dies. When Israel reached the wilderness of Zin, there was no water there. Israel proceeded – that's right – to assemble themselves against Moses and Aaron. Moses and Aaron are instructed to speak to a rock for water, but out of anger toward the people, Moses struck the rock instead, misrepresenting God. Thus, they are both banned from entering the Promised Land (Nu. 20:2-13). Yes, after all that. Moses and Aaron did not uphold God as holy in the eyes of the people, so they were punished. Aaron is then told to ascend Mount Hor where he will die.

After defeating the Canaanites in battle, Israel once again becomes impatient and speaks against Moses and God. Fiery serpents are sent to bite and kill them until Moses is instructed to create a serpent out of bronze for their healing, which would come to be known as *N'chushtan* (2 Ki. 18:4).

In the valley of the Arnon, God gathers Israel at a well to give them drink, and all Israel sings to the well:

> *"Gather the people together and I will give them water." 17 Then Israel sang this song: "Spring up, O well! Sing about it, 18 about the well that the princes dug, that the nobles of the people sank — the nobles with scepters and staffs."*
> *Numbers 21:16b-18a (NIV)*

Israel is trying to pass through lands peacefully on the King's Highway, but they are attacked on occasion, forcing them to fight. They are victorious and begin to settle in the cities they possess.

We encounter the prophet Balaam who is paid by Moab's king with "the fees for divination" to curse Israel. You can read this account in Numbers 22 – 24.

In 1 Corinthians 10 (our premise), Paul references Numbers 25 in verse 8 when Israel began to whore with the daughters of Moab; sacrificed, ate and bowed to Baal of Peor; "and 23,000 fell in a single day." Here we are introduced to Phinehas – Eleazar the Priest's son, Aaron's grandson and Moses' great nephew.

Israel was committing spiritual adultery by worshiping the Baal of Peor, angering God. Moses is instructed to hang all the chiefs of the people before ADONAI Himself –

> *"that the fierce anger of the LORD may turn away from Israel."*
> *Numbers 25:4b*

Moses then instructs the judges of Israel to kill any men under their charge that "have yoked themselves to Baal of Peor." False pagan worship, also known as spiritual adultery, is a serious offense! Meanwhile, while all of this is happening, an Israeli man brings a Midianite woman to meet his family – *in the sight of Moses and the entire assembly of Israel!* – while the people are weeping at the entrance to the tent of meeting, because they've been busted for Baal worship, and another plague has broken out!! Can you say, "Muppet?!?"

> *When Phinehas the son of Eleazar, son of Aaron the priest, saw it, he rose and left the congregation and took a spear in his hand and went after the man of Israel into the chamber and pierced both of them, the man of Israel and the woman through her belly. Thus the plague on the people of Israel was stopped. Nevertheless, those who died by the plague were twenty-four thousand.*
> *Numbers 25:7-9*

Oh, my gosh… I just can't with these people… And they still exist today! I promised you a look at an example of *how* to be like Israel in the midst of pagan worship and disobedience. I introduce to you, Phinehas.

> *"Phinehas the son of Eleazar, son of Aaron the priest, has turned back my wrath from the people of Israel, in that he was jealous with my jealousy among them, so that I did not consume the people of Israel in my jealousy."*
> *Numbers 25:11*

Wow. What a great testimony about him – *from God!*

Phinehas is given God's covenant of peace. How amazing is that?!? I want God's covenant of peace! And this covenant of a perpetual priesthood was bestowed upon him and all his descendants *"because he was jealous for his God* (that's the key here) and made atonement for the people of Israel."

Before dying, Moses is instructed to war against the Midianites to avenge Israel. Phinehas is sent to this war by Moses "with the vessels of the sanctuary and the trumpets for the alarm in his hand" (Nu. 31:6b). You can read about Phinehas all the way through the 20th chapter of Judges.

On this amazing journey from exodus to ingathering, in this desert campaign with Israel on their way to their prophetic inheritance, the Promised Land of Canaan, are you looking for an example of *how* to be like them?

Take Phinehas, Moses' great nephew, who was given God's covenant of peace – he and his descendants forever – a perpetual priesthood before God, because he was jealous for his God and made atonement for the people of Israel.

Be jealous with God's jealousy by being the atoning catalyst for the people around you.

○ FIELD NOTES

DATE: / / TIME: : AM/PM PLACE:

○		A±
○		
○		
○		
○		
○		
○		
○		
○		
○		
○		
○		
○		
○		
○		
○		
○		
○		
○		
○		

ARMOR CHECK: Ephesians 6:10-18

Belt of Truth	S ☐ M ☐ T ☐ W ☐ T ☐ F ☐ S ☐
Breastplate of Righteousness	S ☐ M ☐ T ☐ W ☐ T ☐ F ☐ S ☐
Shoes / Gospel of Peace	S ☐ M ☐ T ☐ W ☐ T ☐ F ☐ S ☐
Shield of Faith	S ☐ M ☐ T ☐ W ☐ T ☐ F ☐ S ☐
Helmet of Salvation	S ☐ M ☐ T ☐ W ☐ T ☐ F ☐ S ☐
Sword of the Spirit / Word of God	S ☐ M ☐ T ☐ W ☐ T ☐ F ☐ S ☐

No weapon formed against you will prosper. This is the heritage of the servants of ADONAI.
Is. 54:17

○ WEEK 17
POSSESSION NOT OCCUPATION (NUMBERS 33:50-53, 55-56)

On the plains of Moab by the Jordan across from Jericho the LORD said to Moses, "Speak to the Israelites and say to them: 'When you cross the Jordan into Canaan, drive out all the inhabitants of the land before you. Destroy all their carved images and their cast idols, and demolish all their high places. Take possession of the land and settle in it, for I have given you the land to possess.

But if you do not drive out the inhabitants of the land, those you allow to remain will become barbs in your eyes and thorns in your sides. They will give you trouble in the land where you will live. And then I will do to you what I plan to do to them.'"

"...then I will do to you what I plan to do to them." Yikes!

Possess: Strong's #H03423
vry yarash, yaw-rash' or yaresh {yaw-raysh'}; a primitive root;

1. to occupy (by driving out previous tenants, and possessing in their place);
2. by implication, to seize, to rob, to inherit;
3. also to expel, to impoverish, to ruin: --cast out, consume, destroy, disinherit, dispossess, drive(-ing) out, enjoy, expel, without fail, (give to, leave for) inherit(-ance, -or) + magistrate;
4. be (make) poor, come to poverty, (give to, make to) possess, get (have) in (take) possession, seize upon, succeed, utterly

1 Corinthians 10:1-12 is our premise and the objective, if you will, of our expedition – to get to the other side: from the desert to the Promised Land, from orphanhood to sonship, from bondage (Egypt) to freedom (Canaan), from death to life, from dark to Light, from this life to the ingathering of the Marriage Supper of the Lamb! Hallelujah!!

And all along this journey, Father God is teaching us how to live according to His will and Way:

> *And the LORD directed me [Moses] at that time to teach you the decrees and laws you are to follow in the land that you are crossing the Jordan to possess.*
> *Deuteronomy 4:14 (NIV)*

And we are learning His ways so that we will do them (Ja. 1:22-25, 2:14-26) in the land, our territory, that God has given us as a prophetic inheritance. Israel refused to learn and walk in these statutes and rules, and Paul warned us not to do the same. The endgame was "possession," possession of their promised inheritance, and this should also be your endgame:

> *You shall therefore be careful to do the commandment and the statutes and the rules that I command you today. And because you listen to these rules and keep and do them, the LORD your God will keep with you the covenant and the steadfast love that he swore to your fathers.*
> *Deuteronomy 7:11-12*

I don't see anything legalistic about that. Didn't Jesus say if we loved Him, we would keep His commandments? Yes. Yes, He did, and that's all this is about, and here are the results of keeping covenant and His steadfast love (Dt. 7:13):

1. He will love you.
2. He will bless you.
3. He will multiply you.
4. He will bless the fruit of your womb.
5. He will bless the fruit of your ground (farming: provision / wealth).
6. He will increase your herds (ranching: provision / wealth).

> *You shall be blessed above all peoples. There shall not be male or female barren among you or among your livestock. And the LORD will take away from you all sickness, and none of the evil diseases of Egypt, which you knew, will he inflict on you, but he will lay them on all who hate you.*
> *Deuteronomy 7:14-15*

We've been taught that some of this will only happen in the afterlife when we die. God says this is our portion *now*, in *this* life. *This* is our covenant with Him and the fruit of His steadfast love

- *If* we are careful to do the commandments,
- *If* we are careful to do the statutes, and
- *If* we are careful to do the rules that He commands us today.

And because you listened to these rules and keep and do them, Jesus says you will hear "Well done, good and faithful servant!" I see obedience to God and His commandments as the right thing to do, and who doesn't want to hear "well done!" at the end of their game?!

> *As it is said, "Today, if you hear his voice, do not harden your hearts as in the rebellion." For who were those who heard and yet rebelled? Was it not all those who left Egypt led by Moses? And with whom was he provoked for forty years? Was it not with those who sinned, whose bodies fell in the wilderness? And to whom did he swear that they would not enter his rest, but to those who were disobedient?*
>
> *So we see that they were unable to enter because of unbelief.*
>
> *Hebrews 3:15-19*

POSSESSION

In order for us to inherit our prophetic destiny, unlike Israel, we have to believe. We have to believe, and we have to take possession of – not occupy – the territory God has given us. And the only way we can survive our time in the land and fully possess it – and *not* be coerced by the local inhabitants – is to be careful to *do* all that God teaches us on the journey to our land of promise.

So then, we need to determine three things:

1. What / where is my territory?
2. Who / what are the giants in my territory that need to be dispossessed?
3. How do I possess my territory?

NOTE: Utilize the Journal and Prayer Modules / Strategies in your *Amazing Journey* devotional section for this exercise. If you already know the answer, follow along and ask for even deeper revelation(s).

1. What / where is my territory?

What do you do that brings you joy, excitement, fulfillment, challenge, peace, accomplishment, destiny, etc.?

Is it cooking, painting, spending time with children, mathematics, language, politics, writing, caring for animals, etc.?

As you narrow down these answers through prayer and fasting, keep a running log. Drill down as much as you can for details, clarity, definition, etc. Some of these things will overlap. You're looking for what Lance Wallnau calls a "gift cluster."

2. Who / what are the giants in my territory that need dispossessing?

These could be generational or based on personality, self-worth and self-esteem... They could be geographical, financial or relational. "Giants" are obstacles – emotional, physical, psychological, spiritual or otherwise – designed to foster fear, doubt and unbelief. Your job is to conquer them and make them your provisional supply to prosper you in your land of inheritance!

It's Jesus' upside-down Kingdom: first is last, last is first, etc. These giants are bread for you! They're there for you to utilize like a chameleon that adapts to any environment or economy and creates the resources necessary for their own success.

3. How do I possess my territory?

Prayer, fasting, praying in the Spirit, worship, fellowship, worship in the Spirit, more fasting, resources like this one... stir, mix and repeat.

There's also planning, strategizing, tenacity, asking, seeking, knocking, more fasting, more praying, networking, marketing, sharing, praying, (have I mentioned fasting?) ...

Christians have been taught to occupy territory instead of possessing territory. We're basically squatters. And please don't misquote the "not of this world" passage in your head. That's not what it's talking about, and that will only serve to keep you impotent and in atrophy instead of actually doing something about possessing your inheritance. Don't be like Israel.

So, until the time comes when He actually does return, there's an entire world full of people who are literally dying to meet Him – people on your "Promised Land" – people in your territory that need to be "possessed" by Him and "dispossessed" by their own "giants."

Remember the challenge from last week about being the catalyst to someone's atonement and the challenge from a few weeks ago about preparing yourself because He *is* coming? That all has more to do about "them" than it does about us. The Marriage Supper always has room for a few more…

○ FIELD NOTES

DATE: / / **TIME:** : AM/PM **PLACE:**

○		A±
○		
○		
○		
○		
○		
○		
○		
○		
○		
○		
○		
○		
○		
○		
○		
○		
○		
○		
○		

ARMOR CHECK: Ephesians 6:10-18

Belt of Truth	S ☐	M ☐	T ☐	W ☐	T ☐	F ☐	S ☐
Breastplate of Righteousness	S ☐	M ☐	T ☐	W ☐	T ☐	F ☐	S ☐
Shoes / Gospel of Peace	S ☐	M ☐	T ☐	W ☐	T ☐	F ☐	S ☐
Shield of Faith	S ☐	M ☐	T ☐	W ☐	T ☐	F ☐	S ☐
Helmet of Salvation	S ☐	M ☐	T ☐	W ☐	T ☐	F ☐	S ☐
Sword of the Spirit / Word of God	S ☐	M ☐	T ☐	W ☐	T ☐	F ☐	S ☐

No weapon formed against you will prosper. This is the heritage of the servants of ADONAI.
Is. 54:17

○ WEEK 18
IDENTITY PROMISE VS IDENTITY CRISIS (MATTHEW 24:9-14)

"Then you will be handed over to be persecuted and put to death, and you will be hated by all nations because of me. At that time many will turn away from the faith and will betray and hate each other, and many false prophets will appear and deceive many people.

Because of the increase of wickedness, the love of most will grow cold, but the one who stands firm to the end will be saved. And this gospel of the kingdom will be preached in the whole world as a testimony to all nations, and then the end will come." (NIV)

Next week will be my "born again" birthday – I've never really used that term before to describe it – but, I got saved 40 years ago next week. It makes more sense to me to say it like that.

A lot of people have left the faith in that amount of time. In fact, *too many* have left the faith since I started this walk with Jesus, Yeshua (His Hebrew name). Even my first spiritual father, the man that shaped my foundation, is no longer one of us.

There is something about Christianity in the last 30 to 40 years that has caused it to lose its soundness and longevity. People just aren't sticking around like they used to or believing what many still call "orthodoxy." There are all sorts of reasons why, and we will barely be scratching the surface of it, but do know that this challenge of staying in the faith has always been there. It just seems more prominent when it's your time period here on earth going through it. One thing we do know, though, is that it doesn't surprise Jesus. He called it. Our job is to determine the hows and whys and to avoid the same demise.

Christianity in 2020 is not the same Christianity from the mid-1980s. The fact that Christianity has changed so drastically in 35 years only confirms what many of us don't necessarily like to think about, and that's just how much Christianity has changed in *2000* years. That thought is shockingly worrisome.

How does something that is supposedly "absolute" change with time, cultural and popular opinion? Well, that happens when you're not the influencer or agent of cultural change. You then become what the Change Agent is advocating. Let's face it – Christianity has had very little-to-no cultural influence since the Renaissance. And, any cultural relevance it might be starting to have today is demonized by the vast majority of its "members," i.e. "the church." (Clue: Jesus is coming back for the Bride, not a church. That's an erroneous concept created by "the church.")

Let's go back a second: "How does something that is supposedly 'absolute' change with time, culture and popular opinion?" It doesn't. Now, religion, on the other hand, will and does. Literally. It changes with the slightest breeze, or, should I say, "with every wind of doctrine?" Heh.

Look at all the ways Israel tried to steer "God" and Moses away from doing God. It never worked, and all the religious imposters with their false narratives and insurgencies were getting everybody killed. That's what religion does.

So to clarify, we are essentially talking about two separate things:

1. Christianity the religion / belief system
2. Christianity the word used to describe what the God of Abraham, Isaac and Jacob is doing with mankind through His Son, Jesus of Nazareth

Those are two drastically different things. One is the construct hijacked, assimilated and constantly being rebuilt by man – the other, the absolute of what it is man is attempting to control. Yup, I said it.

The extreme liberalism that has crept into the church in the last ten years or so is just the other side of the same coin of, let's say, the extreme legalism of the Judaizers of the first century. And for the record, not a single definition online or a casual Google search will yield the correct biblical definition of a Judaizer. And that's essentially my point.

The false narratives, false theologies, false doctrines, false understandings, false teachings and false explanations that define a false "liberal gospel" or exegesis come from the same false spirit that define a false "legalistic gospel" or exegesis. And yes, the same holds true for any biblical falsehood coming from any camp.

Once you allow feelings, prejudices, human understanding and reasoning, social status, era, geographical location, culture, gender, sexual preference, agenda, politics – once you allow *humanity* into the equation when addressing, understanding, reasoning and explaining scripture, the biblical text, you're in trouble.

"That's impossible not to do," too many will shout. They seriously believe that it's impossible *not* to factor in the human element. I adamantly disagree. Again, isn't the whole reason behind "salvation" to be saved from ourselves and our human condition? Isn't that entirely the purpose of Jesus? So why would we rely on our humanity to guide us in such things? That doesn't make any sense.

Aren't we also instructed not to be carnally (human) minded, and in fact, are not our carnal minds in enmity with God? Yes, yes, the scriptures do say that as well. Using our humanity to understand and explain spirituality is as futile as depending on our humanity to do spiritual exploits. They reside in two separate dimensions. Besides, the sound and "orthodox" teaching is that, because of and through Jesus, we are shedding our human / mortal coil, by daily dying on the cross, replacing our human, mortal mind, reasoning, etc., with the Spirit. That's the doctrine – exchanging "corruptible" for "incorruptible."

Two-thirds of the Old Testament is an account of how Israel got everything wrong in regard to God. Everything. And it clearly states that this was the cause and effect of them insisting on depending and relying upon their humanity instead of submitting to the spirituality of God and allowing their humanity to be made spiritual. God literally told them not to do this! He has also, literally, repeated this instruction in the New Testament. Regardless, the Apostle Paul is warning us from the Old Testament, the scriptures, as our premise tells us. So why then, won't we listen?!

Because. We're. Exactly. Like. Israel.

Anyone that defends the use or rationale of the human condition to understand, comprehend and expound on spiritual matters does so because they themselves are not spiritual.

Translated: Not spiritual = Not Godly.

Translated: Not spiritual = Does not have the God of Abraham, Isaac and Jacob living inside of them through the one and only exclusive gatekeeper: Jesus of Nazareth.

Is that clear enough for everyone? Heh.

Go back and remember when you first became born again. If you had used your human reasoning, it never would have happened – not until you gave up all human rationale did Messiah make sense. Why? Because it's a spiritual thing. This whole thing is spiritual.

Resorting back to our human intellect and reasoning regarding matters of the spirit is why so many of us have either left the faith or are stuck in a fruitless cycle of religious routine. That's not life and life more abundantly. You've been deceived somewhere along your journey. Take back your territory and your life!

I want to pray for us right now. May I?

May ADONAI rebuke any lying spirit of division, confusion and religion that would attempt to raise its ugly head right now – right here. I speak healing, wholeness and soundness of spirit, heart and mind. I break off anything caused by an irresponsible word spoken by a parent, family member, youth pastor, pastor, seminary professor – you name it – anyone that has ever spoken an untruth as biblical authority over and into our lives. We declare the Spirit of Soundness of God's Word, over and into us. In Jesus' name. Amen.

Jesus said that many will turn away from the faith and will betray and hate each other.

The enemy enthusiastically desires for us to stay on his turf, limited in our understanding, and trapped in his territorial domain of

- A religious spirit;
- Fear, doubt and unbelief;
- Bad theology and doctrine; and
- Spiritual powerlessness.

I could keep going, but you get my drift. Lucifer wants us living on *his* land / in *his* territory, **as squatters**. He does *not* want us possessing our inheritance – God's destiny for our lives, our territory, our land, *our prophetic rightful role as joint heirs!*

Furthermore, our receiving of our inheritance is greatly determined by our identity. This is where the meat lies.

Israel wasn't able to walk in their identity *promise*, because they had a horrific identity *crisis* – an identity crisis that plagues them even to this day. God knows this. Look:

> *When Pharaoh let the people go, God did not lead them by way of the land of the Philistines, although that was near (closer / shorter). For God said, "Lest the people change their minds when they see war and return to Egypt."*

But God led the people around by the way of the wilderness toward the Red Sea. And the people of Israel went up out of the land of Egypt equipped for battle.
Exodus 13:17-18

God took Israel the long way around to avoid a fight with the Philistines, just in case the Philistines picked one. He knew that Israel would more than likely cower and run back to the familiarity and false safety of Egypt in fear. Nevertheless, God had Israel dressed up and equipped for battle anyway: identity!

In Numbers 22, where we were introduced to the prophet Balaam, do you know why the King of Moab, Balak, paid divination fees to have Israel cursed?

And Balak the son of Zippor saw all that Israel had done to the Amorites. And Moab was in great dread of the people, because they were many. Moab was overcome with fear of the people of Israel. And Moab said to the elders of Midian, "This horde will now lick up all that is around us, as the ox licks up the grass of the field."

So Balak calls for Balaam, saying,

"Behold, a people has come out of Egypt. They cover the face of the earth, and they are dwelling opposite me. Come now, curse this people for me, since they are too mighty for me."
Numbers 22:2-4a, 5b-6a

Moab was terrified of Israel!

While Israel is crying themselves to sleep in horrific and habitual rebellion and believing they were victims of a terrible plight against them, being dragged out into the desert by God and Moses to be killed – "How long will this people despise me? And how long will they not believe in me, in spite of all the signs that I have done among them? I will strike them with the pestilence and disinherit them…" – while Israel insisted on tormenting herself, because of a lack of proper godly identity, her enemies were in total fear of *her!*

To reestablish his rightful identity, the father dressed his prodigal son in rich clothing (Lk 15:11-24). Identity.

Our Heavenly Father is constantly reaffirming who we are in Him, just as He did for Israel in the desert:

Yet the LORD says, "During the forty years that I led you through the wilderness, your clothes did not wear out, nor did the sandals on your feet."
Deuteronomy 29:5 (NIV)

I see this as another sign of identity, of how Israel has always been the recipient of the Father's care as His children. What Father wouldn't provide their children with shoes and clothes?

Identity…

○ FIELD NOTES

DATE: / / TIME: : AM/PM PLACE:

○		A±
○		
○		
○		
○		
○		
○		
○		
○		
○		
○		
○		
○		
○		
○		
○		
○		
○		
○		
○		

ARMOR CHECK: Ephesians 6:10-18

Belt of Truth	S ☐	M ☐	T ☐	W ☐	T ☐	F ☐	S ☐
Breastplate of Righteousness	S ☐	M ☐	T ☐	W ☐	T ☐	F ☐	S ☐
Shoes / Gospel of Peace	S ☐	M ☐	T ☐	W ☐	T ☐	F ☐	S ☐
Shield of Faith	S ☐	M ☐	T ☐	W ☐	T ☐	F ☐	S ☐
Helmet of Salvation	S ☐	M ☐	T ☐	W ☐	T ☐	F ☐	S ☐
Sword of the Spirit / Word of God	S ☐	M ☐	T ☐	W ☐	T ☐	F ☐	S ☐

No weapon formed against you will prosper. This is the heritage of the servants of ADONAI.
Is. 54:17

○ WEEK 19
A CHOSEN PEOPLE (DEUTERONOMY 7:6)

"For you are a people holy to the Lord your God. The Lord your God has chosen you to be a people for his treasured possession, out of all the peoples who are on the face of the earth."

Have you noticed how God is constantly reminding Israel about their identity – who they are in Him, what He believes and says about them, the responsibilities they have because of Him and His name's sake?

I wanted to remind us a little bit today about our identity promise again – who we are in the Lord, what He believes and says about us and the responsibilities we have because of Him and His name's sake.

Have you ever wondered why God was always reminding Israel – just like He's always reminding us (if we're listening) – about Himself, His commandments and our identity in Him? The answer is really quite simple: because He knows how forgetful we are.

In the desert, Israel repeatedly broke God's commandments, and He was constantly creating reminders in order to help them to remember. Those reminders, by the way, always included actions on their part to assist and provoke that remembrance. James, the brother of Jesus and the leader of the church in Jerusalem, said this about our forgetfulness:

> *But be doers of the word, and not hearers only, deceiving yourselves. For if anyone is a hearer of the word and not a doer, he is like a man who looks intently at his natural face in a mirror. For he looks at himself and goes away and at once forgets what he was like. But the one who looks into the perfect law, the law of liberty, and perseveres, being no hearer who forgets but a doer who acts, he will be blessed in his doing.*
> *James 1:22-25*

"...being no hearer who forgets but a doer who acts, he will be blessed in his doing." I love it.

One of the main causes to impede the continual belief in God is the simple decision to *stop* believing

- In who He says He is and
- In who He says we are.

I know that might sound silly, but disbelief is a contributing factor to doubt, and doubt facilitates the seduction of our mind. Our identity plays into all of this more than many of us are comfortable admitting to.

As soon as we stop believing that what God is doing and saying is true, we begin the process of human reasoning. Thus begins the seduction of our minds to another lover, another belief system. God uses these metaphors of love, seduction, jealousy, harlotry and spiritual adultery when discussing these matters because of how intimate this process is.

The goal of our enemy is to destroy us psychologically, emotionally, physically and spiritually. When done intimately, the trauma produced has longer lasting results. Take Israel after the spies returned, for example – coupled with their propensity for fear and doubt, the news of the Nephilim not only being alive but living where they were going and that physical battle would be required triggered them into a state of catatonic unbelief

- In who God was
- In who God had previously proven Himself to be,
- In what God was doing and
- In who God said they were and could be.

This had deep, lasting and grave consequences. It exposed them to their core.

After Israel's refusal to enter the Promised Land because of the spies' report, they are instructed to return towards the Red Sea. The assembly, on the other hand, rose early the following morning and made their way high up into the hill country.

> *"Now we are ready to go up to the land the LORD promised. Surely we have sinned!"*
> *Numbers 14:40 (NIV)*

They're in disobedience, yet again, because of this habitual, passive-aggressive, rebellious behavior. Now, because they've had this "revelation" that they've sinned, they'll go up into the heights of the hill country where the giants live – "the place that God has promised" – and fight the Nephilim, even though God has already told them to go in the opposite direction. See what I mean? What's shocking to me is how prevalent this same behavior is today among people of faith.

This is also what I meant by intimate. If the enemy can decimate you intimately, the effects will be much more far-reaching. This is also what I meant by identity being a factor. If our identity isn't functioning soundly psychologically, emotionally and spiritually, we'll exhibit these sorts of behavioral patterns as well. Of course, we're just scratching at the surface of this subject matter.

Peter knew that his identity lay in his Rabbi. So, when Peter saw Jesus walking on the water, he didn't hesitate to ask if he could join Him. Peter knew that whatever his Rabbi could do, *he* could also do. This is commonly known as "The Rabbi Principle."

Take a look at Peter when he was walking on the water. He was literally walking on water. It wasn't until he saw a wave coming that he realized that he shouldn't be doing what he was actually doing – *walking on water*. He *saw*, in the physical, a wave coming and rescinded his spiritual authority in the matter, causing him to sink. He stopped believing that he was doing what he was actually doing – walking on the water.

Knowing what God believes about us and aligning ourselves to believe the same is paramount to this process and crucial for walking in this paradigm – the reality of who we are physically and spiritually in Messiah. Personally, I believe Peter walked back to the boat after Messiah reached out for him.

One more thought. When my crisis of faith occurred, it wasn't over what He said about Himself or who He said I was. It was because of the fear of the responsibility of what He said about *me*. I didn't stop believing, but I stopped obeying. See, that makes sense to the human rationale, but in *His* reality, to *His* rationale, I stopped obeying, because I *did* stop believing. Otherwise, why would I stop obeying? I understand this now.

Don't get tangled up in the wordplay of the enemy like Eve did in the garden when he seduced her. Keep it simple:

As soon as we stop believing that what God is doing and saying is true, we begin the process of human reasoning.

Don't let the enemy seduce you.

> *But you are a chosen people, a royal priesthood, a holy nation, God's special possession, that you may declare the praises of him who called you out of darkness into his wonderful light. Once you were not a people, but now you are the people of God; once you had not received mercy, but now you have received mercy.*
> *1 Peter 2:9-10*

These things are all true. They're not "fake news." They're the Good News! Meditate on these things. Journal about them and include them in your prayer strategies:

You are chosen.
You are a Kingly Priest.
You are holy.
You are God's special possession.
You were called out of darkness.
You are no longer a spiritual orphan.
You are the people of God.
You have mercy.

The enemy wants to raise up a counterfeit church, a counterfeit Christianity, a counterfeit Bride. It's known as an "Ishmael" and is made out of the will of the flesh, not the will of the Spirit. The first thing one does to create a counterfeit is to undermine the identity: "You're not real!"

Eliminating the counterfeits in your life and within your territory is a great strategy to avoid seduction. When Israel was brought in to possess their land, God cleared the seven nations before them, but then Israel had to devote themselves to their complete destruction. TIsrael was forbidden to make covenants with the seven nations, show them mercy or intermarry with them.

Israel was instructed in these things so that theyl would not position their children or themselves to turn away from ADONAI and begin serving other gods. Otherwise, God would have to destroy them for doing so. It was for Israel's benefit.

Israel was also instructed to break down the altars of the inhabitants of Canaan, dash to pieces their pillars, chop down their Asherim poles and burn their carved images with fire. Of course, Israel didn't do all of this…

Maintaining your Identity of Promise takes a lot of work. It takes all this work, because we're lazy. Maybe some of us are afraid to fail. Whatever your "giant" may be, we don't want to do the work of working against the things that are inside of us, let alone the things outside of ourselves, to maintain His identity. So, listen up!

- You are forbidden to make covenants with them.
- Show them no mercy.
- Do not intermarry.
- Do not position your children or yourselves to turn away from God and serve other gods – *their* gods.
- Break down their altars.

- Dash to pieces their pillars.
- Chop down their Asherim poles.
- Burn their carved images with fire.

This. Is. Your. Identity.

○ FIELD NOTES

DATE: / / **TIME:** : AM/PM **PLACE:**

		A±
○		
○		
○		
○		
○		
○		
○		
○		
○		
○		
○		
○		
○		
○		
○		
○		
○		
○		
○		
○		

ARMOR CHECK: Ephesians 6:10-18

Belt of Truth	S ☐ M ☐ T ☐ W ☐ T ☐ F ☐ S ☐
Breastplate of Righteousness	S ☐ M ☐ T ☐ W ☐ T ☐ F ☐ S ☐
Shoes / Gospel of Peace	S ☐ M ☐ T ☐ W ☐ T ☐ F ☐ S ☐
Shield of Faith	S ☐ M ☐ T ☐ W ☐ T ☐ F ☐ S ☐
Helmet of Salvation	S ☐ M ☐ T ☐ W ☐ T ☐ F ☐ S ☐
Sword of the Spirit / Word of God	S ☐ M ☐ T ☐ W ☐ T ☐ F ☐ S ☐

No weapon formed against you will prosper. This is the heritage of the servants of ADONAI.
Is. 54:17

○ WEEK 20
THE TESTING OF OUR HEARTS (DEUTERONOMY 8:2)

"And you shall remember the whole way that the Lord your God has led you these forty years in the wilderness, that he might humble you, testing you to know what was in your heart, whether you would keep his commandments or not."

If you've done this Christian walk for any amount of time and with any seriousness, you'll recall the times that the Father has humbled you – testing you in order to expose your heart – to see whether or not you would obey Him.

In July of 1994, I temporarily moved my family into my in-laws' home in Dallas while I went on a three-month national tour. When I arrived in October to take them back to Southern California, the Father told me to stay and make a life for ourselves there and that He would bless it. We did, and He did, after no small temper tantrum on my part. Texas? I'm from Los Angeles!

We became friends with a family from Portland, OR that we met at the church we were going to – a family that are still dear friends today. When I asked how long they had been in Texas, they both sort of looked at each other, and with a bit of a grimace on their faces said, "Nine years." "Nine years!?" I exclaimed. "Oh, man. What did the two of *you* do to get *that* long of a sentence" I commented. We would be in Dallas a total of 18 years. They left around our year seven, and I *know* what *I* did to be there for so long.

In all actuality, our time in Dallas was amazing. What the Father did for, with and through us was incredible, but it required, once again, an alignment with our identity, and it required humility on my part. It is only because we allowed that shift to occur that I can say that our Dallas years were fruitful and life-altering.

God is trying to do the same with Israel in the desert, and they're not getting it. To teach them the importance of living by the Spirit, the Word of God, and not just in the flesh, by bread alone, He humbled them by letting them hunger and by feeding them manna. Just like Jesus in *His* desert experience, He's teaching us the same through this resource.

Your clothing did not wear out on you and your foot did not swell these forty years. Know then in your heart that, as a man disciplines his son, the Lord your God disciplines you. So you shall keep the commandments of the Lord your God by walking in his ways and by fearing him.
Deuteronomy 8:4-6

Doesn't it seem like I'm beginning to sound like a broken record player?

- God tells Israel to obey.
- Israel rebels.
- God punishes Israel.
- God reminds Israel of the covenant promise.
- God reminds them of the importance of keeping His commandments.
- God forewarns them of their destruction.
- Israel disobeys.
- God tells Israel to obey.
- Israel rebels some more.
- God punishes Israel.
- Repeat...

But that's literally what's happening on this journey from exodus to ingathering. Literally. And it doesn't get better.

- Israel doesn't succeed in completely possessing the land.
- Israel doesn't completely rid the land of the demonic strain of humanity that resides there.
- Israel adapts all the paganism of Canaan into their lives and into the worship of God.
- Israel never truly repents.
- Judges are raised up to bring Israel back to repentance when they would get to the end of their collective ropes.
- Having a king fared no better.
- Every single king of the Northern Kingdom was Godless.
- They killed the prophets of God.
- God *still* bothers with them.
- They eventually kill Messiah.

It's depressing. And we do the very same thing. We just throw "Jesus" into the mix. Nothing's really changed. Amazing.

This resource is designed to help you avoid these pitfalls, but in order to do so, we're going to have to do some repeating of ourselves. We're going to have to attack the same points from multiple angles so that you can fully understand how this all ties in contextually. The more angles from which you can see things, the more adept you'll become in dividing the Word of God correctly, contextually and proficiently. Make sense?

Let's unpack the "I'm testing you to know what is in your heart – whether you will keep My commandments or not" deal. The idea of God testing us to expose our hearts to determine whether or not we'll obey Him might be a new concept for some of us.

The manna that was given Israel to eat in the desert was a test from God to see if they would walk in obedience or not (Ex. 16:4). Israel was to go out in the morning and gather enough manna for the day. They were not to keep any overnight until morning. Those that didn't obey woke up to stinky manna full of worms. Again, basic obedience.

They were to gather manna six days a week, and on the sixth day, they would gather twice as much for the Sabbath. Because the Sabbath is holy, they were not to gather on that day. The extra manna gathered on the sixth day was to be set aside, and it wouldn't go bad. But some people went out to gather on the seventh day anyway, in disobedience, causing God to instruct them to stay in their tents on the Sabbath. Manna was a test that they failed the first time out in week one.

By Judges 2, after Joshua had died, we see that because of their continual sin God is no longer driving out the inhabitants of the land before Israel. God is also going to use these not-entirely-human people groups that Israel was supposed to exterminate to test them, to see whether or not Israel would walk in His ways. We all know the answer to that. Le sigh…

Can you think of any instances where God deliberately set up a test to determine your heart? To determine whether or not you would obey His commandments? Use the Journal and Prayer Modules in *The Amazing Journey from Exodus to Ingathering* for this exercise.

We see Jesus testing the faith of the disciples all throughout the gospels. I think the parables were some of those tests. In the feeding of the 5000, in John's account (Jn 6), it states that Jesus tested Philip:

> *Lifting up his eyes, then, and seeing that a large crowd was coming toward him, Jesus said to Philip, "Where are we to buy bread, so that these people may eat?" He said this to test him, for*

he himself knew what he would do.
John 6:5-6

In a test similar to those seen in the desert campaign, a man and his wife sell some land for a certain amount but only bring part of the money to the Apostles as a gift, claiming that it was all of the proceeds (Ac 5). The man is killed by God for lying to the Holy Spirit, and when his wife is tested with a similar line of questioning – tested to see if she would herself keep God's commandments and speak truth – she too is killed. Like in the desert campaign, the death of those claiming to be a part of us – but who actually aren't – is designed to put fear in the rest of the assembly to dissuade them from sinning themselves.

We see this same premise when it comes to correction within the body. You are to take a brother aside privately and correct him. If he continues in his way, bring another brother or two that can substantiate the infraction and confront him. If he still refuses, bring him in front of the entire assembly. If that doesn't persuade him to repent, then you expel him (Jesus in Mt. 18:15-17).

As for those who persist in sin, rebuke them in the presence of all, so that the rest also may stand in fear.
I Timothy 5:20 (NRS)

God has, does and will test us to expose our hearts, to determine whether or not we will walk in His ways, keep His commandments and obey His voice. That's what this entire exercise called "life on Earth" is all about. Hopefully, you've figured that out by now.

Ever since the Garden of Eden, it has been about one thing: obedience.

Jesus in the wilderness with Lucifer? Obedience.

"If you love Me," Jesus said, you'll do what? Keep His commandments: obedience.

Jesus in the Garden of Gethsemane? Obedience.

You and I, right now, at this very moment? As for me and my house... Obedience.

You see, keeping God's commandments has never been an issue of "could we" but rather an issue of "would we."

Will you?

○ FIELD NOTES

DATE: / / TIME: : AM/PM PLACE:

○		A±
○		
○		
○		
○		
○		
○		
○		
○		
○		
○		
○		
○		
○		
○		
○		
○		
○		
○		
○		

ARMOR CHECK: Ephesians 6:10-18

Belt of Truth	S ☐ M ☐ T ☐ W ☐ T ☐ F ☐ S ☐
Breastplate of Righteousness	S ☐ M ☐ T ☐ W ☐ T ☐ F ☐ S ☐
Shoes / Gospel of Peace	S ☐ M ☐ T ☐ W ☐ T ☐ F ☐ S ☐
Shield of Faith	S ☐ M ☐ T ☐ W ☐ T ☐ F ☐ S ☐
Helmet of Salvation	S ☐ M ☐ T ☐ W ☐ T ☐ F ☐ S ☐
Sword of the Spirit / Word of God	S ☐ M ☐ T ☐ W ☐ T ☐ F ☐ S ☐

No weapon formed against you will prosper. This is the heritage of the servants of ADONAI.
Is. 54:17

○ WEEK 21
I AM THE BREAD OF LIFE (JOHN 6:35)

Jesus said to them, "I am the bread of life; whoever comes to me shall not hunger, and whoever believes in me shall never thirst."

The feeding of the 5000 (Jn 6:1-14) is the only miracle recorded by all four Gospels, creating a precise marker for the synchronization of the Gospel accounts. This is also the backdrop for the messianic declaration made by Jesus that He was the Bread of Life, the true eternal manna (Bread) sent from heaven.

After the miraculous feeding,

Perceiving then that they were about to come and take him by force to make him king, Jesus withdrew again to the mountain by himself.
Verse 15

Later that evening, the disciples took a boat across the Galilee to Capernaum. Three or four miles out into the lake, a storm came upon them. It was dark.

Mark states that Jesus saw them struggling because of the wind from land. Matthew and Mark give the account of the disciples seeing what they believed was a phantom walking on the water towards them. Only the Gospel of Matthew (chapter 14) has Peter walking on the water. John says that as soon as Jesus got into the boat, they transported immediately to the other side of the lake where they were heading.

That's a lot of supernatural activity for one day:

- 5000 men, not including women and children, were fed with five barley loaves and two fishes.
- 12 baskets of leftovers were gathered.
- Jesus appears out of thin air, walking on water.
- *Peter* is now walking on water.
- They were just transported, in a flash, across the lake.

Remember, this day happened after returning from their first "missionary journey" where they were casting out demons and healing many who were sick. Even still, these were new concepts and paradigms for them, and after Jesus got into the boat,

> *[...] they were utterly astonished, for they had not gained any insight from the incident of the loaves, but their heart was hardened.*
> *Mark 6:51b-52 (NASB)*

Le sigh...

It's important to note that the disciples' fear of the storm and fear that a phantom was walking on the water towards them – after casting out demons, healing the sick and feeding over 5000 – are considered "hardness of heart" here. Other translations have "stubborn," "their minds were closed," "their hearts were blind," "their minds could not grasp it," "their minds were dull," and "they resisted God's ways." Either way, it was a rebuke.

We need to understand that these are the parameters from which God works. To us, their behavior could be considered normal, logical and even acceptable. Who would blame them, right? But to Jesus, this was unacceptable and hardness of heart.

The next day, Jesus was in the synagogue of Capernaum teaching (Jn 6:22-59). It's a bit of a difficult discourse. Jesus tells them that the only reason why they were looking for Him was because He had fed them for free (the feeding of the 5000) the previous day. He warns them against pursuing the food that perishes and tells them to pursue the food that produces eternal life, which He could give them.

The following is, once again, indicative of their generational condition:

> *Then they said to him, "What must we do, to be doing the works of God?" Jesus answered them, "This is the work of God, that you believe in him whom he has sent."*
> *Verses 28-29*

Jesus knows the difficulty that they'll have simply believing over "doing." He knows how difficult it was for them to simply believe the Father in the desert, even with the signs that He did on their behalf and within their midst. To simply believe wasn't a trait of theirs.

To further incriminate themselves, they ask Jesus what sign He would be doing for them in order to persuade them to believe in Him. See the generational attitude?

"Our ancestors ate manna in the wilderness," they said, as if to trump whatever sign He might produce. "As it is written, 'He gave them bread from heaven to eat.'"

Jesus tells them, "It wasn't Moses that gave you bread from heaven, it was my Father. And He wants to give you the true bread from heaven, the bread that came down that gives life to the world," speaking of Himself.

It's a bit of a "war of wits" between Creator and creation, sort of like the dialog in *The Voyage of the Dawn Treader* between the Duffers and Prince Caspian's party before the Duffers are made visible and the exchange with Coriakin after the Duffers are given back their visibility. Silly.

> *Jesus said to them, "I am the bread of life; whoever comes to me shall not hunger, and whoever believes in me shall never thirst. But I said to you that you have seen me and yet do not believe.*
> *John 6:35-36a*

So they began grumbling about Jesus, because He said that He was the bread come down from heaven. What a surprise – they're grumbling!

They said, "Is this not Jesus, the son of Joseph, whose father and mother we know? How can he now say, 'I came down from heaven'?"

> *"Stop grumbling among yourselves," Jesus answered.*
> *John 6:43 (NIV)*

It would be comical if it wasn't so tragic. But Jesus is just getting started with them. He tells them that no one can come to Him unless the Father draws them and that Jesus will raise that person up on the last day. This isn't acceptable stuff here that He's saying…

He quotes the Prophets, and in verse 46, tells them that

> *No one has seen the Father except the one who is from God; only he has seen the Father. (NIV)*

Oh, man. He just told them… wait, He's not finished…

> *I am the bread of life. Your ancestors ate the manna in the wilderness, yet they died. But here is the bread that comes down from heaven, which anyone may eat and not die.*
> *John 6:48-50 (NIV)*

Jesus just made the Messianic declaration that He was the living bread come down from heaven versus the manna in the desert they were championing. Yikes! He unapologetically continues with, "Whoever eats *this* bread (Himself) lives forever." Manna-eating Israel in the desert? They all died.

> *"This bread is my flesh, which I will give for the life of the world."*
> *Verse 51c (NIV)*

There's no going back now.

They begin arguing angrily among themselves.

> *"How can this man give us his flesh to eat?"*
>
> *Jesus said to them, "Very truly I tell you, unless you eat the flesh of the Son of Man and drink his blood, you have no life in you. Whoever eats my flesh and drinks my blood has eternal life, and I will raise them up at the last day. For my flesh is real food and my blood is real drink. Whoever eats my flesh and drinks my blood remains in me, and I in them. Just as the living Father sent me and I live because of the Father, so the one who feeds on me will live because of me. This is the bread that came down from heaven. Your ancestors ate manna and died, but whoever feeds on this bread will live forever." He said this while teaching in the synagogue in Capernaum.*
> *Verses 52b-59 (NIV)*

He said this while teaching in the synagogue in Capernaum! Brutal!!

This has got to be one of the most incriminating things He could have said... ever. He's describing "cannibalism," and that's definitely not "kosher!" Oh. My. Goodness.

Not only is this cryptic, He's not even offering an explanation! Go back and re-read the passage slowly and deliberately. He just lost a good majority of His disciples. Even his original 12 are grumbling about it!

Funny thing this, believing that the carpenter from Nazareth, the son of Mary and Joseph, could possibly be the Promised Messiah. But He just told all of us that we would have to eat His flesh and drink His blood...

God's thoughts are not our thoughts. They're outside of our "wheelhouse." This means that every revelation of Jesus should be offensive to us to some degree, because they're outside of our realm of thinking. That day, Jesus offended every reasonable thinker in the synagogue in Capernaum with His thoughts and words – words He said were full of the Spirit and life (verse 63).

Jesus asked the 12 if they wanted to leave Him as well. Peter asked where else would they go, and besides, Jesus had the words of eternal life, and they just knew He was the Messiah. Jesus replied, "Didn't I choose you?"

What separates the called from the chosen?

A religious spirit that paralyzes the called from being able to wrap their heads around a concept or thought from God.

The chosen trust and discern the concept or thought and then go with it, no matter how crazy it sounds. Just like the 12 with the "eat my flesh, drink my blood" revelation. It didn't "sound right," but they trusted Jesus and what Jesus was saying and doing because they saw the Kingdom in it.

Imagine for a second the peer pressure not to continue going forward with that crazy Rabbi Jesus after that?!

The chosen trust that the Father will reveal the revelation to them; whereas, a religious spirit never crosses that line…

○ FIELD NOTES

DATE: / / TIME: : AM/PM PLACE:

		A±
○		
○		
○		
○		
○		
○		
○		
○		
○		
○		
○		
○		
○		
○		
○		
○		
○		
○		
○		
○		

ARMOR CHECK: Ephesians 6:10-18

Belt of Truth	S ☐ M ☐ T ☐ W ☐ T ☐ F ☐ S ☐
Breastplate of Righteousness	S ☐ M ☐ T ☐ W ☐ T ☐ F ☐ S ☐
Shoes / Gospel of Peace	S ☐ M ☐ T ☐ W ☐ T ☐ F ☐ S ☐
Shield of Faith	S ☐ M ☐ T ☐ W ☐ T ☐ F ☐ S ☐
Helmet of Salvation	S ☐ M ☐ T ☐ W ☐ T ☐ F ☐ S ☐
Sword of the Spirit / Word of God	S ☐ M ☐ T ☐ W ☐ T ☐ F ☐ S ☐

No weapon formed against you will prosper. This is the heritage of the servants of ADONAI.
Is. 54:17

WEEK 22
THE RABBI PRINCIPLE
(JOHN 14:12)

"Truly, truly, I say to you, whoever believes in me will also do the works that I do; and greater works than these will he do, because I am going to the Father."

John 14 begins what has become known as the "Farewell Discourse." It is immediately following Judas leaving the last supper and runs through chapter 17, ending before Jesus and the remaining 11 disciples go to the garden where they frequently met when in Jerusalem.

Jesus knew what would transpire that night, the following day at Passover and in the next 72 hours. I'm pretty sure He chose every word carefully. This would be the last time, while still in His mortal body, that He would be teaching them the things they needed to hear and understand.

He tells them how He's going to leave, return to His Father's house, prepare a place for them and come back for them. He tells them that they know where He's going, to which Thomas says, "No, we don't know where you're going or the way to get there."

Jesus answered, "I am the way and the truth and the life. No one comes to the Father except through me."
John 14:6 (NIV)

"*I* am..."

Jesus' statement above is crucial to our faith, and it's also where we lose a lot of people. There's a meme out there depicting various spiritual leaders like Gandhi, Buddha and Jesus, all saying similar things – or even the very same thing. The quaint inspirational one-liners are all met with praise and acceptance except for Jesus'. His is met with criticism and even hostility.

Suggesting that Jesus is the only exclusive access point to truth, life and God has never been very popular. It's especially unpopular in today's polarizing climate of inclusion. In fact, to state that Jesus is the only absolute gatekeeper or doorway to a "God," or a "higher power," is politically incorrect, inflammatory and on a fast track to becoming illegal.

Regardless, this claim that Jesus makes of Himself is a market differentiator. It separates us from everybody else. Many are willing to accept that there is a god of some sort, but few are willing to embrace the exclusivity of Jesus as "*the* only way" *to* that God. They cannot – will not – reconcile the narrowness of that entry point. Jesus Himself stated that this path was narrow, restrictive and that few would find it, so this shouldn't be a surprise to any of us. It is easier for the majority to conclude that Jesus is only one of many teachers or prophets than to concede that He is *the* One – the *Only* One. It's less offensive.

When John the Baptist was imprisoned, he sent some of his disciples to ask Jesus if He was the One or if they should wait and look for another. Jesus answered by listing His various works and concluded with, "And blessed is he that is not offended by Me" (Mt. 11:4-6). So many are offended by Him. So many in the *faith* are offended by Him. Yet, He stands there with the openness of His gentle arms to receive you…

Philip asks Him to show them the Father. Jesus replies, "If you have seen Me, you have seen the Father." I love this revelatory answer. It takes a lot out of the Old Testament mystery of who, what and how God is: that controversial Jesus is how the God of heaven is.

In Rabbi Schneur Zalman's Code of Jewish Law he writes: "When a child begins to speak, the father should begin teaching him verses of Torah."

Perhaps the child does not yet comprehend what he is saying, yet he begins to build an appreciation and respect for the Torah. The age of three marks another milestone in a child's education— at this age it is customary to begin training a boy to wear tzitzit, and a girl to light Shabbat and holiday candles. Children are then taught to recite the morning blessings, the Grace after Meals, and the Shema before retiring. Halachically speaking, the obligation to start training children to do all mitzvot begins somewhere between the age of 6 and 9— depending on the nature of the child.

At the age of 13, for a boy, or 12 for a girl, the time the child reaches Bar or Bat Mitzvah, respectively, the child – or actually, the new adult – becomes obligated to fulfill all of G d's commandments.

(Source: Shmuel Kogan. *At what age does a child's Torah education begin?* https://www.chabad.org/library/article_cdo/aid/585406/jewish/At-what-age-does-Torah-education-begin.htm)

According to Judah ben Tema, "At five years the age is reached for studying Mikra (written Torah), at ten for studying the Mishnah (oral Torah), at thirteen for fulfilling the mitzvoth (Bar or Bat Mitzvah), at fifteen for studying Talmud" (Avot 5:21).

(Source: Moses ben Maimon, Maimonides. *Mishne Torah. Laws of Torah,* Study 1:13)

Jewish males begin studying Torah in an organized educational setting by age five. Between the ages of 13 to 16, a decision to begin vocational training is made. Those that show promise are encouraged to continue their studies in a *yeshiva* – a seminary, if you will. The idea is to attract the attention of a rabbi to then further your education and career.

Rabbis in the first century would select an elect few that showed promise from the crop of potential recruits. A rabbi would select those he thought would fully measure up to his standards, meaning the rabbi would only choose a disciple based on the rabbi's determination that he could duplicate himself into that disciple – the Rabbi Principle. When a rabbi determined that a potential disciple had the capability to become like himself, the rabbi would then tell the budding hopeful, "Follow me."

Jesus was/is a proper Rabbi with a capital "R." Thus, Jesus hand-picked His disciples, you and I, and He hand-picked us believing that He could duplicate Himself into us

- Mentally,
- Emotionally,
- Intellectually and
- Spiritually.

Every aspect of Himself:

- His personality
- How He reasons
- How He processes information
- How he emphasizes
- How He interprets scripture
- How He comes to His conclusions

...what makes Him tick, and what ticks Him off. Rabbi chose us, because He saw that we demonstrated the potential to live out and exemplify to others God's Word. Just like He did/does.

The Jewish disciple understood all this. They understood the principle. He knew that if he was chosen by Rabbi that Rabbi believed he was going to be able to duplicate himself into that disciple. That's the entire relationship – to make a disciple of yourself.

We had no idea of this when we accepted the invitation of "Follow Me." The majority of us *still* don't understand that this is what we signed up for, and we're not all being taught this. This is why it is essential to understand the basic scriptural and Hebrew foundations of our faith. Things would make a lot more sense if we knew and understood these things.

So when Peter sees Jesus walking on the water, Peter *knows* that if Rabbi can walk on water, *he* can walk on water. Asking Jesus if he could join Him wasn't that far-fetched when you understand the relationship. This was incredibly pleasing and satisfying to Jesus! This meant that Peter was growing in the faith to walk in the dust of his Rabbi!

Whatever Rabbi says and whatever Rabbi does, the disciple knows and understands that he's going to be able to say and do those same things.

Jesus says that if you believe in Him, believe that He's the Promised Messiah of Israel, you will do the same works that He does. We will do the same miracles, the same signs and wonders. In fact, Jesus says that we will do *greater* signs and wonders, works and miracles than He did, because He's going to the Father.

I know this might still sound crazy to some of you… I also know that this is starting to make sense to some of you. Some of you can now begin to understand why Jesus would say this in light of this Rabbi Principle and the parameters of the relationship.

We're going to do greater works than Jesus and He's leaving the planet. It's a transference of spiritual responsibility and spiritual authority.

Therefore, greater works than this (the "this" being the works that Jesus personally did here on earth) will you and I do, Jesus said, because – now get this – the sign of a great rabbi is that his disciple surpasses him. That's the goal of the entire rabbi / disciple relationship.

And Jesus is the Ultimate Rabbi.

○ FIELD NOTES

DATE: / / TIME: : AM/PM PLACE:

		A±
○		
○		
○		
○		
○		
○		
○		
○		
○		
○		
○		
○		
○		
○		
○		
○		
○		
○		
○		
○		

ARMOR CHECK: Ephesians 6:10-18

Belt of Truth	S ☐	M ☐	T ☐	W ☐	T ☐	F ☐	S ☐
Breastplate of Righteousness	S ☐	M ☐	T ☐	W ☐	T ☐	F ☐	S ☐
Shoes / Gospel of Peace	S ☐	M ☐	T ☐	W ☐	T ☐	F ☐	S ☐
Shield of Faith	S ☐	M ☐	T ☐	W ☐	T ☐	F ☐	S ☐
Helmet of Salvation	S ☐	M ☐	T ☐	W ☐	T ☐	F ☐	S ☐
Sword of the Spirit / Word of God	S ☐	M ☐	T ☐	W ☐	T ☐	F ☐	S ☐

No weapon formed against you will prosper. This is the heritage of the servants of ADONAI.
Is. 54:17

○ WEEK 23
AS IT WAS IN THE DAYS OF NOAH (MATTHEW 24:37)

"Remember how it was in the days of Noah. It will be the same when the Son of Man comes." (NIRV)

At the top of Matthew 24, Jesus prophesies the destruction of the temple. The disciples ask Jesus when the temple would be destroyed and what the signs of His return and the end of the age would be.

You can read the entire discourse on your own, but part of what is to come is an increase in "lawlessness," ("iniquity" in other translations) among believers. The Greek word here is "*anomos*", Strong's #G459, meaning:

1. destitute of (the Mosaic) law
    - of the Gentiles
2. departing from the law, a violator of the law, lawless, wicked

in other words, "*Torahless*," or "*Torahlessness*:" void of the "Law of Moses."

Because of the lack of Torah observance among believers, the love of many grows cold. There is a great falling away, believers are betraying and hating each other, and all the while, false prophets and false messiahs are rising up, functioning in supernatural signs and wonders, deceiving many.

Sounds about right.

Israel was to obey God's commandments – the Torah, the Mosaic "law" – in order to love God and each other, as He prescribed, so that they would have the discernment not to follow false prophets and false "messiahs" (like Korah) and fall away, betray and hate one another. In the same exact way, Jesus is telling us that *we* need to obey God's commandments – His Torah – to avoid the same fate, just like the Apostle Paul warned in our premise, 1 Corinthians 10:1-12.

Now keep in mind, Jesus is going to answer their questions and tell them the signs that *we* are to be looking for, the signs *we're* to be aware of, that will show us the season of His return. We're going to break it down to its three main parts:

- The days of Noah
- "No one knows the day or hour"
- The lesson of the fig tree

AS IT WAS IN THE DAYS OF NOAH

The common teaching on this is that there wasn't anything special about the days of Noah. Besides, Jesus describes the days of Noah in verses 38-39 (NIV):

> *For in the days before the flood, people were eating and drinking, marrying and giving in marriage, up to the day Noah entered the ark; and they knew nothing about what would happen until the flood came and took them all away. That is how it will be at the coming of the Son of Man.*

The only difference here from, say, any other ordinary day or age / time period, is the use of the words "flood," "Noah" and "ark." Seemingly. People eating, drinking and marrying happens every day. It happened in the days of Adam, it happened in the days of Abraham, and it happened in the days of Moses. So then, why mention specifically the days of Noah? How *was it* in the days of Noah that made them different?

> *[...] the sons of God saw that the daughters of humans were beautiful, and they married any of them they chose. The Nephilim were on the earth in those days — and also afterward — when the sons of God went to the daughters of humans and had children by them. They were the heroes of old, men of renown.*
> *Genesis 6:2, 4 (NIV)*

Remember the Nephilim, that demonic strain of humanity in the land of Canaan that weren't entirely human? The days of Noah were when the transgression of the Watchers, the 200 Sons of God, came to a head – causing the flood and the extermination of all life on earth.

The Watchers were 200 Sons of God – sentinels, if you will – that protected our airspace, our planet. They saw the daughters of men, thought them beautiful and made a unanimous pact to descend from their godly place, their "proper sphere," as Jude 1:6 puts it, for the sole and disobedient act of procreation. They wanted to sire offspring, like humans, with our women. They created a semi-human race on earth, the Nephilim, and both the Watchers and the Nephilim coexisted with man, teaching us everything we were never supposed to know.

To add to their unfathomable infraction, the Watchers start experimenting with genetics, mixing the DNA of human, plant and animal life in search of immortality for their offspring and breaking the most basic of God's commands in the process – *everything after its own kind* (Gn. 1:11, 12, 21, 24; 6:20; 7:14) – perverting creation at its DNA level, thus causing the flood.

Enoch, Noah's great grandfather, was the patriarch assigned to bring judgment on the Watchers and their Nephilim children. The spirits of the original Nephilim were disembodied, spawning demons, while the Watchers were imprisoned in the bottomless pit. The Watchers are believed to be those released at the Fifth Trumpet in Revelation 9. Hence, as it was in the days of Noah…

NO ONE KNOWS THE DAY OR HOUR

It's important to note that Jesus is bouncing around in this dialog in chapter 24. I think that's the biggest cause of confusion here when trying to understand what He's saying. For example, why would He tell us the signs of His return and then blurt out that no one can know the day or the hour unless He's talking about various scenarios with different timetables?

In verse 36, He makes the statement that all of Christendom has been banking on:

> *"But about that day or hour no one knows, not even the angels in heaven, nor the Son, but only the Father." (NIV)*

Not knowing and never having the ability to know takes a pretty big load off of our plates, right? It would also lessen the responsibilities Jesus says are ours when determining His coming. Maybe?

- Do not be led astray.
- Do not be alarmed.
- Endure to the end.
- Let the reader understand.
- Flee to the mountains.
- Leave behind your belongings.
- Pray that your flight isn't in winter or on the Sabbath.
- Do not believe fake news about Jesus.
- Do not heed false prophets and/or false messiahs.
- Learn the fig tree lesson.
- Stay vigilant.
- Be the faithful and wise servant.

It's so much easier to just trust in His merciful goodness than to actually be proactive like the wise and faithful servant that He literally references in verses 46-51! But no, let's bank on what He said in verse 36, because, you know...

This single, standalone verse, if it's saying what we teach it is saying, contradicts the intent of the other 50 verses in the chapter, as well as the parable of the Ten Virgins in chapter 25. Here's what I mean:

Verses 4-31 are clear instruction on what to look for and what to expect as the signs of the end of the age and of His coming. Verses 32-35 are the lesson of the fig tree.

In verse 36, He says "no one can know the day or hour," but He says this after the lesson of the fig tree, which clearly tells us that, yes, we *can* know the season of His return. Then we have the two verses about Noah, and *then* we're back to tribulation, rapture-esque type stuff that sounds like it should be around verses 16-26.

I see two things being talked about here:

1. Jesus' second coming

The beginning of the Millennium Reign, an event we are completely expected to know the season of its coming, and

2. The end of the age

The end of the Millennium Reign.

Look at what Jesus says in verse 35, between the fig tree lesson and the "no one knows" verse 36, contextually:

> *"Heaven and earth will pass away, but my words will never pass away. But about that day or hour no one knows, not even the angels in heaven, nor the Son, but only the Father." (NIV)*

Test what I'm saying here for yourself against the other Gospel accounts found in Mark 13:24-37 and Luke 12:35-43.

THE LESSON OF THE FIG TREE

> *"Now learn this lesson from the fig tree: As soon as its twigs get tender and its leaves come out, you know that summer is near.*
>
> *Even so, when you see all these things, you know that it is near, right at the door.*
> *Matthew 24:32-33 (NIV)*

Know the season of His return in the same way you know that summer is near because of the fig leaves.

You've heard the term "thief in the night," right?

> *"Therefore be on the alert, for you do not know which day your Lord is coming. But be sure of this, that if the head of the house had known at what time of the night the thief was coming, he would have been on the alert and would not have allowed his house to be broken into. For this reason you also must be ready; for the Son of Man is coming at an hour when you do not think He will." Matthew 24:42-44 (NASB)*

Peter refers to His coming as a thief at the end of the age, not the second coming, in 2 Peter 3:10-13. Jesus refers to coming like a thief to the church of Sardis because they were not awake in Revelation 3:2-3 and again in Revelation 16:15.

But Paul had this to say about it:

> *Now, brothers and sisters, about times and dates we do not need to write to you, for you know very well that the day of the Lord will come like a thief in the night. But you, brothers and sisters, are not in darkness so that this day should surprise you like a thief. 1 Thessalonians 5:1-2, 4 (NIV)*

Make sure to keep doing all those things Jesus told us to do, the things that keep us living in the Light. Because we don't live in darkness, brethren, so that day won't catch us by surprise like a thief.

○ FIELD NOTES

DATE: / / TIME: : AM/PM PLACE:

○		A±
○		
○		
○		
○		
○		
○		
○		
○		
○		
○		
○		
○		
○		
○		
○		
○		
○		
○		
○		

ARMOR CHECK: Ephesians 6:10-18

Belt of Truth	S ☐ M ☐ T ☐ W ☐ T ☐ F ☐ S ☐
Breastplate of Righteousness	S ☐ M ☐ T ☐ W ☐ T ☐ F ☐ S ☐
Shoes / Gospel of Peace	S ☐ M ☐ T ☐ W ☐ T ☐ F ☐ S ☐
Shield of Faith	S ☐ M ☐ T ☐ W ☐ T ☐ F ☐ S ☐
Helmet of Salvation	S ☐ M ☐ T ☐ W ☐ T ☐ F ☐ S ☐
Sword of the Spirit / Word of God	S ☐ M ☐ T ☐ W ☐ T ☐ F ☐ S ☐

No weapon formed against you will prosper. This is the heritage of the servants of ADONAI.
Is. 54:17

○ WEEK 24
THE ZION OF THE HOLY ONE OF ISRAEL (ISAIAH 60:14C)

[...] they shall call you the City of the LORD, the Zion of the Holy One of Israel.

THE FIRSTFRUITS OFFERING - A PARAPHRASE DEUTERONOMY 26:1-11

This is one of the most beautiful things we do as a community. There is nothing like making covenant and declarations with and for the brethren.

When you enter the territory Father God has set aside for you, you will take it and possess it.

Then, take the first share, the first fruits, of everything you produce, of everything you make in your new territory. Put it in a basket and take it to the place where He has told you to worship, with whom He has told you to worship.

Tell your pastor, your spiritual covering, your spiritual authority, "Today I declare to ADONAI, my God, that I possess the territory He has given me; my prophetic inheritance that I was promised."

Your leader will then take the basket from you and place it in front of the altar. You will have the following conversation with God as He listens to you:

"Our spiritual ancestor, Jacob, was a wandering Aramean. He went to Egypt with a few people, lived there and became a great nation. They were treated badly in Egypt – made to suffer as slaves.

"We cried out to ADONAI, the God of our people, and He didn't have a deaf ear towards us but heard our voice – He didn't have a blind eye towards us but saw our suffering under the heavy yoke of the Egyptians.

"ADONAI raised His mighty hand and extended his expansive arm of deliverance, bringing us out of Egypt with great and terrible supernatural signs and wonders. It was miraculous.

"He brought us here and gave us this territory – a land flowing with His goodness and provision like milk and honey.

"Now, Lord, I bring to you the first portion, the firstfruits of what I have produced. After all, You're the one that gave them to me."

Place the basket before the LORD your God and bow to Him.

Now you will enjoy all the blessings that the LORD has given you and your family. You, the assembly and the strangers among you.

BLESSINGS FOR OBEDIENCE - A PARAPHRASE DEUTERONOMY 28:1-14

This is the "Gospel of Prosperity." Obedience is everything. Disobedience is rebellion. Rebellion is witchcraft. Witchcraft is Godlessness.

> *"And if you faithfully obey the voice of the Lord your God, being careful to do all his commandments that I command you today, the Lord your God will set you high above all the nations of the earth. And all these blessings shall come upon you and overtake you, if you obey the voice of the Lord your God."*
> *Deuteronomy 28:1-2*

Live in the city? You will be blessed. Live in the country? You will be blessed.

Your children will be blessed. Your crops, even your young livestock will be blessed. And your bread baskets and bread pans will be blessed, too.

It doesn't matter where you go, you will be – that's right – blessed.

When enemies come against you? God will help you win that fight. They'll come from one direction, and they'll run away in seven directions.

Your barns will be blessed with plenty. Grain, produce – food from God Himself. Everything you do in the territory He gave you He will bless you in.

ADONAI has set you apart, separated you from everyone else, to make you *His* holy people. He swore against Himself that He would do that *if* you keep His commandments – *if* you are obedient and live *exactly* as He instructed you to live – and always for your good.

Everyone else – your neighbors, strangers – will see that you belong to Him and want the life you have.

He'll give you more than you need. You'll have lots of children. Even your livestock will have lots of children. You'll also have the best crops. All of this is promised to you in the territory He promised you, your prophetic inheritance, a promise He made to your spiritual fathers.

He will open up the storehouses of His riches in heaven for you. He will send rain on your land at the right time. HE *WILL* BLESS EVERYTHING YOU DO!

You will be the lender, not the borrower. He will make you leaders, not the followers. Pay attention to this instruction of His that I'm telling you right now. Be vigilant to obey and follow them, then you'll always be on top, never on the bottom.

Please, don't ignore what I'm saying. Stay the course and don't waver left and right. And don't follow other gods, anything that can be considered idolatry, and that includes your attitude. Only worship Him.

GALILEE OF THE GENTILES

> *Leaving Nazareth, he went and lived in Capernaum, which was by the lake in the area of Zebulun and Naphtali — to fulfill what was said through the prophet Isaiah: "Land of Zebulun and land of Naphtali, the Way of the Sea, beyond the Jordan, Galilee of the Gentiles — the people living in darkness have seen a great light; on those living in the land of the shadow of death a light has dawned." [Is. 9:1-2] From that time on Jesus began to preach, "Repent, for the kingdom of heaven has come near."*
> *Matthew 4:13-17 (NIV)*

Israel is a land bridge between three continents and is Africa's only land link to Europe and Asia. Why else would God have Abram move from one end of the fertile crescent to the other? Strategy.

And then you have Capernaum, a fishing village on the northwestern shore of the Galilee – a "frontier town" between the territories of Antipas and Philip; a social hub, if you will, on this all-important land bridge. It became "His own town" (Mt. 9:11) …

This sociological diversity was a cornerstone of his ministry. And this too was due to the geographical position of Capernaum. The village was located right along one of the major international highways of the Ancient Near East: the coastal road, which connected Egypt to Mesopotamia.

At Mount Carmel it turned inland, cutting through Nahal Iron (Wadi Ara), passed beneath the great city of Megiddo, and crossed the Jezreel Valley until it reached the Sea of Galilee. It was here that the highway skirted the modest village of Capernaum.

(Source: Lipnick, Jonathan. "Capernaum By The Sea," Israel Institute of Biblical Studies https://blog.israelbiblicalstudies.com/holy-land-studies/home-capernaum-sea)

I love the water, and I love the mountains. Capernaum has both, so I can easily see the attraction. Tiberias is 15 kilometers away and also became a favorite lakeside location of mine. There's just something in the air in the Galilee of the Gentiles – the land of Naphtali. It has called to me for 40 years now. Maybe one day it'll be *my* own town…

> *And he went throughout all Galilee, teaching in their synagogues and proclaiming the gospel of the kingdom and healing every disease and every affliction among the people. So his fame spread throughout all Syria, and they brought him all the sick, those afflicted with various diseases and pains, those oppressed by demons, those having seizures, and paralytics, and he healed them.*
> *Matthew 4:23-24*

○ FIELD NOTES

DATE: / / TIME: : AM/PM PLACE:

		A±
○		
○		
○		
○		
○		
○		
○		
○		
○		
○		
○		
○		
○		
○		
○		
○		
○		
○		
○		
○		

ARMOR CHECK: Ephesians 6:10-18

Belt of Truth	S ☐	M ☐	T ☐	W ☐	T ☐	F ☐	S ☐
Breastplate of Righteousness	S ☐	M ☐	T ☐	W ☐	T ☐	F ☐	S ☐
Shoes / Gospel of Peace	S ☐	M ☐	T ☐	W ☐	T ☐	F ☐	S ☐
Shield of Faith	S ☐	M ☐	T ☐	W ☐	T ☐	F ☐	S ☐
Helmet of Salvation	S ☐	M ☐	T ☐	W ☐	T ☐	F ☐	S ☐
Sword of the Spirit / Word of God	S ☐	M ☐	T ☐	W ☐	T ☐	F ☐	S ☐

No weapon formed against you will prosper. This is the heritage of the servants of ADONAI.
Is. 54:17

○ WEEK 25
THE SECRET THINGS REVEALED (DEUTERONOMY 29:29)

"Things which are hidden belong to ADONAI our God. But the things that have been revealed belong to us and our children forever, so that we can observe all the words of this Torah." (CJB)

We're so predisposed to disobedience that we actually believe that God would instruct us, command us and demand from us, because He's some egotistical monster.

At the same time, the religious believe that obedience to almost everything is legalism. We have become so deluded in our reasoning, our understanding, in regard to obedience that obedience itself is wrong and somehow bad for us. I mean, doesn't reading that last line alone smack of the enemy? Hasn't that been his tactic from the garden?

We credit our "freedom" from obedience, our freedom from "legalism," our "right" to be lawless as "Believers," all this "liberty from obligation and responsibility," to the Blood of Jesus… Just typing those words was difficult, because it's such a demonic thought.

If Lucifer's goal was to deceive Eve in the garden by seducing her with twisted words, wouldn't Lucifer's goal be to deceive you and me by seducing us with twisted words, twisted theology and doctrine? Yes, yes it would, and that's exactly what he's done and what all the epistles in the New Testament warn against.

This is why, on this journey from exodus to ingathering, you're constantly seeing the reminder and instruction to keep God's law, God's commandments, His Torah. Because if we don't, we're essentially keeping Lucifer's way.

Moses' time is coming to an end, and Deuteronomy 29 is Moses reiterating the terms of the covenant and imploring Israel to *follow* the terms of the covenant. The terms are actually quite simple:

Follow the terms of the covenant and live. Disobey the terms of the covenant and die.

Jesus Himself said that not a jot or tittle of this covenant would be done away with. It would be easier for heaven and earth to pass away before that would happen (Mt. 5:18-19; 24:35; Mk 13:31; Lk 16:17; 21:33), but we simply don't believe Him. Instead, we've created theologies and doctrines that literally contradict this truth that Jesus spoke and conclude that the terms of the covenant – obedience to God's laws, His Torah – were done away with and replaced by Jesus Himself! This is an absolute lie from the enemy.

> *These are the words of the covenant that the LORD commanded Moses to make with the people of Israel [...] Therefore keep the words of this covenant and do them, that you may prosper in all that you do. [...] that he may establish you today as his people, and that he may be your God, as he promised you [...]*
>
> *It is not with you alone that I am making this sworn covenant, but with whoever is standing here with us today before the LORD our God, and with whoever is not here with us today.*
> *Deuteronomy 29:1, 9, 13a-15*

That "and with whoever is not here with us today" means you and me.

God wants to prosper us in everything that we do. This is the life more abundant that Jesus spoke about. God wants to establish us as His people and to establish Himself as our God. His desire is to restore what was lost – no, given away by Adam to the enemy – but it requires our obedience to His precepts and mandates.

The entire New Testament narrative supports this. Everything Jesus taught teaches obedience to God's Word, the Torah. Everything that Paul taught was obedience to God's Word, the scriptures, the Torah. It's like a secret hidden in plain sight...

So, now that we've gotten that out of the way, let's continue.

When Israel lived in Egypt, and when they trekked through the various countries in their 40-year exodus, they were exposed to the various idols and altars of the gods of the land of Canaan. Your personal journey from your personal Egypt to salvation took you through some places in your life that were also riddled with false gods and idols. The Lord *hates* those false gods and idols.

> *"I am making this covenant with you so that no one among you— no man, woman, clan, or tribe— will turn away from the LORD our God to worship these gods of other nations, and so that no root among you bears bitter and poisonous fruit."*
> *Deuteronomy 29:18 (NLT)*

That can't be any clearer, and to suggest that Jesus did away with these things is extremely doubtful. It is our responsibility to make sure that no one in our families or communities turns away from the Lord. No one is to be involved with the worship of the false gods of Canaan, and we're to make sure that this sin doesn't spread like poison throughout our numbers.

Well, like Israel, we haven't done very well in this regard, corporately or personally. Why? For starters, we believe in a religion that teaches that our Messiah liberated us from such nonsense, such "legalism." We're free not to obey the covenant, remember?

> *"If there is such a person, when he hears the words of this curse, he will bless himself secretly, saying to himself, 'I will be all right, even though I will stubbornly keep doing whatever I feel like doing; so that I, although "dry," [sinful,] will be added to the "watered" [righteous].'"*
> *Deuteronomy 29:19 (CJB)*

Le sigh...

Again, the Apostle Paul warns us in 1 Corinthians 10:1-12 to avoid every blunder Israel made in the desert. Those errors all stemmed from the belief that it wasn't entirely necessary for them to follow, obey, regard, keep and/or do God's commandments, precepts, and mandates. His Torah.

When Paul wrote this warning, there were people going around teaching the Sanhedrin lie, the lie that none of this was necessary – that, because of Jesus, we weren't expected or needed to keep God's Torah, just like we are being taught today. Paul himself was accused of teaching this as we see in Acts 21:24.

THE SANHEDRIN LIE

The Sanhedrin did everything they could to prove Jesus a false prophet as outlined in Deuteronomy 13. If they could prove Him to be a false prophet, then there was no validity to the claim of His being Messiah. They were never able to achieve that, so at His illegal trial, they paid for false witnesses to lie about Jesus in order to persuade Rome to give them an execution order. Having false witnesses to prompt a stoning also happened to the disciple Stephen in Acts 6-7.

Stephen is accused of speaking blasphemy against Moses (i.e. Torah) in Acts 6:11, and the following is stated in verses 13-14:

> *[...] and they set up false witnesses who said, "This man*

never ceases to speak words against this holy place and the law, for we have heard him say that this Jesus of Nazareth will destroy this place and will change the customs that Moses delivered to us."

Stephen is accused of speaking against the temple and the Torah and of preaching that Jesus changed – threw out – the customs and practices of Moses, i.e. the Torah.

This is, in essence, what is literally taught in churches everywhere today. The Sanhedrin Lie is Christianity's Truth. That's a concern.

The LORD will never be willing to forgive those people. His burning anger will blaze out against them. All of the curses I've written down in this scroll will fall on them. And the LORD will wipe out their names from the earth.

He will find those people in all of the tribes of Israel and give them nothing but trouble. That will be in keeping with all of the curses of the covenant. They are written down in this Scroll of the Law.

Deuteronomy 29:20-21 (NIRV)

It hardly matters whether we agree or not, whether this teaching and belief fits within our denominational backgrounds or not. This is what God established, and Jesus only says what He hears the Father say. Again, this isn't to condemn or judge. We are only sticking to our premise of the warning from these very writings that the Apostle Paul said he didn't want us to be ignorant about.

Surely, we all understand and believe that the blessings of the Bible also come with curses, right?

God "will repay each person according to what they have done." (Jb. 34:11; Ps. 62:12; Pr. 24:12; Je. 17:10, 32:19; Mt. 16:27)

To those who by persistence in doing good seek glory, honor and immortality, he will give eternal life. But for those who are self-seeking and who reject the truth and follow evil, there will be wrath and anger.

There will be trouble and distress for every human being who does evil: first for the Jew, then for the Gentile; but glory, honor and peace for everyone who does good: first for the Jew, then for the Gentile.

Romans 2:6-10 (NIV)

It's passages like the one above and the one below that really bring to the forefront the ministry of Paul, the Apostle to the Gentiles.

This is why Paul – "circumcised the eighth day, of the nation of Israel, of the tribe of Benjamin, a Hebrew of Hebrews; as to the Law, a Pharisee; as to zeal, a persecutor of the church; as to the righteousness which is in the Law, blameless" (Philippians 3:4-6) – was the Apostle to the Gentiles. Besides this amazing Jewish pedigree, Paul, possibly an up-and-comer for the Jewish high council and more than likely on a fast track for High Priest, was also a Roman citizen. Who else could unpack this nebulous "Old Testament" to pagan Gentiles? The fishermen or tax collector? I think not.

Paul is teaching Gentiles in his letters / epistles the proper way to live out the Scriptures in light of the Messianic fulfillment of Jesus as a Jewish Rabbi would, not as a Roman Citizen.

(Source: Aguirre, Allan R. "Introduction," In *The Feasts Unlocked*, ix. Park City, Utah: Planet Blue Media, 2018. http://planetbluemedia.com)

> *For it is not merely the hearers of Torah whom God considers righteous; rather, it is the doers of what Torah says who will be made righteous in God's sight.*
>
> *For whenever Gentiles, who have no Torah, do naturally what the Torah requires, then these, even though they don't have Torah, for themselves are Torah!*
>
> *For their lives show that the conduct the Torah dictates is written in their hearts. Their consciences also bear witness to this, for their conflicting thoughts sometimes accuse them and sometimes defend them on a day when God passes judgment on people's inmost secrets. (According to the Good News as I proclaim it, he does this through the Messiah Yeshua.)*
>
> *Romans 2:13-16 (CJB)*

"...when God passes judgment on people's inmost secrets." There's that word, "secret," again.

> *The secret things belong to the LORD our God, but the things revealed belong to us and to our children forever, that we may follow all the words of this law.*
>
> *Deuteronomy 29:29 (NIV)*

○ FIELD NOTES

DATE: / / TIME: : AM/PM PLACE:

○		A±
○		
○		
○		
○		
○		
○		
○		
○		
○		
○		
○		
○		
○		
○		
○		
○		
○		
○		
○		

ARMOR CHECK: Ephesians 6:10-18

Belt of Truth	S ☐ M ☐ T ☐ W ☐ T ☐ F ☐ S ☐
Breastplate of Righteousness	S ☐ M ☐ T ☐ W ☐ T ☐ F ☐ S ☐
Shoes / Gospel of Peace	S ☐ M ☐ T ☐ W ☐ T ☐ F ☐ S ☐
Shield of Faith	S ☐ M ☐ T ☐ W ☐ T ☐ F ☐ S ☐
Helmet of Salvation	S ☐ M ☐ T ☐ W ☐ T ☐ F ☐ S ☐
Sword of the Spirit / Word of God	S ☐ M ☐ T ☐ W ☐ T ☐ F ☐ S ☐

No weapon formed against you will prosper. This is the heritage of the servants of ADONAI.
Is. 54:17

○ WEEK 26
FEAST OF TRUMPETS / YOM TERUAH (LEVITICUS 23:23-25)

> *And the LORD spoke to Moses, saying, "Speak to the people of Israel, saying, In the seventh month, on the first day of the month, you shall observe a day of solemn rest, a memorial proclaimed with blast of trumpets, a holy convocation (a High Sabbath). You shall not do any ordinary work, and you shall present a food offering to the LORD."*

"It's the first of the three Fall Feasts: The Feast of Trumpets / Yom Teruah.

"Yom Teruah is the only feast day that falls on a Rosh Chodesh. In Chapter 2 of *The Feast Unlocked*, we discuss Israel's knowledge of the lunar conjunction to determine when their Rosh Chodesh feasting should begin and that three days for feasting were set aside for the New Moon observance. We also determined that it wasn't until the visible crescent was seen that Rosh Chodesh was officially started as we looked at the following:

> *David said to Jonathan, "Behold, tomorrow is the new moon, and I should not fail to sit at table with the king. But let me go, that I may hide myself in the field till the third day at evening." Then Jonathan said to him, "Tomorrow is the new moon, and you will be missed, because your seat will be empty. On the third day..." And when the new moon came, the king sat down to eat food. But on the second day, the day after the new moon, David's place was empty.*
>
> *1 Samuel 20:5; 18-19; 24, 27*

"They knew when the New Moon was coming but set aside three days for feasting. On seeing the visible crescent, the elders would declare it in order to alert the people that Rosh Chodesh, the beginning of the month, had commenced. Accordingly, since Yom Teruah falls on a Rosh Chodesh, "Rosh Hashanah" is observed as a two-day holiday to accommodate the determination of Rosh Chodesh. The Torah on the other hand, ordains only a one-day observance for Yom Teruah: *"on the first of the month," "a day of remembrance."*

"*Teruah* literally means "shout" or "to make a loud noise," so Yom Teruah would translate to "Day of Making a Loud Noise" or the more suitable "Day of Shouting." On the first day of the seventh month of Ethanim, on Rosh Chodesh, we are to keep a solemn High Shabbat: *"you shall observe a day of solemn rest," "a holy convocation."* It is also a memorial day. "Memorial" here in the Hebrew is Strong's #H2146 *"zikrown"*:

1. memorial, reminder, remembrance

"We're also to mark / announce this memorial day of shouting with shofar blasts (a memorial proclaimed with blast of trumpets.) And because it is a High Sabbath, you shall not do any ordinary work, and you shall present a food offering to ADONAI.

"Essentially, the instruction found in Leviticus 23:23-25 is telling us that on this specific Rosh Chodesh, it is to be a High Shabbat of remembrance, a reminder marked or announced with shouts and blasts of the shofar along with a food offering.

> *This day shall be for you a memorial day, and you shall keep it as a feast to the LORD; throughout your generations, as a statute forever, you shall keep it as a feast.*
> *Exodus 12:14*

"A High Shabbat of remembrance. A solemn reminder announced with blast of shofars." "A reminder of what?" you might ask. It's a reminder of the blowing of a shofar that occurred four months ago at Mount Sinai!

> *On the morning of the third day there were thunders and lightnings and a thick cloud on the mountain and* ***a very loud trumpet (shofar) blast****, so that all the people in the camp trembled. Then Moses brought the people out of the camp to meet God, and they took their stand at the foot of the mountain.*
>
> *Now Mount Sinai was wrapped in smoke because ADONAI had descended on it in fire. The smoke of it went up like the smoke of a kiln, and the whole mountain trembled greatly. And as* ***the sound of the trumpet (shofar) grew louder and louder****, Moses spoke, and God answered him in thunder.*
> *Exodus 19:16-19 [Emphasis mine]*

"Yom Teruah is God instructing us to remember how, when, where and *why He* approached us with His life-giving precepts! Remember?

"In Chapter 4 of *The Feasts Unlocked* we discuss the reason behind bringing Israel out from under the burden of Egypt, the reasons for Israel's deliverance...

"We discuss how Passover's deliverance and salvation from physical slavery and death and the resulting exodus from Egypt occurred with one single goal in mind: an encounter 50 days later with the Living God – Shavuot!

"We discuss how Shavuot prophetically speaks of the marriage between man and God and how Israel never consummated the marriage vows at Sinai and how Jesus is man's final hope for that consummation; the consummation of "I will take (marry) you (the bride) to be my people (my wife), and I (the Bridegroom) will be your God (our Husband).

"He wants us to remember His Shofar blast of Exodus 6:7!!!

> ***I will take you to be my people, and I will be your God,***
> *and you shall know that I am ADONAI your God, who has brought you out from under the burdens of the Egyptians.*

"He wants us to remember that this is the gospel unto salvation; His "Master Plan;" that He loves us, desires us and is our Bridegroom!

"This is what we're supposed to be remembering on Yom Teruah, this holy Rosh Chodesh, this solemn day of remembrance marked with the blasts of shofars, this High Shabbat. Not a civil "New Year's celebration" ...

> *Blessed are the people who know the festal shout (teruah),*
> *who walk, O LORD, in the light of your face...*
> *Psalm 89:15*

"Yom Teruah is better known by its popular and erroneous Babylonian inspired name, "Rosh Hashanah" and it's meaning of "head of the year / new year." In reality, Yom Teruah is a Rosh Chodesh, a High Shabbat of solemn rest, a holy convocation of remembrance when no ordinary work is done. A reminder announced with shouts and blasts of the shofar and a food offering presented to ADONAI. On this Day of Remembrance, we are to remember the Shofar Blast of Mount Sinai and the Covenant of Torah that took place at Shavuot.

"Yom Teruah is not a Rosh Hashanah "New Year's – head of the year" celebration that takes place two weeks before the Feast of Tabernacles (Sukkot) – described in Exodus 23:16 as the "End of the Year".

(Taken from "Feast of Trumpets (Yom Teruah)," In *The Feasts Unlocked.* Park City, Utah: Planet Blue Media, 2018. http://planetbluemedia.com)

○ FIELD NOTES

DATE: / / TIME: : AM/PM PLACE:

○		A±
○		
○		
○		
○		
○		
○		
○		
○		
○		
○		
○		
○		
○		
○		
○		
○		
○		
○		
○		

ARMOR CHECK: Ephesians 6:10-18

Belt of Truth	S☐ M☐ T☐ W☐ T☐ F☐ S☐
Breastplate of Righteousness	S☐ M☐ T☐ W☐ T☐ F☐ S☐
Shoes / Gospel of Peace	S☐ M☐ T☐ W☐ T☐ F☐ S☐
Shield of Faith	S☐ M☐ T☐ W☐ T☐ F☐ S☐
Helmet of Salvation	S☐ M☐ T☐ W☐ T☐ F☐ S☐
Sword of the Spirit / Word of God	S☐ M☐ T☐ W☐ T☐ F☐ S☐

No weapon formed against you will prosper. This is the heritage of the servants of ADONAI.
Is. 54:17

○ WEEK 27
THE VOW OF A NAZIRITE (NUMBERS 6:1-4)

> *And the LORD spoke to Moses, saying, "Speak to the people of Israel and say to them, When either a man or a woman makes a special vow, the vow of a Nazirite, to separate himself to the LORD, he shall separate himself from wine and strong drink. He shall drink no vinegar made from wine or strong drink and shall not drink any juice of grapes or eat grapes, fresh or dried. All the days of his separation he shall eat nothing that is produced by the grapevine, not even the seeds or the skins."*

The two most famous Nazirites (Hebrew *nazir*, meaning *consecrated, holy, devoted one*) from the Bible are Samson the Judge and John the Baptist, the Levitical priest and cousin of Jesus. The third but not-so-famous one would be Samuel, the prophet and judge who was also a Levitical priest. All three men are recorded to have been Nazirites from the womb. Yeah. How awesome is that?

Along with not being allowed to eat or drink anything harvested from the grape (today, almost every condiment has vinegar), a Nazirite was also to avoid dead bodies. And then there's the hair (verse 5):

> *"All the days of his vow of separation, no razor shall touch his head. Until the time is completed for which he separates himself to the LORD, he shall be holy. He shall let the locks of hair of his head grow long."*

Many, including myself, believe that because the word "locks" is used for hair, the Nazirites dreaded their hair:

> *"If you weave the seven locks of my head [...]"*
> *Samson in Judges 16:13*

It doesn't say "seven braids" like many interpret and depict this passage as meaning. It clearly states "locks."

The male character in the Song of Solomon (that portrays Solomon in the story), his hair is referred to as "locks" and described as "a cluster of dates" in SOS 5:11 (NAS). That's what dreadlocks look like. And, ancient Ethiopian iconography depicts Moses with dreadlocks. By the way, I'm not suggesting that every dreadlocked individual is aware of this nor that they are a Nazirite. I do want to be clear about that.

When explaining the Nazirite vow, I usually describe it as "Torah observance on steroids." Not cutting your hair, abstaining from wine and strong drink (liquor) and not touching anything dead is relatively easy to do. So is avoiding anything from the grape – fresh or dried, the seeds and skin, the juice… it's the no vinegar or anything produced by the grapevine that's the challenge.

I mentioned that most condiments have vinegar in them. Try cooking a meal without anything that has vinegar in it. If you're from Texas, that means saying no to barbeque sauce, most salsas and most sauces in general (unless you can determine that the vinegar in that particular food is not sourced from grapes.)

Many consider the Nazirite vow as trivial, whereas I find it fascinating that God would see this sort of self-denial and dedication as "holy." Because it's usually so outside of our scope of things, I'm always fascinated by how and what God determines and deems holy.

Take the eating of matzah, for example, during the Feast of Unleavened Bread. How could *not* eating leavened bread for a week be such a big deal? Have you tried it?

It states that the *covenant* is made by the *eating* of matzah, the eating of unleavened bread (Ex. 13:7-9). That's *"covenant with God,"* in case you didn't catch that… and that's why it's so difficult. It's spiritual! And the enemy doesn't like it when you obey an instruction, especially a *covenant-making* instruction of God's like eating matzah!

Something like eating matzah as an act of covenant with God really puts meat on that passage that says, "My ways are not your ways," doesn't it? We really need to be that careful – that vigilant.

The Nazirite Vow…

There are more verses regarding how to *complete* the vow than there are verses on how to *keep* the vow – twelve, in all.

Here's what the Nazirite was to do to complete his or her solemn vow to the Lord if (a.) A human death occurred beside them,

- They were to shave their head on the seventh day;
- They were to bring two turtledoves or two pigeons to the priest, to the entrance of the tent of meeting, on the eighth day; and
- They had to bring a year-old male lamb for a guilt offering;

(b.) The time of their vow had been completed,

- They were brought to the entrance to the tent of meeting;
- They brought one year-old male lamb without blemish as a gift to ADONAI for a burnt offering;
- They also brought one year-old ewe lamb without blemish as a sin offering;
- One ram without blemish for a peace offering; and
- A basket of unleavened bread, loaves of fine flour mixed with oil, and unleavened wafers smeared with oil along with their corresponding grain and drink offerings.

The priest would then bring these items before the LORD and offer up the Nazirite's sin and burnt offerings. The ram was sacrificed as a peace offering to the LORD along with the basket of unleavened bread and its corresponding grain and drink offerings.

The Nazirite would shave their consecrated head at the entrance of the tent of meeting and then take their hair and place it into the fire under the peace offering sacrifice.

> *And the priest shall take the shoulder of the ram, when it is boiled, and one unleavened loaf out of the basket and one unleavened wafer, and shall put them on the hands of the Nazirite, after he has shaved the hair of his consecration, and the priest shall wave them for a wave offering before the LORD. They are a holy portion for the priest, together with the breast that is waved and the thigh that is contributed. And after that the Nazirite may drink wine.*
> *Numbers 6:19-20*

Isn't that beautiful? How amazing is that?!

You know, not all of this "Old Testament" stuff is lost in the New Testament narrative. Let me show ya.

All firstborn Israeli males must present themselves before God three times a year in Jerusalem at three specific pilgrimage feasts. In Acts 21, we find

Paul traveling to Jerusalem in preparation of presenting himself before God on Shavuot, the second pilgrimage feast of the year. Shavuot is when God gave Moses the "law" / the Torah on Mount Sinai. It's also the 50th day of the Omer Count and when the Holy Spirit came down on the 120 disciples in the upper room: Pentecost. I love how God does those things!

In Acts 21:17, we find Paul going to visit with his church leader, James, the brother of Jesus and the leader of the church in Jerusalem, along with all the church elders.

> *After greeting them, he related one by one the things that God had done among the Gentiles through his ministry. And when they heard it, they glorified God. And they said to him,*
>
> *"You see, brother, how many thousands there are among the Jews of those who have believed. They are all zealous for the law, and they have been told about you that you teach all the Jews who are among the Gentiles to forsake Moses, telling them not to circumcise their children or walk according to our customs (the Torah).*
>
> *What then is to be done? They will certainly hear that you have come. Do therefore what we tell you. We have four men who are under a vow; [...]"*
>
> *Acts 21:19-23*

The Apostle Paul is in great standing with the church leaders in Jerusalem, but there are malicious rumors circulating that Paul teaches against the observance of "the law" / the Torah. The believers that have come to Jerusalem from all over the world for the pilgrimage feast are going to not only know about these rumors, but they're also going to know that Paul is actually in town. So, we have an idea... we have these four guys that are completing a vow... Yup. You guessed it!

In order to quash the rumors that Paul doesn't teach Torah observance, four of our guys are completing their Nazirite vow. Not only *join them* in completing their vow but *pay* for their temple service as well. This will

1. Diffuse any and all rumors against you in regard to your theological and doctrinal position on the observance of Torah, and
2. Show that you yourself live in observance of Torah

> *Take them with you, be purified with them, and pay the expenses connected with having their heads shaved. Then everyone*

will know that there is nothing to these rumors which they have heard about you; but that, on the contrary, you yourself stay in line and keep the Torah.
Acts 21:24 (CJB)

Then Paul took the men, and the next day he purified himself along with them and went into the temple, giving notice when the days of purification would be fulfilled and the offering presented for each one of them.
Acts 21:26

Remember that list we went through that a Nazirite had to do to complete their vow? That's what Paul and these four other guys were about to do.

Yes, born-again Christians were going into the temple; submitting themselves to the rabbinical priests; and were involved with ritual bathing, cleansing, and the shaving of their hair – head, beard and body; as well as offering the animal sacrifices that also accompanied the completion of this vow from Numbers 6.

It was during this week-long temple service of sacrificing animals, etc., in Jerusalem's Temple that Paul was attacked and imprisoned.

When the seven days were almost completed, the Jews from Asia, seeing him in the temple, stirred up the whole crowd and laid hands on him, crying out, "Men of Israel, help! This is the man who is teaching everyone everywhere against the people and the law and this place."
Acts 21:27-28

Nothing like getting jumped in church...

It was this incarceration that would take Paul to Rome and eventually lead to his death. As you may know, this had been prophesied over him prior to his trip to Jerusalem on several occasions. They had tried to stop Paul from going, but he insisted, saying:

"I am ready not only to be imprisoned but even to die in Jerusalem for the name of the Lord Jesus."
Acts 21:13b

"This is the law of the Nazirite. But if he vows an offering to the LORD above his Nazirite vow, as he can afford, in exact accordance with the vow that he takes, then he shall do in addition to

the law of the Nazirite."
Numbers 6:21

I think Paul could not only afford it but also had the wherewithal to pay for it… in full. Thank you, brother.

○ FIELD NOTES

DATE: / / TIME: : AM/PM PLACE:

○		A±
○		
○		
○		
○		
○		
○		
○		
○		
○		
○		
○		
○		
○		
○		
○		
○		
○		
○		
○		

ARMOR CHECK: Ephesians 6:10-18

Belt of Truth	S ☐ M ☐ T ☐ W ☐ T ☐ F ☐ S ☐
Breastplate of Righteousness	S ☐ M ☐ T ☐ W ☐ T ☐ F ☐ S ☐
Shoes / Gospel of Peace	S ☐ M ☐ T ☐ W ☐ T ☐ F ☐ S ☐
Shield of Faith	S ☐ M ☐ T ☐ W ☐ T ☐ F ☐ S ☐
Helmet of Salvation	S ☐ M ☐ T ☐ W ☐ T ☐ F ☐ S ☐
Sword of the Spirit / Word of God	S ☐ M ☐ T ☐ W ☐ T ☐ F ☐ S ☐

No weapon formed against you will prosper. This is the heritage of the servants of ADONAI.
Is. 54:17

○ WEEK 28
DAY OF ATONEMENT / YOM KIPPUR (LEVITICUS 23:27-28)

"Now on the tenth day of this seventh month is the Day of Atonement. It shall be for you a time of holy convocation (a High Sabbath), and you shall afflict (humble) yourselves and present a food offering to the LORD. And you shall not do any work on that very day, for it is a Day of Atonement, to make atonement for you before the LORD your God."

"In traditional Judaism, Yom Kippur is the culmination of the "Days of Awe," the ten-day period of repentance that started with Yom Teruah and the culmination of the Season of Teshuvah (repentance), the 40-day period that started on Elul 1.

"According to the Jewish sages, seven weeks after the Exodus, on the 6th of Sivan (the Omer Count based on Pharisaical tradition), Moses ascended Sinai to receive the Torah – Shavuot. On the 17th of Tammuz, forty days later, Moses destroyed the tablets with the Ten Commandments that had been written with the Finger of God (Ex. 31:18) out of anger for Israel's sin of idolatry of the golden calf. It is then suggested that Moses interceded on Israel's behalf for an additional forty days until being called back up to Sinai (Ex. 34:1-4) on Elul 1, the start of the Season of Teshuvah. After receiving the new tablets, tradition states that Moses descended Mount Sinai on Tishri 10, Yom Kippur, the zenith of the Season of Teshuvah and the Days of Awe.

"Also according to the sages, Yom Teruah is when the righteous are written in the Book of Life and the wicked are written in the Book of Death. During the Days of Awe, however, you have 10 days to atone for your sins and "turn back" to God prior to your fate being sealed on Yom Kippur.

"This tradition of the books is based on Moses' conversation with God (Ex. 32:30-33) the day after Israel's sin of idolatry, when Moses offered to be removed from "the Book you have written:"

The next day Moses said to the people, "You have sinned a great sin. And now I will go up to the LORD; perhaps I can make atonement for your sin." So Moses returned to the LORD and said, "Alas, this people has sinned a great sin. They have made for themselves gods of gold. But now, if you will forgive their sin – but if not, please blot me out of your book that you have written." But the LORD said to Moses, "Whoever has sinned against me, I will blot out of my book."

"How amazing is that? Moses was willing to be blotted out of God's Book – as the penalty for sin – on behalf of a stiff-necked people. This Levite, this Egyptian noble, this warrior, this Nephilim killer... this Prophet that precedes the Messiah Jesus just offered himself up on Israel's behalf. This is who God calls the humblest man that ever walked the face of the earth, and he just gave a mighty prophetic picture of Messiah.

"Yom Kippur is considered Judaism's holiest and most solemn day of the year. To fully appreciate the significance and "back story" of Yom Kippur, a study of Leviticus chapters 8 - 10 and 16 is where you'd want to go.

"Contextually, chapter 16 starts with chapter 8 when Aaron and his sons are presented to serve ADONAI as priests. In chapter 9, Aaron and his sons begin the ministry of priesthood. In chapter 10 you'll find the tragic deaths of Aaron's sons at the Hand of God for offering unauthorized fire before ADONAI.

"The death of Aaron's two sons is the setting for Leviticus 16. Here you'll find the actual instructions for the sacrificial atonement / the cleansing of sins and the commandment to observe Yom Kippur repeated after those instructions.

"The prescribed way for Aaron to enter the temple included bathing and his priestly garments. A bull for a sin offering for himself and the Levites, two goats taken from the congregation for a sin offering for the people and 2 rams for burnt offerings on behalf of himself and the people. Atonement, or "Kippur," means "to cleanse," and this is what Aaron was doing in verses 12-20 of Leviticus 16. Verse 16 says:

Thus he shall make atonement for (kippur) the Holy Place, because of the uncleannesses of the people of Israel and because of their transgressions, all their sins. And so he shall do for the tent of meeting, which dwells with them in the midst of their uncleannesses.

"Aaron is cleansing, "decontaminating" from spiritual and physical impurities, the Holy of Holies, the Tent of Meeting and the Altar (verse 20). Thus, the reason for Yom Kippur is the cleansing of our temples from our sins:

> *For on this day shall atonement (kippur) be made for you to cleanse you. You shall be clean before the LORD from all your sins.*
> *Leviticus 16:30*

> *But when Christ appeared as a high priest of the good things that have come, then through the greater and more perfect tent (not made with hands, that is, not of this creation) he entered once for all into the holy places, not by means of the blood of goats and calves but by means of his own blood, thus securing an eternal redemption.*
> *Hebrews 9:11-12*

"Yom Kippur is the Day of Cleansing. It is a High Shabbat, a holy convocation when no ordinary work is done. It is a day of repentance, self-examination and atonement – "At-One-Ment" with the Living God. We are to "afflict" ourselves; busy ourselves with bowed down humility, and present a food offering to ADONAI.

> *Therefore, brothers, since we have confidence to enter the holy places by the blood of Jesus, by the new and living way that he opened for us through the curtain, that is, through his flesh, and since we have a great priest over the house of God, let us draw near with a true heart in full assurance of faith, with our hearts sprinkled clean from an evil conscience and our bodies washed with pure water.*
> *Hebrews 10:19-22*

(Taken from "Day of Atonement (Yom Kippur)," In *The Feasts Unlocked.* Park City, Utah: Planet Blue Media, 2018. http://planetbluemedia.com)

○ FIELD NOTES

DATE: / / TIME: : AM/PM PLACE:

○		A±
○		
○		
○		
○		
○		
○		
○		
○		
○		
○		
○		
○		
○		
○		
○		
○		
○		
○		
○		

ARMOR CHECK: Ephesians 6:10-18

Belt of Truth	S ☐ M ☐ T ☐ W ☐ T ☐ F ☐ S ☐
Breastplate of Righteousness	S ☐ M ☐ T ☐ W ☐ T ☐ F ☐ S ☐
Shoes / Gospel of Peace	S ☐ M ☐ T ☐ W ☐ T ☐ F ☐ S ☐
Shield of Faith	S ☐ M ☐ T ☐ W ☐ T ☐ F ☐ S ☐
Helmet of Salvation	S ☐ M ☐ T ☐ W ☐ T ☐ F ☐ S ☐
Sword of the Spirit / Word of God	S ☐ M ☐ T ☐ W ☐ T ☐ F ☐ S ☐

No weapon formed against you will prosper. This is the heritage of the servants of ADONAI.
Is. 54:17

○ WEEK 29
FEAST OF INGATHERING / SUKKOT (LEVITICUS 23:34-36)

"Speak to the people of Israel, saying, On the fifteenth day of this seventh month and for seven days is the Feast of Booths to the LORD.

On the first day shall be a holy convocation (a High Sabbath); you shall not do any ordinary work. For seven days you shall present food offerings to the LORD. On the eighth day you shall hold a holy convocation (a High Sabbath) and present a food offering to the LORD. It is a solemn assembly; you shall not do any ordinary work."

"It is the Feast of Ingathering, the Feast of Tabernacles, the Feast of Booths: *Sukkot*! We've made it to the end of the year! (Ex. 23:16)

"The Feast of Tabernacles, *Sukkot* (the plural of *"sukkah"*), signifies our wandering in the desert wilderness, His provision on our behalf and our dependence on His care all along the way (Dt. 29:5). This feast, which is also known as "The Feast," reminds us that He had Israel "dwell in booths" after their deliverance from Egypt. These temporary dwelling places, these booths, are individually known as a *"sukkah."*

"*Sukkah* (Strong's #H5521) is the Hebrew word used in the TaNaKh (Old Testament); whereas the Greek word equivalent used in the New Testament is *"skēnoō"* (Strong's #G4637). We find this Greek word used as "dwelling" when referring to Jesus' dwelling or tabernacling among us in John 1:14 and in reference to God dwelling among us in Revelation 7:15, 12:12, and 13:6. Some translations use this word as "tabernacle" in regard to our physical bodies as seen in 2 Peter 1:13-14 and especially in 2 Corinthians 5:1-10. The theme of "temporary dwelling place" and "temporary physical body" also speaks to our temporary journey through this earth as pilgrims on our way to the final Spiritual Sukkah (Re 21:1-3).

"Sukkot brings us from Yom Kippur, the most solemn day of the year to, just five days later, the most festive eight days of the year – from repentance to rejoicing redemption! Because of this, Sukkot is commonly referred to in traditional Jewish prayers and literature as "The Season of our Rejoicing."

"Sukkot is the last of the Three Pilgrimage Festivals (Dt. 16:16-17) and carries the dual historical / spiritual and agricultural significance we've seen in the other pilgrimage feasts. Sukkot commemorates forty years of wandering in the desert wilderness while living in temporary dwellings. Agriculturally, Sukkot celebrates the gathering of the end of the year harvest known as *Chag ha-Asif*: "of the harvest" – the Festival of Ingathering.

> *You shall keep the Feast of Harvest, of the firstfruits of your labor, of what you sow in the field. You shall keep the Feast of Ingathering at the end of the year, when you gather in from the field the fruit of your labor.*
> *Exodus 23:16*

"Agriculturally, Passover paralleled the planting and harvesting of the barley season, Shavuot the wheat harvest, while Sukkot is the season for harvesting produce. Physically and spiritually, all the crops for the year have been harvested and gathered. God's provision is a time for rejoicing!

"This ongoing theme of harvesting, reaping and sowing is one of God's "Love Languages" towards us; the increase of Himself, in and through us, returned to Him as fruit. Just like in the parables of the minas and the talents, He expects a return from our stewardship of His increase. Sukkot, this appointed time of "ingathering," is that reaping of the harvest in and of our lives of His sowing.

> *He calls to the heavens above and to the earth, that he may judge his people: "Gather to me my faithful ones, who made a covenant with me by sacrifice!"*
> *Psalm 50:4-5*

"God's calendar being an agricultural one, the Feasts are intricately connected to the land. This is why Jesus used agricultural metaphors as often as He did in the Gospels. Words like planting, seeds and reaping within concepts of sowing, seasons and harvesting, etc.

"The first three spring feasts are connected to barley, the first crop in Israel's yearly harvest. Seven weeks later (50 days), the assembly is gathered for the wheat harvest and to participate in the receiving of Torah and the baptism of Pentecost on their way to the ingathering of the produce harvest of Booths / Sukkot.

"As we've seen, the feasts are a massive part of Israel's identity; individually, corporately, physically and spiritually. So imagine again the richness these yearly experiences brought to families and individuals. Jesus knew this, so the agricultural symbolism in His discourses rang true to His listeners. See also Deuteronomy 16:13-15.

"If there was one way to describe the purposes of God through religion and the biblical text, it would be the theme of God's desire to dwell with man. This theme of "dwelling together" is at the core of our journey from Passover to Tabernacles, from Exodus to Ingathering and at the very heart of everything God has orchestrated on our behalf. It's the reason behind placing Adam in the Garden.

"All throughout the scriptures, we see these physical and spiritual "types and shadows" of this desire, the Feast of Sukkot being the end result:

> *And let them make me a sanctuary, that I may dwell (sukkah) in their midst.*
> *Exodus 25:8*

> *I am the LORD your God from the land of Egypt; I will again make you dwell in tents, as in the days of the appointed feast.*
> *Hosea 12:9*

"The Feast of Tabernacles, the Feast of Booths, this Feast of Ingathering, Sukkot, is the culmination and the designed desired end result of the exodus from Egypt. We've been gathered by Him, for Him and in Him. We remember this by dwelling in a temporary physical place that speaks of and calls us to an eternal dwelling place, in and with Him (Re 21:1-3).

"Sukkot signifies our wandering in the desert wilderness, His provision on our behalf and our dependence on His care all along the way (Dt. 29:5). We've been taken from deliverance and repentance to redemption!

"The physical, prophetic and ultimately spiritual significance of Sukkot is this ingathering of His people unto Himself – the "dwelling among" – the "being in His Rest" as we've seen represented throughout all of the Feasts. Sukkot, this appointed time of "ingathering," is the reaping of the fruit harvest in and of our lives of His sowing. It would behoove us to be well versed in this appointed expression of celebratory worship and rejoicing unto our God as we continue ever forward in our earthly sukkah to the spiritual sukkah that awaits us."

(Taken from "Feast of Tabernacles (Sukkot)," In *The Feasts Unlocked*. Park City, Utah: Planet Blue Media, 2018. http://planetbluemedia.com)

○ FIELD NOTES

DATE: / / TIME: : AM/PM PLACE:

○		A±
○		
○		
○		
○		
○		
○		
○		
○		
○		
○		
○		
○		
○		
○		
○		
○		
○		
○		
○		

ARMOR CHECK: Ephesians 6:10-18

Belt of Truth	S ☐ M ☐ T ☐ W ☐ T ☐ F ☐ S ☐
Breastplate of Righteousness	S ☐ M ☐ T ☐ W ☐ T ☐ F ☐ S ☐
Shoes / Gospel of Peace	S ☐ M ☐ T ☐ W ☐ T ☐ F ☐ S ☐
Shield of Faith	S ☐ M ☐ T ☐ W ☐ T ☐ F ☐ S ☐
Helmet of Salvation	S ☐ M ☐ T ☐ W ☐ T ☐ F ☐ S ☐
Sword of the Spirit / Word of God	S ☐ M ☐ T ☐ W ☐ T ☐ F ☐ S ☐

No weapon formed against you will prosper. This is the heritage of the servants of ADONAI.
Is. 54:17

WEEK 30
THE GREATEST LOVE STORY NEVER TOLD (JEREMIAH 31:3, 9B)

"I have loved you with an everlasting love; therefore I have continued my faithfulness to you. [...] for I am a father to Israel, and Ephraim is my firstborn."

It's called "The Greatest Love Story Never Told" and you've probably never heard it.

Before he died, King Solomon made an enemy with a man named Jeroboam. Jeroboam had fled to Egypt during Solomon's reign, because Solomon sought to kill him due to a prophetic word that Jeroboam had received from the prophet Ahijah.

The prophecy was about how God was going to tear the Kingdom of Israel away from Solomon because of the pagan worship he was involved with. Jeroboam would receive 10 of the 12 tribes to rule over. This wouldn't occur during Solomon's reign because of God's love for King David, but it would occur during the reign of Solomon's son, Rehoboam.

So, in the reign of Rehoboam, the Kingdom of Israel was divided. The ten northern tribes, calling themselves the Northern Kingdom of Israel, made Jeroboam their king. In the Southern Kingdom of Judah, retaining Jerusalem as its capitol in the south, Rehoboam reigned over the tribes of Judah and Benjamin that lived in the cities of Judah.

Remember in Week 10 when we studied the Samaritan woman at the well? The Tribe of Ephraim led the ten northern tribes, which is why they were also collectively known as Ephraim and/or Samaria.

About 1000 years before this, Jacob, also known as Israel, would pray and bless his son Joseph's two sons, Manasseh and Ephraim (Gn. 48).

When Israel prayed blessing over the boys, he crossed his arms, placing his right hand on the head of the younger brother, Ephraim, and placing his left hand on the head of the older brother, Manasseh. Thinking that his father was making a mistake, due to his old eyes and failing sight, Joseph corrected his father. Israel said:

"I know, my son, I know. He also shall become a people, and he also shall be great. Nevertheless, his younger brother shall be greater than he, and his offspring shall become a multitude of nations." So he blessed them that day, saying, "By you Israel will pronounce blessings, saying, 'God make you as Ephraim and as Manasseh.'" Thus he put Ephraim before Manasseh.
Genesis 48:19-20

The Hebrew word used for nations in verse 19, "a multitude of *nations*", is *gowy*, where the word *goyim* (nations) comes from: *gentile* nations. Jacob/Israel prophesied that his grandson, Ephraim, would be the father of Gentile nations.

Jeroboam is afraid that if the ten tribes obey God by going up to Jerusalem to worship, that they'll reject him and return to Rehoboam. Jeroboam has two golden calves made. He tells the people they won't be going back to Jerusalem to worship God anymore, instead, they'll worship the new golden calves at Dan and Bethel, essentially breaking every possible commandment in one fell swoop.

Jeroboam is causing all ten northern tribes to commit spiritual adultery through syncretism; the mixture of the holy and the profane, with this new edict. We hold to the position that syncretism is highly frowned upon by God (Dt. 12:1-4, 28-32) and strictly forbidden and yet, Israel's faith, our faith, isriddled with it.

Israel had 42 kings, and its divided kingdom had a total of 38 kings and one queen. All 19 kings of Israel (the ten northern tribes collectively known as Ephraim, or Samaria) were evil. Eight out of the 19 kings of Judah were good. This was determined by who kept God's commandments (Torah, the "law") and who didn't. In time, God was forced to divorce Israel (Ephraim):

The LORD said to me in the days of King Josiah: "Have you seen what she did, that faithless one, Israel, how she went up on every high hill and under every green tree, and there played the whore?

And I thought, 'After she has done all this she will return to me,' but she did not return, and her treacherous sister Judah saw it. She saw that for all the adulteries of that faithless one, Israel, I had sent her away with a decree of divorce. Yet her treacherous sister Judah did not fear, but she too went and played the whore.

Because she took her whoredom lightly, she polluted the

land, committing adultery with stone and tree. Yet for all this her treacherous sister Judah did not return to me with her whole heart, but in pretense, declares the LORD."
Jeremiah 3:6-10

Ephraim is also known as the Ten Lost Tribes of Israel, because they would be scattered and dispersed throughout Assyria as punishment for their spiritual adultery, paganism, and failure to obey and keep God's Torah – God's commandments. Collective Ephraim was dispersed, scattered and assimilated, accounting for their eventual disappearance; their being lost into *a multitude of Gentile nations.*

Because of this divorce and the eventual dispersion, the Northern Kingdom were no longer a people (Is. 7:8); technically, they were no longer God's people. Judah would also follow in her sister's footsteps:

Because the Lord was very angry with Israel, he swept them away from his presence. Only the tribe of Judah remained in the land. But even the people of Judah refused to obey the commands of the Lord their God, for they followed the evil practices that Israel had introduced.
2 Kings 17:18-19 (NLT)

Israel / Ephraim is assimilated and lost into the Gentile nations as prophesied, and Judah is taken into Babylonian captivity for 70 years. This is why Israel, as a whole, has been known as the Southern Kingdom of Judah only, even if God has always intended to restore Ephraim. But how can He when He's already given her a letter of divorce?

[...] the first husband may not marry her again, for she has been defiled. That would be detestable to the Lord. You must not bring guilt upon the land the Lord your God is giving you as a special possession.
Deuteronomy 24:4

And according to Hosea 6:10, Ephraim / Israel was defiled. According to His Torah, His own law, there's only one way that God can legally restore Israel, remarry Ephraim, and bring her back into the fold: death.

For a married woman is bound by law to her husband while he lives, but if her husband dies she is released from the law of marriage.
Romans 7:2

God, in the person, death and resurrection of Jesus of Nazareth, is released from His letter of divorce with Ephraim, the Gentiles, and is free to marry her again! This is the mystery of the Gospel talked about by Paul.

In Matthew 15:24 (NIV), Jesus says

"I was sent only to the lost sheep of Israel."

The Northern Kingdom of Israel, Ephraim, the Gentile nations.

When we read the exchange between Jesus and the Samaritan woman, there's a reason that I think this is the most engaging conversation found in the Gospels. Was it simply because she was a Daughter of Ephraim? A Lost Daughter of the Nations, *goyim*? The Samaritan woman was clearly honored by Jesus and in Week 34 we'll discuss some other aspects of this interview, of this mystery of the Gospel.

(Inspirational source: 119 Ministries. "The Lost Sheep": https://vimeo.com/82312937)

○ FIELD NOTES

DATE: / / **TIME:** : AM/PM **PLACE:**

○		A±
○		
○		
○		
○		
○		
○		
○		
○		
○		
○		
○		
○		
○		
○		
○		
○		
○		
○		
○		

ARMOR CHECK: Ephesians 6:10-18

Belt of Truth	S ☐ M ☐ T ☐ W ☐ T ☐ F ☐ S ☐
Breastplate of Righteousness	S ☐ M ☐ T ☐ W ☐ T ☐ F ☐ S ☐
Shoes / Gospel of Peace	S ☐ M ☐ T ☐ W ☐ T ☐ F ☐ S ☐
Shield of Faith	S ☐ M ☐ T ☐ W ☐ T ☐ F ☐ S ☐
Helmet of Salvation	S ☐ M ☐ T ☐ W ☐ T ☐ F ☐ S ☐
Sword of the Spirit / Word of God	S ☐ M ☐ T ☐ W ☐ T ☐ F ☐ S ☐

No weapon formed against you will prosper. This is the heritage of the servants of ADONAI.
Is. 54:17

○ WEEK 31 HIS STEADFAST LOVE (ISAIAH 54:10)

> *"For the mountains may depart and the hills be removed, but my steadfast love shall not depart from you, and my covenant of peace shall not be removed," says the LORD, who has compassion on you.*

"Steadfast love" (Hebrew *chesed*) appears 196 times in the Old Testament in the English Standard Version – with 127 of those times in the Psalms alone. The Psalmist of Psalm 136 reminds us in 26 ways how God's steadfast love endures forever.

"Abounding in steadfast love..." what a defining characteristic. *Chesed* is a love based on covenantal commitment, a loyal and faithful love. It translates into kindness, *philia* and *agape* love, and the loving mercy the Father has toward His creation – man.

The word hesed...[is] the descriptor par excellence of God in the Old Testament. The word speaks of a completely undeserved kindness and generosity done by a person who is in a position of power. This was the Israelites' experience of God. He revealed himself to them when they were not looking for him, and he kept his covenant with them long after their persistent breaking of it had destroyed any reason for his continued keeping of it. ...Unlike humans, this deity was not fickle, undependable, self-serving, and grasping. Instead he was faithful, true, upright, and generous— always.

(Source: Oswalt, John. *The Bible Among the Myths*)

> *"The Lord, the Lord, a God merciful and gracious, slow to anger, and abounding in steadfast love and faithfulness, keeping steadfast love for thousands, forgiving iniquity and transgression and sin [...]"*
> *Exodus 34:6-7a*

The story of Ruth is a good example of *chesed* between humans as depicted in Ruth 1:16-17:

But Ruth said (to Naomi), "Do not urge me to leave you or to return from following you. For where you go I will go, and where you lodge I will lodge. Your people shall be my people, and your God my God. Where you die I will die, and there will I be buried. May the Lord do so to me and more also if anything but death parts me from you."

I'm sitting here, trapped by my own decision to title and make the subject of this devotional two words – "steadfast love" – that have been used over and over and over again in lyrics, articles, sermonettes and, yes, devotionals. It's not like me to give in to conformity so easily...

It's over 16 hours later, and I have resorted to social media as my out by asking others what they think of when they hear the term "steadfast love." Here are some of the responses:

- Just as a word association. Long suffering. Patience. Kindness even in frustration.
- Yah's agape love is longsuffering. If we're impatient, then we're unlike Yeshua (John 13:1). Agape is longsuffering – it forgives 70 times 7, and then keeps right on.
- Covenant love. It never stops flowing.
- I looked up the meaning of "steadfast" a few days ago after reading Psalm 107, and the similar words say so much about the intense love the Father has for us.
- I think of the words Unconditional and Unselfish. Wife says through mood swings.
- Enduring patience, kindness, loyalty and faithfulness
- "No matter what u do, I will always love u."
- Covenant loyalty
- Through our human ups and downs, His love is pure, reliable, continuous, everlasting.
- Steadfast love endures ups and downs and never questions.

And then my friend, Randy, commented with Ezekiel 16.

The premise for our *Exodus to Ingathering Series* (*E2iS*) is the Apostle Paul's warning in regard to Israel's journey – their exodus from Egypt to their ingathering in the Promised Land – from 1 Corinthians 10:1-12 where Paul states:

Now these things happened to them ***as an example****, but they were* ***written down for our instruction (warning)****, on whom the end of the ages has come.*
1 Corinthians 10:11 (Emphasis mine)

Paul states what happened to our older brother Israel (and make no mistake about it, Israel is our older brother.) We were adopted into Israel, as sons – joint heirs – through the shed Blood of Jesus. What happened to Israel in the desert – as recorded in the books of Exodus, Leviticus, Numbers and Deuteronomy – was written down as a warning and for our instruction – "our" being the end-times, New Testament church, and "written down so that we don't repeat their mistakes," as the Message Bible aptly puts it.

Their "mistakes" cost them their lives, physically and spiritually. In fact, Paul says in verse five of 1 Corinthians 10 that with most of them, God was not pleased... and they never made it to their prophetic destiny – their prophetic inheritance: the Promised Land.

So, what did Israel do?

Ezekiel 16 is a difficult read – 58 verses of detailed harlotry on Israel's part.

God tells Jerusalem, through the Prophet Ezekiel, that when she was born, her umbilical cord hadn't been cut, and she wasn't washed or cleaned. No one showed her sympathy or compassion in that vulnerable state to wash or clean her and instead, she was thrown out into a field – she was hated from birth.

> *I passed by you, and saw you flailing about in your blood. As you lay in your blood, I said to you, "Live! and grow up like a plant of the field." You grew up and became tall and arrived at full womanhood; yet you were naked and bare.*
>
> *I passed by you again and looked on you; you were at the age for love. I spread the edge of my cloak over you, and covered your nakedness: I pledged myself to you and entered into a covenant with you, says the Lord God, and you became mine. Then I bathed you with water and washed off the blood from you, and anointed you with oil.*
>
> *Ezekiel 16:6-9 (NRS)*

"... and you became Mine..."

God goes on to tell her how He bathed her, washed the blood off of her and anointed her with oils. He clothed her with embroideries, dressed her in fine linen and lavished her with expensive clothes and jewelry – bracelets, a necklace, rings on her nose and ears and a beautiful crown for her head. Sounds so much like what the Father did with His prodigal son...

She becomes a very beautiful queen – so beautiful that she becomes famous among the nations. The glory given her by ADONAI our King "made her beauty perfect."

> *"But you trusted in your beauty, and played the whore because of your fame, and lavished your whorings on any passer-by.*
>
> *You took your sons and your daughters, whom you had borne to me, and these you sacrificed to them to be devoured. As if your whorings were not enough!*
>
> *You slaughtered my children and delivered them up as an offering to them. And in all your abominations and your whorings you did not remember the days of your youth, when you were naked and bare, flailing about in your blood.*
>
> *Ezekiel 16:15, 20-22 (NRS)*

Then we hear Him say things like, "How terrible it will be for you" because of her continual sin against Him.

He begins to detail her whoring: her places of pagan worship, her misuse of her body on every street corner where she offered herself to anyone that passed by over and over again; and her shameful acts with Egypt, Assyria and Babylon. He continues on about how they didn't satisfy her and how it only angered Him against her:

> *"Adulterous wife, who receives strangers instead of her husband! You took your clothes off and made love to them. You did it again and again. You worshiped other gods. I hate them. You even sacrificed your children to them. My anger burns against you so much that I will sentence you to death for everything you have done."*
>
> *Verse 32, 36b, 38*

God explains how He's going to strip her in front of her lovers and how they will turn on her. Verses 40 and 41 are especially not pretty:

They strip her, remove her jewelry and leave her naked and bare. It really isn't pleasant, what's done to her, what God does to Israel for her spiritual adultery – what God does to *us* for *our* spiritual adultery.

> *Then my burning anger against you will die down. My jealous anger will turn away from you. I will be calm. I will not be angry anymore.*
>
> *"You did not remember the days when you were young. The things you did made me very angry. So anything that happens*

to you will be your own fault," announces the LORD and King. "You added impure conduct to all of the other evil things you did. I hate all of those things.
Verses 42-43 (NIRV)

And it keeps going...

I have always found it fascinating how the Romanized Western Church (that would be everything from Catholicism to Protestantism, including Evangelicalism) believes that they are absolutely immune to this side of God, regardless of their position with Him, because of "Jesus." That's not even sound theology. (We should come up with a buzz word for that: "Sacrosanct Privilege," maybe?)

We believe that we have a "pass" because of Jesus, *regardless* of whether or not our lives actually reflect Him and *regardless* of whether or not our lives bear the fruit that Jesus Himself says is the sign of one that truly is *known* by Him.

Funny, Israel thought and said the same thing about God (Ezk. 8-9) ...

Do not be deceived: God is not mocked, for whatever one sows, that will he also reap. For the one who sows to his own flesh will from the flesh reap corruption, but the one who sows to the Spirit will from the Spirit reap eternal life.
Galatians 6:7-8

But I digress...

My point is this, and it will always be this: more than half of the Old Testament is the account of Israel's gross disobedience towards God. They had everything they required to serve Him successfully (Jesus says this at least twice: Lk 16:29, 31; Jn 5:46-47), but Israel still decided to make the choice to *not* be obedient.

Contrary to everything you have ever been taught and/or told, we are *exactly* like Israel and will suffer the same *consequences* as Israel, because we have the same *laissez-faire* attitude as Israel. We just throw Jesus into the mix.

To clarify: Paul says perfectly clearly in our premise (1Co. 10:1-12) that Israel was saved in the desert. ***Regardless***, God still killed them off because of their disobedience, and this is what Paul – not me – is warning you about in 1 Co. 10. So...

To avoid any and all possibility of being on the wrong side of all this, all we have to do is make sure that we're not committing spiritual adultery in our lives and that we are actually keeping God's commandments.

If you have any doubt about *that*, read the letters of Paul, and be sure that you're not doing the things that he lists in his letters that will *definitely* keep you out of heaven and lead you into death. Pretty simple, right? Because…

> *Yes, thus says the Lord God: I will deal with you as you have done, you who have despised the oath, breaking the covenant; yet I will remember my covenant with you in the days of your youth, and I will establish with you an everlasting covenant.*
>
> *Then you will remember your ways, and be ashamed, but not on account of my covenant with you.*
>
> *I will establish my covenant with you, and you shall know that I am the Lord, in order that you may remember and be confounded, and never open your mouth again because of your shame, when I forgive you all that you have done, says the Lord God.*
> *Ezekiel 16:59-63 (NRS)*

That's *chesed*. That's God's steadfast love towards you!

> *For you, O Lord, are good and forgiving, abounding in steadfast love to all who call on you.*
> *Psalm 86:5 (NRS)*

○ FIELD NOTES

DATE: / / TIME: : AM/PM PLACE:

		A±
○		
○		
○		
○		
○		
○		
○		
○		
○		
○		
○		
○		
○		
○		
○		
○		
○		
○		
○		
○		

ARMOR CHECK: Ephesians 6:10-18

Belt of Truth	S ☐ M ☐ T ☐ W ☐ T ☐ F ☐ S ☐
Breastplate of Righteousness	S ☐ M ☐ T ☐ W ☐ T ☐ F ☐ S ☐
Shoes / Gospel of Peace	S ☐ M ☐ T ☐ W ☐ T ☐ F ☐ S ☐
Shield of Faith	S ☐ M ☐ T ☐ W ☐ T ☐ F ☐ S ☐
Helmet of Salvation	S ☐ M ☐ T ☐ W ☐ T ☐ F ☐ S ☐
Sword of the Spirit / Word of God	S ☐ M ☐ T ☐ W ☐ T ☐ F ☐ S ☐

No weapon formed against you will prosper. This is the heritage of the servants of ADONAI.
Is. 54:17

WEEK 32
BEFORE ABRAHAM WAS, I AM (JOHN 8:56)

"Your father Abraham rejoiced that he would see my day. He saw it and was glad."

In Genesis 14, we read about nine kings and how Chedorlaomer king of Elam and the three kings that were allied with him successfully attacked the Rephaim, the Zuzim, the Emim, the Amalekites and the Amorites – all Nephilim giants that inhabited the land of Canaan. These are four formidable armies that were able to subdue Nephilim warriors.

Afterward, the kings of Sodom and Gomorrah went into battle with their three allies against Chedorlaomer and his allied forces, four kings against five. Chedorlaomer was the victor, and the inhabitants of Sodom and Gomorrah were the bounty – including a man named Lot, the nephew of Abram.

A man who had escaped came and told Abram the Hebrew that his nephew and all of his belongings had been taken captive by these four pagan kings:

> *Now when Abram heard that his brother was taken captive, he armed his three hundred and eighteen trained servants who were born in his own house, and went in pursuit as far as Dan. He divided his forces against them by night, and he and his servants attacked them and pursued them [...] So he brought back all the goods, and also brought back his brother Lot and his goods, as well as the women and the people.*
> *Genesis 14:14-15a (NKJV)*

Three hundred and eighteen trained servants born in Abram's house... trained in battle, apparently. They just took out the four kings that the top of the chapter was clear in noting had themselves taken out five Nephilim tribes. Lance Wallnau calls these 318 "killer sheep."

Abram, and his precursor to "Mossad," liberated the captives. It says that the king of Salem came out to meet Abram in a valley named the King's Valley "after his return from the defeat of Chedorlaomer and the kings who were with him."

Then Melchizedek king of Salem brought out bread and wine; he was the priest of God Most High. And he blessed him [...] Genesis 14:18-19a

We know absolutely nothing about this "king of Salem, Melchizedek" except for the fact that Jesus is a priest in His order (Ps. 110:4). Crazy that the guy I'm betting everything on, Jesus, is a priest in the order of this king that we know absolutely nothing about. Melchizedek blesses Abram, who in turn gives Melchizedek a tenth of everything (Heb. 7:4-10).

For this Melchizedek, king of Salem, priest of the Most High God, met Abraham returning from the slaughter of the kings and blessed him, and to him Abraham apportioned a tenth part of everything. He is first, by translation of his name, king of righteousness, and then he is also king of Salem, that is, king of peace. He is without father or mother or genealogy, having neither beginning of days nor end of life, but resembling the Son of God he continues a priest forever.
Hebrews 7:1-3

The writer of Hebrews continues to unpack this meeting between Abram, the father of our faith, and this supernatural Kingly Priest – the two foundational cornerstones of our faith. The letter to the Hebrews notes that Abram tithed to Him before the Torah instruction of tithing was established and that Levi (only the tribe of Levi is to receive tithes) made the tithe through Abram by proxy, because Levi was in Abram's loins. Melchizedek's blessing over Abram would transcend over 400+ years just in that account, and a couple thousand years beyond that to you and me, since, because of Jesus, we are now able to hold the offices of both kings and priests.

"[...] a priest forever after the order of Melchizedek."
Psalm 110:4

There is so much going on right here. We have the two foundational cornerstones of our faith meeting for the first time (that we know of). One of these cornerstones, Melchizedek, has neither father nor mother. He lacks human / Terran (earthly) genealogy – He's not human! (Heb. 7:3). The other is the son of an idol maker. Abram is a Gentile from present-day southern Iraq!

So, how does God create a people unto Himself – the Hebrews / Israel – with two Gentiles, Abram and Sarai?

It began with Abram's simple belief that God was speaking the truth regarding him having his own son and countless descendants:

> *And he believed the LORD, and he counted it to him as righteousness.*
> *Genesis 15:6*

Abram believed God regarding this, and that simple act of belief and trust was considered an act of righteousness on Abram's account. It's still that simple today, if we would only believe and trust Him, too.

God also told Abram that he would possess all the land of Canaan. This was a little harder to believe than being the father of countless thousands, so God was going to prove it to him.

God asked for a young cow, a goat and a ram, all three years of age, along with a dove and a young pigeon. Abram did as he was told, brought them before God and cut them in half, except for the birds. He laid the halves opposite of each other.

When large birds of prey came down to eat the animal carcasses, Abram chased them away. He fell into a deep sleep as the sun was going down, and a thick and dreadful darkness engulfed him.

God proceeds to prophesy about how Abram's descendants would be sojourners in a foreign country as slaves for 400 years but that they would be delivered "after the sin of the Amorites had come to maturity."

> *When the sun had gone down and it was dark, behold, a smoking fire pot and a flaming torch passed between these pieces.*
>
> *On that day the LORD made a covenant with Abram, saying, "To your offspring I give this land, from the river of Egypt to the great river, the river Euphrates*
> *Genesis 15:17-18*

> *When Abram was ninety-nine years old the LORD appeared to Abram and said to him, "I am God Almighty; walk before me, and be blameless, that I may make my covenant between me and you, and may multiply you greatly."*
>
> *No longer shall your name be called Abram, but your name shall be Abraham, for I have made you the father of a multitude of nations.*
> *Genesis 17:1-2, 5*

At the age of 75, Abram was called by God to begin to walk the territorial boundaries of what would be the Promised Land of Israel, the land promised by God for Abram's countless descendants.

At the age of 86, Abram would jump the gun and have a child out of his practical reasoning – a child from his flesh and not the child that was the spiritual "son of promise" that the Father had promised him – and he named that child Ishmael.

At 99, God made a covenant with Abram – predicated by the command that Abram was to *walk before God, blameless* (Mt. 5:48) – so that God could *make* that covenant with him and multiply him greatly. With that covenant came the breath of God's Holy Spirit – the "hhhhhaaa" of God – changing his name from Abram to Abra*HA*m. The birth of Abraham's son is promised, and the covenant is made and sealed with circumcision, as it is today.

> *This is my covenant, which you shall keep, between me and you and your offspring after you: Every male among you shall be circumcised. You shall be circumcised in the flesh of your foreskins, and it shall be a sign of the covenant between me and you. Genesis 17:10-11*

In Genesis 21, Abraham's son, Isaac, was born – the "son of promise" and of the Spirit. Abraham was 100 years old.

In the first part of Genesis 18, there are two things I would like for you to ponder, journal and pray about. The first is Abraham's life cadence of offering, sacrifice and giving, as we saw him do with Melchizedek.

God appears to Abraham as he was sitting at the entrance to his tent in the heat of the day. He looked up and saw three men standing there before him. He runs to meet them and bows low to the ground – discernment – and says (verse three):

> *"O Lord, if I have found favor in your sight, do not pass by your servant."*

This acknowledgement is key to aligning yourself with and for an interaction with the Father. Abraham offers water with which to wash, a place to rest in the shade and food to eat, which the three accept. While they ate, they asked about Sarah, who was eavesdropping on the conversation. This is the second thing I want us to understand.

God begins to explain how this time next year, Sarah would have a son. On hearing this, she laughed to herself. Then the LORD asked Abraham,

"Why did Sarah just laugh? Next year, Sarah will have a son." Verse 15:

> *But Sarah denied it, saying, "I did not laugh," for she was afraid. He said, "No, but you did laugh."*

This is an extremely common thing I see constantly when God confronts us with ourselves:

"No, I didn't."
"No, but you did…"

Don't do that.

○ FIELD NOTES

DATE: / / TIME: : AM/PM PLACE:

○		A±
○		
○		
○		
○		
○		
○		
○		
○		
○		
○		
○		
○		
○		
○		
○		
○		
○		
○		
○		

ARMOR CHECK: Ephesians 6:10-18

Belt of Truth	S ☐	M ☐	T ☐	W ☐	T ☐	F ☐	S ☐
Breastplate of Righteousness	S ☐	M ☐	T ☐	W ☐	T ☐	F ☐	S ☐
Shoes / Gospel of Peace	S ☐	M ☐	T ☐	W ☐	T ☐	F ☐	S ☐
Shield of Faith	S ☐	M ☐	T ☐	W ☐	T ☐	F ☐	S ☐
Helmet of Salvation	S ☐	M ☐	T ☐	W ☐	T ☐	F ☐	S ☐
Sword of the Spirit / Word of God	S ☐	M ☐	T ☐	W ☐	T ☐	F ☐	S ☐

No weapon formed against you will prosper. This is the heritage of the servants of ADONAI.
Is. 54:17

○ WEEK 33
ELISHA AND THE SHUNAMMITE WOMAN (2 KINGS 4:9-10)

And she said to her husband, "Behold now, I know that this is a holy man of God who is continually passing our way. Let us make a small room on the roof with walls and put there for him a bed, a table, a chair, and a lamp, so that whenever he comes to us, he can go in there."

I love this account of the prophet Elisha. Here's why:

- He's a traveling prophet.
- A well-to-do woman gives him hospitality.
- A child is born out of the Spirit of Prophecy.
- She trusts in the prophet.
- She has a habit of seeking out the prophetic on the New Moon and Sabbath.
- The dead are risen back to life.

Let's unpack the different aspects of this story and learn how we can apply them to our own lives.

THE TRAVELING PROPHET

Let's say that Elisha is on an "overland speaking excursion" that takes him to the town of Shunem. A wealthy woman lives there, and various translations state that she invited, urged, begged, persuaded and pressed him to stay at her home for a meal. So then, every time he came into town, he stopped by there to eat.

She had the wherewithal to determine that by blessing and honoring this man, a man that she already discerned was a man of God, blessing and favor would continue to come and fall on her and her family. And she tells her husband this very thing:

And she said to her husband, "Behold now, I know that this is a holy man of God who is continually passing our way.
Let us make a small room on the roof with walls and put

there for him a bed, a table, a chair, and a lamp, so that whenever he comes to us, he can go in there."
2 Kings 4:9-10

The Shunammite woman was so serious in her convictions that she persuades her husband to build a studio apartment for Elisha on the property, and they do.

- She acknowledged the prophet of ADONAI.
- She and her husband had agreement in the gift of hospitality towards the prophet.
- They aligned their finances, territory and charitable hearts with the Spirit of Prophecy.

A CHILD IS BORN

On one of his visits, Elisha had his servant, Gehazi, summon the Shunammite woman. As she stood in front of Elisha, he said to his servant,

"Tell her, 'You have gone to all this trouble for us. Now what can be done for you? Can we speak on your behalf to the king or the commander of the army?'"
2 Kings 4:13 (NIV)

She replied, "I have everything I need here."

The prophet of God had good standing with the Government Mountain and was in a position to put in a good word for her with the king and the commander of the army.

On a side note: there's a growing sect out there today, that I have had the displeasure of encountering, that believes that any favor a believer may have with the government, in business, the entertainment industry, the PTA, etc., is probably

a. Not a true believer and
b. Should be dealt with cautiously and suspiciously, because
c. They are more than likely a Luciferian plant.

I'm serious. As comical and unscriptural as all of that was, it's equal parts delusional and tragic. I can't make this stuff up.

After the Shunammite woman leaves, Elisha asks his servant, "What can we do for her?" Gehazi says,

"Well, she has no son, and her husband is old."

He said, "Call her." And when he had called her, she stood in the doorway. And he said, "At this season, about this time next year, you shall embrace a son." And she said, "No, my lord, O man of God; do not lie to your servant." But the woman conceived, and she bore a son about that time the following spring, as Elisha had said to her.

2 Kings 4:14b-17

Consider Gehazi's "normal" when asked what could be done for the Shunammite woman as thanks for her generous hospitality:

"Well, she has no son, and her husband is old."

Calling out into existence the fruit of a barren womb needs to become *our* "normal."

I hear a tinge of fear in hoping for something that hasn't happened thus far in the Shunammite woman's reaction. Has she longed and desired for this so badly that she given up all hope for a child of her own?

TRUSTING IN THE SPIRIT OF PROPHECY

One day, after the child had grown, he was out in the fields where his father was working and started shouting, "My head! My head hurts!" The boy is carried to his mother where he sits on his mother's lap until about noon and then dies.

I have three adult children and four grandchildren between the ages of one and nine. I spend quite a lot of time with my grandchildren. I've been accused of being a "helicopter grandpa." Heh. I can't tell you how difficult it was to write the words "then dies..."

If you're a parent, you know...

This poor Shunammite woman. She goes up into Elisha's studio apartment, where she lays the boy "on the bed of the man of God," shuts the door and goes out.

As far as we can tell by the narrative, this woman is more than likely a Proverbs 31 woman. She's proactive. She gets things done. This situation is no different.

She sends for her husband and requests a servant and a donkey so that she can go immediately to the man of God. She has assessed the situation, and she's activating alignment: Go to where the Spirit of the Lord, the Spirit of Prophecy is.

I love the husband's response in verse 23:

> *"Why do you want to go to him today?" he asked. "It isn't the time for the New Moon Feast. It isn't the Sabbath day." (NIRV)*

His response tells us that she had a habit of going to the prophet and seeking the prophetic of God on both the beginning of every month, on the New Moon, and every week on the Sabbath. And yes, I believe this is a key here.

Her answer is priceless (verse 23):

> *"Don't let that bother you," she said.*

"Don't worry about it, old man! Just get me the donkey and a servant to accompany me!"

> *So she set out and came to the man of God at Mount Carmel. When the man of God saw her coming, he said to Gehazi his servant, "Look, there is the Shunammite. Run at once to meet her and say to her, 'Is all well with you? Is all well with your husband? Is all well with the child?'" And she answered, "All is well."*
>
> *And when she came to the mountain to the man of God, she caught hold of his feet. And Gehazi came to push her away. But the man of God said, "Leave her alone, for she is in bitter distress, and the LORD has hidden it from me and has not told me."*
> *2 Kings 4:25-27*

She told Gehazi, "All is well," but clung to Elisha's feet. She had self-control and understood authority. Also, notice that even Elisha, at least in this regard, could only "see in part" (1 Co. 13:9). Verses 28-29:

> *Then she said, "Did I ask my lord for a son? Did I not say, 'Do not deceive me?'"*

Another translation puts it: "Did I ask you for a son? Didn't I tell you not to get my hopes up?"

> *He said to Gehazi, "Tie up your garment and take my staff in your hand and go. If you meet anyone, do not greet him, and if anyone greets you, do not reply. And lay my staff on the face of the child."*

Looks like the prophetic kicked in pretty fast there. Another key about proximity and alignment: as Gehazi leaves, she tells Elisha, "As ADONAI lives, I'm not leaving here without you." I don't hear franticness in her voice. I hear cool, calm, collective assurance.

THE DEAD ARE MADE TO RISE

Gehazi gets to the boy ahead of Elisha and the Shunammite, he lays Elisha's staff on the boy's face, but there was no sound or any movement at all. Gehazi goes back to Elisha and tells him that the boy hasn't awakened… I hear "hope" in that.

Elisha arrives to find the boy still dead and lying on Elisha's bed. Elisha goes into the studio apartment, shuts the door and begins to pray. He then gets *into* the bed, lays down *on* the boy – his mouth touching the boy's mouth, his eyes touching the boy's eyes, his hands touching the boy's hands – the boy's body starts to grow warm as Elisha is laying on him.

Elisha gets up, *turns away* and paces back and forth in the studio apartment before getting back into the bed again. He lays down on the boy once more, and this time, the boy begins to sneeze – seven times – and then opens his eyes.

Elisha tells Gehazi to go and get the Shunammite woman. When she arrives, Elisha tells her to take her son. Verse 37:

> *She came and fell at his feet, bowing to the ground. Then she picked up her son and went out.*

She honors the God of the Living by first honoring the man of God, the prophet – *then* she picks up her son…

○ FIELD NOTES

DATE: / / **TIME:** : AM/PM **PLACE:**

		A±
○		
○		
○		
○		
○		
○		
○		
○		
○		
○		
○		
○		
○		
○		
○		
○		
○		
○		
○		
○		

ARMOR CHECK: Ephesians 6:10-18

Belt of Truth	S ☐	M ☐	T ☐	W ☐	T ☐	F ☐	S ☐
Breastplate of Righteousness	S ☐	M ☐	T ☐	W ☐	T ☐	F ☐	S ☐
Shoes / Gospel of Peace	S ☐	M ☐	T ☐	W ☐	T ☐	F ☐	S ☐
Shield of Faith	S ☐	M ☐	T ☐	W ☐	T ☐	F ☐	S ☐
Helmet of Salvation	S ☐	M ☐	T ☐	W ☐	T ☐	F ☐	S ☐
Sword of the Spirit / Word of God	S ☐	M ☐	T ☐	W ☐	T ☐	F ☐	S ☐

No weapon formed against you will prosper. This is the heritage of the servants of ADONAI.
Is. 54:17

○ WEEK 34
GIVE ME A DRINK…
(JOHN 4:6)

Jacob's well was there; so Jesus, wearied as he was from his journey, was sitting beside the well. It was about the sixth hour.

Remember in Week 10 and Week 30 when we studied the Samaritans and the Samaritan woman at the well? We talked about how the Samaritans were originally the ten northern tribes of the Northern Kingdom of Israel. The tribe of Ephraim led the ten northern tribes, which is why they were collectively known as Ephraim and/or Samaria. These ten tribes would be scattered, lost and assimilated, prophetically becoming the Gentile nations of Ephraim as we saw in Genesis 48.

The Samaritans were a disenfranchised people when it came to the Southern Kingdom of Judah, the two tribes that were taken into Babylonian captivity but returned to the Land because of all of the above.

We're going to take another look at what I called "one of the most engaging conversations found in the Gospels" in Week 10. I want to look at a couple other aspects of this encounter. Are you seated comfortably?

This Samaritan woman was further disenfranchised for two main reasons:

- She's a woman.
- She's been married five times.

"Give Me a drink," Jesus asks her.

This was a loaded question, and He knew it.

Jesus has been made out to be a gentle, passive and completely docile character – when in reality, He's quite confrontational, almost manipulative (in the best sense of the word), self-assured, aggressive, a bit abrasive and a provoker. In the parable of the talents and minas, one of the servants is absolutely *terrified* of Jesus. Be certain of this: Jesus is in no way a pushover, and I wouldn't want to cross Him.

Jesus is well aware of what He's doing when He asks this woman at the well for a drink. He's creating an awkward and unacceptable social disruption. He's a Jewish Rabbi, she's a woman, she's a *Samaritan* woman, and they're in a public place – and then there's the matter of her reputation.

She's at the well at the hottest time of the day, because, like I mentioned earlier, she's disenfranchised, and this includes being disenfranchised within her own local community. She's avoiding the social gathering of the other women at the well, and it's more than likely because of the gossip, slander and ridicule she's subjected to for having had five husbands, and, as Jesus prophetically tells her, the man that she's living with isn't her husband. Take a look.

After a little conversational parley about water, Jesus tells her that whomever drinks the water *He* has to offer will never thirst again, to which she replies:

> *"Sir, give me this water, so that I will not be thirsty or have to come here to draw water."*
>
> *Jesus said to her, "Go, call your husband, and come here."*
>
> *The woman answered him, "I have no husband." Jesus said to her, "You are right in saying, 'I have no husband'; for you have had five husbands, and the one you now have is not your husband. What you have said is true."*
>
> *John 4:15-18*

"Go, call your husband, and come here."

This still isn't "passive Jesus." This is "confrontational Jesus" taking "give me a drink" to the next level. I love "confrontational Jesus." This is, after all, His reason for coming to earth – to proclaim "Repent, for the Kingdom of Heaven is at hand!" (Mt. 3:2)

This is, as we see (especially all throughout the Gospel of Matthew), *exactly* what the Kingdom of Heaven looks like – "at hand" – here on earth. Confronting humanity's humanity head on – addressing it, correcting it, instructing it, equipping it – "for those that have ears to hear and eyes to see." This is God's love for your fellow man!

Let me repeat that:

The Kingdom of Heaven on earth is about confronting humanity's humanity head on – addressing it, correcting it, instructing it, equipping it – "for those that have ears to hear and eyes to see."

The conundrum is the majority of us just aren't interested in having these layers pulled back and exposed.

> *"Indeed, in their case the prophecy of Isaiah is fulfilled that*

says: 'You will indeed hear but never understand, and you will indeed see but never perceive. For this people's heart has grown dull, and with their ears they can barely hear, and their eyes they have closed, lest they should see with their eyes and hear with their ears and understand with their heart and turn, and I would heal them.'" Matthew 13:14-15 [Jesus quoting Is. 6:9-10]

Confrontational Jesus tells a woman – a *Samaritan* woman, no less – to fetch Him a drink. This is socially unacceptable. To escalate the situation, He tells her to go and get her husband and come back, knowing full well that she's an adulteress *five times over!*

My wife and I led a home church / Bible study for many years when we lived in Dallas. One evening, a young couple that had been invited were being introduced to me. They sat down, introductions were made, and within a couple minutes, I told them point blank that they were fornicating; that they were sexually immoral.

Now, this doesn't go over very well with a lot of people. They think it inappropriate, "politically incorrect," rude, abrasive, lacking "love, mercy and grace." Well, those people are wrong and are more than likely terrified of their *own* sin being exposed.

I will always defer to and go with the example and model of Jesus. If the Holy Spirit is going to go out of His way to reveal things, who am I not to cooperate?

> *[...] the word of the LORD came to me, saying, "Son of man, I have appointed you a watchman to the house of Israel; whenever you hear a word from My mouth, warn them from Me.*
>
> *When I say to the wicked, 'You will surely die,' and you do not warn him or speak out to warn the wicked from his wicked way that he may live, that wicked man shall die in his iniquity, but his blood I will require at your hand.*
>
> *Yet if you have warned the wicked and he does not turn from his wickedness or from his wicked way, he shall die in his iniquity; but you have delivered yourself.*
>
> *Again, when a righteous man turns away from his righteousness and commits iniquity, and I place an obstacle before him, he will die; since you have not warned him, he shall die in his sin, and his righteous deeds which he has done shall not be remembered; but his blood I will require at your hand.*

However, if you have warned the righteous man that the righteous should not sin and he does not sin, he shall surely live because he took warning; and you have delivered yourself."
Ezekiel 3:16b-21 (NAS - See also Ezekiel 33:1-9)

And speaking of God's steadfast love...

Jesus tells the woman, "Believe Me, the hour is coming, the hour is now here..." to which she replies, "I know that Messiah is coming..." and then, for the very first time, the dimensional realms of the natural and the spiritual are merged with the proclamation / declaration / confession of *Ani Hu: I He – I AM He.*

The first human being to whom Jesus reveals that He is indeed the promised Messiah is a disenfranchised Gentile. A disenfranchised *adulterous Samaritan woman* who is broken emotionally, relationally, socially, religiously, spiritually... That's my Jesus.

Many Samaritans believed in Him that day, because of the woman's testimony and even more because of His words.

○ FIELD NOTES

DATE: / / TIME: : AM/PM PLACE:

○		A±
○		
○		
○		
○		
○		
○		
○		
○		
○		
○		
○		
○		
○		
○		
○		
○		
○		
○		
○		

ARMOR CHECK: Ephesians 6:10-18

Belt of Truth	S ☐ M ☐ T ☐ W ☐ T ☐ F ☐ S ☐
Breastplate of Righteousness	S ☐ M ☐ T ☐ W ☐ T ☐ F ☐ S ☐
Shoes / Gospel of Peace	S ☐ M ☐ T ☐ W ☐ T ☐ F ☐ S ☐
Shield of Faith	S ☐ M ☐ T ☐ W ☐ T ☐ F ☐ S ☐
Helmet of Salvation	S ☐ M ☐ T ☐ W ☐ T ☐ F ☐ S ☐
Sword of the Spirit / Word of God	S ☐ M ☐ T ☐ W ☐ T ☐ F ☐ S ☐

No weapon formed against you will prosper. This is the heritage of the servants of ADONAI.
Is. 54:17

○ WEEK 35
SEEING THE FACE OF GOD (GENESIS 33:10)

"For I have seen your face, which is like seeing the face of God."

Years ago, the Lord told me that being "Christlike" wasn't being a pushover; a doormat. I wasn't to let people take advantage of me, and I didn't have to put up with that sort of treatment. But if that person should come back, apologize and ask forgiveness, I was to receive them with no questions asked, unconditionally and with no strings attached.

He also told me that sometimes He might deliberately send people to mess with me, and that in those cases, He was working out things with *them* and to allow them to do their thing. Again, if they came back, apologized and asked for forgiveness, I was to receive them with no questions asked, unconditionally, no strings attached. That's "Christlike."

It's made for an interesting and challenging time. It has also cost me a lot of "friendships" with other believers that either don't like my supposed "insensitivity," "lack of grace and/or mercy," "rudeness" or "arrogance." Sometimes, it was the exact opposite: they don't like how "gullible" I am, that I would entertain reconciliation with those that have "spitefully used me," my willingness to position myself to be taken advantage of over and over again, my "lack of backbone..." you get the drift. There's no winning. Heh.

It's not easy, but when God tells you to empty yourself so that He can fill you up anew, so that He can then pour you out as a drink offering to the nations... thank you, Father... Then that's what you do, and you do it willfully and joyfully. Hallelujah!!

You see, I really buy into this whole Jesus thing:

- Take up your cross (Mt. 10:38, 16:24-26; Lk 9:23).
- Deny yourself (Mt. 10:38, 16:24-26; Lk 9:23).
- Throw yourself on the altar willingly (Ro. 12:1).
- Die to yourself (Ro. 6:3; 1 Co. 15:31; Co. 3:3).
- Lose your life for His sake (Mk 8:35).
- Take no thought for your life (Mt. 6:25 KJV).

And here's the one that should do it for all of us:

- Your life is not your own.

You are not your own, for you were bought with a price.
1 Corinthians 6:19b-20a

David Hogan says that because our lives have been bought with Blood, *our* blood belongs to whomever God wills. I believe that, and I have done my best to live up to the arrangement that He requires of me. Right now, my blood belongs to the Utahns that He has sent me to serve.

It becomes an issue of spiritual authority – binding and loosing, actually. Let me explain:

In 1990, I released a record on a major Christian record label. It was quite controversial for the time with the style of music, the way we looked, the themes in our lyrics; nothing like it had ever been seen or heard of – then or since – so it "challenged" a lot of industry people, to say the least. Needless to say, it was a volatile situation. The label fielded inquiries about the album lyrics, and my pastor fielded the calls about our character and my "Christian legitimacy."

A local record buyer for a national chain at the time was dating a girl who was a former friend of my brothers and me. She had some bone to pick with us and decided to tell her boyfriend, the music buyer for this local outlet, that not only did she know us and had known us for years, she had it on the best authority that neither of us were actually Christians. It was his "Christian duty" to report this travesty: a non-Christian band had infiltrated Contemporary Christian Music! Egad!

And so, like the good little whistle blower that he was, the next time the distribution rep stopped by, he told him the whole sordid made-up story. It spread like wildfire, and there was no stopping it. Remember, the entire enterprise was already on shaky ground.

Benson was the distributor, and Zondervan – yes, that Zondervan – was the parent company. Our album was pulled from stores worldwide. Nothing like it had ever been seen or heard of, then or since… It was quite the blow to my career.

Fast forward four years. The Mrs. and I were visiting a friend's home church / bible study. Afterward, during the refreshment portion of the meeting, this man about two or three years younger than I came up to introduce himself.

When I told him my name, he said that he knew. He knew who I was. He looked a bit distraught as he began to unburden himself with the story of how he was dating this girl, he was in love, and she had convinced him that this band – my band – was a bunch of charlatans, imposters that had infiltrated Christian music, and how he needed to set things right. He confessed, "I'm the guy."

Wow... I often wondered what I'd do in this situation.

He proceeded to tell me how he had known he had done wrong and how it ate him up, and when he saw me there that night, he knew that this was his chance to make it right and how relieved he felt from the burden of carrying this weight.

This poor guy... This had been tormenting him this whole time.

"Be free, brother." I heard myself saying.

"Be released in Jesus' name. Be released from everything that has burdened you regarding this all these years," is what came out of my mouth.

He was crying. He had been released, freed, loosed. No longer bound. After thanking me, he left. My wife and I looked at each other.

"Wow..." we thought. "I wonder what this is going to break in the spiritual realm."

The patriarch Jacob (of "Abraham, Isaac and Jacob"), also known as Israel, was a usurper. He had conned his older brother, Esau, out of his birthright (Gn. 25:29-34) and had conned his father, Isaac (of "Abraham, Isaac and Jacob"), into giving him Esau's blessing of the firstborn, causing Jacob to flee for his life in fear of Esau's wrath (Gn. 27:1-45).

Twenty years later, Jacob returns to his homeland, so he makes a "preemptive strike" by reaching out to Esau, hoping to find favor in his sight:

> *And the messengers returned to Jacob, saying, "We came to your brother Esau, and he is coming to meet you, and there are four hundred men with him."*
> *Genesis 32:6*

Jacob was scared. He separated his people, flocks, herds and camels into two camps, thinking that if his brother attacked the one, the other could escape. And then he prayed... a sincere prayer. Read Jacob's prayer in Genesis 32:9-12, and meditate on it during your Journal / Prayer Modules.

Jacob sent five separate caravans of gifts to his brother ahead of himself thinking, "I'll make peace with these gifts that I'm sending ahead of myself, and when I see him, maybe he'll welcome me."

The next morning, there was Esau with 400 men. Jacob approached his brother, bowing seven times. But Esau ran to Jacob, hugging him, throwing his arms around him and kissing him. They cried.

Jacob said, "Seeing your face is like seeing the face of God."

When you offer another forgiveness, mercy, grace, and loving kindness, spiritual authority and binding and loosing come into play. Jacob was well aware of the wrong he had done his brother, but Esau wasn't vindictive. He didn't repay evil for evil or bring against Jacob an insulting charge. Instead, he received him – no questions asked, unconditionally – with no strings attached. "Christlike."

Is there someone to whom you can be "Christlike," as seeing the face of God?

○ FIELD NOTES

DATE: / / **TIME:** : AM/PM **PLACE:**

		A±
○		
○		
○		
○		
○		
○		
○		
○		
○		
○		
○		
○		
○		
○		
○		
○		
○		
○		
○		
○		

ARMOR CHECK: Ephesians 6:10-18

Belt of Truth	S ☐ M ☐ T ☐ W ☐ T ☐ F ☐ S ☐
Breastplate of Righteousness	S ☐ M ☐ T ☐ W ☐ T ☐ F ☐ S ☐
Shoes / Gospel of Peace	S ☐ M ☐ T ☐ W ☐ T ☐ F ☐ S ☐
Shield of Faith	S ☐ M ☐ T ☐ W ☐ T ☐ F ☐ S ☐
Helmet of Salvation	S ☐ M ☐ T ☐ W ☐ T ☐ F ☐ S ☐
Sword of the Spirit / Word of God	S ☐ M ☐ T ☐ W ☐ T ☐ F ☐ S ☐

No weapon formed against you will prosper. This is the heritage of the servants of ADONAI.
Is. 54:17

○ WEEK 36
THE WAYS OF ADONAI ARE RIGHT (HOSEA 14:9)

> *Whoever is wise, let him understand these things; whoever is discerning, let him know them; for the ways of the LORD are right, and the upright walk in them, but transgressors stumble in them.*

In this week's reading, Ephraim / Samaria and the wilderness campaign (the exodus from Egypt) are brought up by the prophet Hosea in chapter 13, which is entitled "God's Relentless Judgment on Israel."

I can only imagine what this resource looks like to an outsider. It looks like a free for all against Israel and a constant, relentless dragging over the coals. But it is.

I deliver you from abject slavery. I show you My power, on your behalf, by taking down the mightiest nation in the world, Egypt, through miraculous and supernatural signs and wonders – that no one can contest aren't supernatural – and then I make an everlasting covenant with you; a marriage proposal – that you accepted – you will be My people, a nation favored above all others of kings and priest unto me, and I will be your God.

> *"Say therefore to the people of Israel, 'I am the LORD, and I will bring you out from under the burdens of the Egyptians, and I will deliver you from slavery to them, and I will redeem you with an outstretched arm and with great acts of judgment.*
>
> *I will take you to be my people, and I will be your God, and you shall know that I am the LORD your God, who has brought you out from under the burdens of the Egyptians.*
>
> *I will bring you into the land that I swore to give to Abraham, to Isaac, and to Jacob. I will give it to you for a possession. I am the LORD.'"*
>
> *Exodus 6:6-8*

Instead, you choose to grumble and complain, disobey Me at every turn, you rise up in mutiny against Me and My servant leaders, Moses and Aaron, that I established for you. You're convinced that I've delivered you from slavery only to harm you, to kill you, to lay waste to you and your little ones:

> *"How long will this people despise me? And how long will they not believe in me, in spite of all the signs that I have done among them? I will strike them with the pestilence and disinherit them" [...]*
> *Numbers 13:11-12*

> *Know then in your heart that, as a man disciplines his son, the LORD your God disciplines you.*
> *Deuteronomy 8:5*

"My servant Moses pleaded on your behalf, reminding Me of how I *am* slow to anger, abounding in steadfast love, forgiving iniquities and transgressions. Even so, *I will not pacify the guilty!* Their sins will be visited on their children, three and four generations down (Nu. 14:15-19)."

> *"But truly, as I live, and as all the earth shall be filled with the glory of the LORD, none of the men who have seen my glory and my signs that I did in Egypt and in the wilderness, and yet have put me to the test these ten times and have not obeyed my voice, shall see the land that I swore to give to their fathers. And none of those who despised me shall see it."*
> *Numbers 14:21-23*

Can you blame Him?

And to make matters worse, when Israel finally enters the Promised Land, they do *exactly* as they were instructed *not* to do and begin to worship the false gods of Canaan.

The entire time they were in the desert, Israel was instructed, coached, prepped, taught and *forewarned* regarding what to do and what not to do when they entered the land. And, as they disobeyed Him while wandering in the wilderness "without food and water" (*they* were the reason they were wandering in the desert, *not* God, and, they *did* have food and water, they just didn't *like* the food and how they got the water), they disobeyed Him when they entered the land.

And it was a good land: streams, rivers, fountains and springs; a land that yielded wheat, barley, produce; a land "flowing with milk and honey" and copper, silver and gold for the taking. There were houses they didn't build, crops they didn't plant, cattle and herds... all at the ready! (You can read all of this for yourself in Deuteronomy 8.) And how do they repay Him? By playing the harlot – whoredom, spiritual adultery. And that's something the prophet Hosea would know a little about ...

THIS. IS. WHAT. PAUL. IS. TRYING. TO. WARN. US. ABOUT.

> *Now these things happened to them **as an example**, but they were **written down for our instruction (warning)**, on whom the end of the ages has come.*
> *1 Corinthians 10:11 [Emphasis mine]*

The term "on whom the end of the ages has come" is also translated as "to us who are living in the 'the last days'" – you and me.

Paul is clearly and plainly telling those of us that will listen that what happened to Israel in the desert was an instructional warning for us.

The Message Bible puts verse 11 like this (emphasis mine):

> *These are all warning markers - danger! - in our history books, **written down so that we don't repeat their mistakes. Our positions in the story are parallel** - they at the beginning, we at the end - and we are just as capable of messing it up as they were.*

"...written down so that we don't repeat their mistakes. Our positions in the story are parallel..."

Read that again, three times. Slowly...

Their "mistakes" cost them their lives, physically and spiritually. They never made it to their prophetic destiny, their prophetic inheritance: the Promised Land. *I want you to make it to **your** prophetic destiny – to **your** Promised Land!*

This is what happened in the desert. This is what Paul is talking about. We need to heed these instructions and avoid making the same mistakes.

I tire of repeating this, so I can only imagine how you feel. But I promise you, it isn't just me! *All* throughout the Old Testament narrative, God is repeating Himself:

- In the desert: either through Himself or through Moses
- In the Promised Land: either through Himself or through the Judges and/or the Prophets

And it happens in the New Testament narrative as well!

- The Red Letters

How many times is Jesus finding new ways to say the same thing in the parables? Lots!

- The Epistles of Paul

In almost every letter Paul writes, he repeats the same warning instructions to his Gentile churches and how they are to keep God's commandments, God's Torah, just like Moses repeatedly instructed Israel, as we have studied these past 35 weeks:

- Romans 1:24-32, 13:13
- 1 Corinthians 5:1-2, 11-12; 6:7-8, 15-18
- Galatians 5:19-21, 25
- Ephesians 4:17-3; 5:3-5
- Colossians 3:5, 8-9
- 1 Timothy 1:8-10; 6:3-5
- 1 Timothy 3:1-9

Hosea came from the northern Kingdom of Israel, also known as Ephraim / Samaria, during the kingdom's tragic final days. The first part of Hosea speaks of his family life as a symbol of what God desires to convey to His people. Hosea was ordered by God to marry an adulterous wife. Each of their three children are given symbolic names in relation to God's prophetic message:

> *"Go, take to yourself a wife of whoredom and have children of whoredom, for the land commits great whoredom by forsaking the LORD."*
> *Hosea 1:2*

His first son was named Jezreel for the house of Jehu and for the blood of Jezreel. God was about to put an end to the kingdom of the house of Israel.

Next, Hosea had a daughter named No Mercy, because God was no longer going to show mercy on the house of Israel. He was no longer going to forgive them.

> *But I will have mercy on the house of Judah, and I will save them by the LORD their God. I will not save them by bow or by sword or by war or by horses or by horsemen."*
> *Verse 7 (He was talking about Jesus)*

Hosea had another son named Not My People (verse 9);

"[…] for you are not my people, and I am not your God."

This makes me want to cry. It's so tragic…

Hosea's entire relationship with his wife and children purposefully echoes that of God and His children both then and now. God loved Israel and desired to take them back. The imagery of the amazing journey from the Exodus from Egypt to the ingathering in Canaan is depicted here with that desire (1:11; 2:14-23; 3:5; 11:10-11; 14:4-7).

This connection, this exodus to ingathering, is found all throughout the biblical narrative, and it carries with it the warning of disobedience and whoredom – spiritual adultery. That's what kills us in the desert. That's what keeps us from our prophetic destiny.

Let those who are wise understand these things.

Let those with discernment listen carefully and know:

The paths of the LORD are true and right, and righteous people live by walking in them.

Sinners? They stumble and fall in those paths.

Prophetically, Hosea proclaims God's compassionate and covenantal love that cannot – will not – let Israel go. This is what we discover on this amazing journey from exodus to ingathering.

○ FIELD NOTES

DATE: / / TIME: : AM/PM PLACE:

		A±
○		
○		
○		
○		
○		
○		
○		
○		
○		
○		
○		
○		
○		
○		
○		
○		
○		
○		
○		
○		

ARMOR CHECK: Ephesians 6:10-18

Belt of Truth	S ☐ M ☐ T ☐ W ☐ T ☐ F ☐ S ☐
Breastplate of Righteousness	S ☐ M ☐ T ☐ W ☐ T ☐ F ☐ S ☐
Shoes / Gospel of Peace	S ☐ M ☐ T ☐ W ☐ T ☐ F ☐ S ☐
Shield of Faith	S ☐ M ☐ T ☐ W ☐ T ☐ F ☐ S ☐
Helmet of Salvation	S ☐ M ☐ T ☐ W ☐ T ☐ F ☐ S ☐
Sword of the Spirit / Word of God	S ☐ M ☐ T ☐ W ☐ T ☐ F ☐ S ☐

No weapon formed against you will prosper. This is the heritage of the servants of ADONAI.
Is. 54:17

○ WEEK 37
GOING BACK TO BETH'EL
(GENESIS 35:1B)

"Make an altar there to the God who appeared to you..."

Bethel is located approximately ten miles north of Jerusalem between the territory of the tribe of Benjamin from the Southern Kingdom of Judah and that of the tribe of Ephraim from the Northern Kingdom of Israel.

King Jeroboam would erect one of his golden calf gods in Bethel and bring in his counterfeit "priests" (1 Ki. 12:28-33) to minister there. Bethel is where the man of God from Judah was sent to curse the altar of Bethel and prophesy 300 years into the future about King Josiah (1 Ki. 13:1-10).

The sin of Jeroboam in Bethel, syncretism (the mixture of the holy and the profane), is completely against everything that God established as true and spiritual in regard to the worship of Him, and will plague every king and subject of the Northern Kingdom of Israel – every single one.

Bethel (previously known as Luz) is first mentioned as the place where Abram stayed and built an altar en route to and from Egypt (Gn. 12, 13). It was the location where Abraham's grandson, Jacob, dreamt of a ladder being used as an angelic portal between heaven and earth. God, standing atop the ladder, promises the land of Canaan to Jacob and to make his descendants as numerous as the stars and sand as He did with his father and grandfather. Jacob awakes, erects the stone that he used for a pillow as a pillar, anoints it with oil and names the place *Beth'El* – "House of El" / "House of God" (Gn. 28:10-22). God instructs Jacob to return to Bethel in Genesis 35 where he is once again visited by God. This time, the covenantal promise is reaffirmed, and God changes Jacob's name to Israel.

Bethel is where the warrior prophetess Deborah lived (Jg. 4). An important religious center at the time, Bethel is where the Ark of the Covenant would reside under the care of Phinehas, grandson of Aaron (Jg. 20:26-28). Also, in I Samuel 10:1-13, the prophet and judge Samuel instructs the future King Saul to go to Bethel and visit the "Hill of God." When Saul arrives, he's met by a group of prophets and begins to prophesy with them.

Bethel is also the place where some young lads mocked the prophet Elisha, saying, "Go up, you baldhead! Go up, you baldhead!" Elisha cursed them in ADONAI'S name, and two she-bears came out of the woods and mauled forty-two of the young men (2 Ki. 2:23-25).

The prophet Jeremiah writes of Bethel's idolatry as Israel's shame, and the prophet Hosea prophesied of Bethel's wickedness (Ho. 10). Hosea 13:1b alludes to Bethel's golden calf worship as graduating into full-blown Baal worship:

> *But the people of Ephraim sinned by worshiping Baal and thus sealed their destruction.*

Hosea had so much righteous indignation and contempt for Bethel that he called it *Beth-aven*, "house of idols," at least four times.

Bethel is where God met Abram and Jacob.

Bethel is where God affirmed, established, reaffirmed and reestablished His covenant with man, giving it its namesake – *Beth'El* (House of God). Bethel – the lost and demonic wasteland of pagan worship and idolatry.

Be careful to guard, protect, cultivate and nurture *your* Beth'El.

That pretty much brings us full circle, doesn't it?

> *God said to Jacob, "Arise, go up to Bethel and dwell there. Make an altar there to the God who appeared to you when you fled from your brother Esau."*
> *Genesis 35:1*

So, he does.

Jacob tells all his people to dispose of all the foreign gods – the idols of false gods – in their possession, purify themselves and change their clothes, because they're going to go to *Beth'El*, the home of the One True God, to honor Him there.

As they travelled to Bethel, it says that the terror of God fell on all the towns and cities that they travelled through so that no one attacked them, chased them or interrupted their journey. One of the ways we pray is we ask God to "make us invisible to the evil one and the evil man."

They arrive at Bethel, and Rebekah's nurse, Deborah, dies. I make note of that, because Deborah is buried under an oak tree just outside Bethel, and they called it "*Al'lon-bacuth*." In Judges 4:5, it says that the warrior prophetess Deborah,

[...] used to sit under the palm of Deborah between Ramah and Bethel in the hill country of Ephraim, and the people of Israel came up to her for judgment.

Once again, God visits Jacob at Bethel. He changes his name from Jacob to Israel, which means "God contends," to contend and to fight. Remember how Jacob "wrestled with an angel"?

And God said to him, "I am God Almighty: be fruitful and multiply. A nation and a company of nations shall come from you, and kings shall come from your own body. The land that I gave to Abraham and Isaac I will give to you, and I will give the land to your offspring after you."
Genesis 35:11-12

Jacob once again erects a pillar, pours out a drink offering on it and anoints it with oil.

Bethel is where God met Abram and Jacob.

Bethel is where God affirmed, established, reaffirmed and reestablished His covenant, giving it its namesake – *Beth'El* (House of God).

Bethel would become known for its pagan worship and idolatry and would be lost and destroyed forever as a demonic wasteland.

Be careful to guard, protect, cultivate, nurture and cherish *your* "*Beth'El*," the *Beth'El* in your heart from the attacks from the enemy.

I thought that warranted repeating.

So how do we, then, protect the "House of God" in our hearts?

"'Oh that they had such a mind as this always, to fear me and to keep all my commandments, that it might go well with them and with their descendants forever!'

You shall be careful therefore to do as the LORD your God has commanded you. You shall not turn aside to the right hand or to the left. You shall walk in all the way that the LORD your God has commanded you, that you may live, and that it may go well with you, and that you may live long in the land that you shall possess."
Deuteronomy 5:29, 32-33

- Be careful; stay vigilant.
- Keep the commandments.
- Don't deviate or turn.
- Walk in all the ways He instructed.

Be the House of God.

○ FIELD NOTES

DATE: / / **TIME:** : AM/PM **PLACE:**

○		A±
○		
○		
○		
○		
○		
○		
○		
○		
○		
○		
○		
○		
○		
○		
○		
○		
○		
○		
○		

ARMOR CHECK: Ephesians 6:10-18

Belt of Truth	S ☐	M ☐	T ☐	W ☐	T ☐	F ☐	S ☐
Breastplate of Righteousness	S ☐	M ☐	T ☐	W ☐	T ☐	F ☐	S ☐
Shoes / Gospel of Peace	S ☐	M ☐	T ☐	W ☐	T ☐	F ☐	S ☐
Shield of Faith	S ☐	M ☐	T ☐	W ☐	T ☐	F ☐	S ☐
Helmet of Salvation	S ☐	M ☐	T ☐	W ☐	T ☐	F ☐	S ☐
Sword of the Spirit / Word of God	S ☐	M ☐	T ☐	W ☐	T ☐	F ☐	S ☐

No weapon formed against you will prosper. This is the heritage of the servants of ADONAI.
Is. 54:17

○ WEEK 38
HERE COMES THE DREAMER
(GENESIS 37:3)

Now Israel loved Joseph more than any other of his sons, because he was the son of his old age. And he made him a robe of many colors.

In Week 01, we discussed God's prophetic word to Abram in Genesis 15 regarding his offspring being sojourners in a land that wasn't their own – Egypt. In Genesis 37, we see Abraham's great grandson, Joseph, begin to fulfill that prophecy:

Then Judah said to his brothers, "What profit is it if we kill our brother and conceal his blood? Come, let us sell him to the Ishmaelites, and let not our hand be upon him, for he is our brother, our own flesh." And his brothers listened to him. Then Midianite traders passed by. And they drew Joseph up and lifted him out of the pit, and sold him to the Ishmaelites for twenty shekels of silver. They took Joseph to Egypt.
Genesis 37:26-28

Joseph was loved by his father Jacob / Israel more than any of his brothers, and they knew it, saw it and hated him for it. The gift of a multicolored coat that their father had made him only compounded the situation.

And if that wasn't enough, Joseph had a couple of prophetic dreams where his family bowed down to him as if he were royalty. Sharing these dreams only made his brothers hate him the more.

One day, Joseph was sent by his father to check up on his brothers while they were tending the flocks. They saw him coming from afar and began to devise a plan. The decision to kill him was made before he even reached them – that's how strong their hatred of him was. Joseph was 17.

Welcome to the dysfunctional family that was to become the twelve tribes of Israel…

They said to one another, "Here comes this dreamer.

Come now, let us kill him and throw him into one of the pits. Then we will say that a fierce animal has devoured him, and we will see what will become of his dreams."
Genesis 37:19-20

Reuben, thinking fast on his feet in order to save the poor kid, heard them and suggested that they throw him into an empty well instead of killing him.

So when Joseph came to his brothers, they stripped him of his robe, the robe of many colors that he wore. And they took him and threw him into a pit. The pit was empty; there was no water in it.
Verses 23-24

Being thrown into an empty pit would have hurt. The brothers, sans Reuben, sat down to eat as a caravan of Ishmaelites (descendants of their great-great uncle), en route to Egypt, was approaching. They pulled Joseph up out of the pit and sold him for eight ounces of silver.

Reuben came back to an empty well. Upset, he tore his clothes and scolded his brothers who proceeded to take Joseph's beautiful coat, dip it in goats blood, and take it to their father saying, "We found this."

Meanwhile, in Egypt, Joseph is sold to a man named Potiphar, one of Pharaoh's officials and captain of the palace guard.

I asked this question Week 01:

Do you ever get the feeling that you're serving someone else's agenda? That the season of your life isn't actually about you but about somebody or something else? That your needs, your "quieros" aren't being met? That you're... inconsequential? Unappreciated – irrelevant, even – and not just by your friends or loved ones, but maybe even by your pastor or by... God Himself...?

For Joseph, the boy with the coat of many colors, the "reward" for sharing a couple of prophetic dreams with his brothers, was to be thrown into a pit and then sold into slavery – to Ishmaelites no less! How was that a "part of God's plan"?

Lance Wallnau says the following: Joseph was not a prisoner of Egypt, he was a prisoner of a prophetic promise. God must deny Josephs [sic] prayer for deliverance because the world needs Joseph to stay where he is.

(Source: Lance Wallnau. https://lancewallnau.com/joseph-prisoner-of-circumstance-or-prophetic-process)

- Are we learning to answer some of these questions in the spiritual realm versus defaulting to our physical realm and practical reasoning?
- Are we learning the spiritual reasoning behind some of these difficult lessons found in the paragraph from Week 01?
- Are you feeling confident that some of these challenges are being addressed and that understanding and revelation are being gained through explanation and scriptural case studies after 37 weeks?

Be sure to utilize the Journal and Prayer Modules for the above exercise. Also, feel free to email us at feedback@E2iSeries.com and let us know your answers.

We will also be discussing this in a Live Q&A over at *Exodus Expedition* next week, giving everyone time to plan for it. If you haven't already, sign up at: https://www.patreon.com/E2iS

The account of Joseph is a great case study for so many biblical principles.

I usually touch on the aspect of Joseph being exalted to Second Pharaoh status and the proof text that it is for the Seven Mountain teaching on government.

I also address how Joseph demands that he be shaved before going before Pharaoh to interpret his dream. This wasn't about Joseph or Judaism. This was all about making sure he had Pharaoh's full and undivided attention. "Make me look like a Gentile Egyptian – shave me – so that Pharaoh is sure to hear and receive the prophetic word of God."

I will mention that the reason Joseph's brothers didn't recognize him as being their Hebrew brother is the same reason Israel (Jews) don't recognize Jesus as their long-awaited and promised Hebrew Messiah. We have Jesus all dressed up like a Gentile Egyptian...

I've always been moved by the account of Joseph in *The Testaments of the Twelve Patriarchs*, a pseudepigraphical work comprised of the dying testimonies of the twelve patriarchs.

And I did nor raise myself (against them) with evil intent, but I honoured my brethren; and out of respect for them, even when I was being sold, I refrained from telling the Ishmaelites that I was a son of Jacob, a great man and a mighty.

(Source: "The Testament of Joseph the Eleventh Son of Jacob and Rachel, Chapter 10," In *The Testaments of the Twelve Patriarchs*)

In this writing, it is suggested that it was blatantly obvious that Joseph wasn't a slave but rather the Hebrew prince that he was.

And when I came to the Indocolpitae with the Ishmaelites, they asked me, saying: Art thou a slave? And I said that I was a home-born slave, ***that I might not put my brethren to shame****. And the eldest of them said unto me: Thou art not a slave, for even thy appearance doth make it manifest. But I said that I was their slave.*
(Emphasis mine)

(Source: ibid. Chapter 11)

And he took me apart from him, and said unto me: Art thou a slave or free? And I said: A slave. And he said: Whose? And I said: The Ishmaelites. And he said: How didst thou become their slave? And I said: They bought me out of the land of Canaan. And he said unto me: Truly thou liest; and straightway he commanded me to be stripped and beaten.

(Source: ibid. Chapter 13)

Now after four and twenty days came the Ishmaelites; for they had heard that Jacob my father was mourning much concerning me.

And they came and said unto me: How is it that thou saidst that thou wast a slave? and lo, we have learnt that thou art the son of a mighty man in the land of Canaan, and thy father still mourneth for thee in sackcloth and ashes.

When I heard this my bowels were dissolved and my heart melted, and I desired greatly to weep, but I restrained myself, ***that I should not put my brethren to shame****. And I said unto them, I know not, I am a slave.*
(Emphasis mine)

(Source: ibid. Chapter 15)

Ye see, therefore, my children, what great things I endured ***that I should not put my brethren to shame****.*
(Emphasis mine)

(Source: ibid. Chapter 17)

"... so as not to shame my brothers."

I read this years ago, and I've never forgotten it. Joseph endured being sold into slavery, beatings, incarceration and resisted the wiles of a beautiful Egyptian woman so as not to bring shame to his brothers. I can't even begin to explain the importance of this amazing attribute and spiritual revelation.

That this is an apocryphal text hardly matters when the essence of this account is mirrored in the canon by Moses, David and Messiah Himself.

Do ye also, therefore love one another, and with long-suffering hide ye one another's faults. For God delighteth in the unity of brethren, and in the purpose of a heart that takes pleasure in love.

(Source: ibid.)

○ FIELD NOTES

DATE: / / **TIME:** : AM/PM **PLACE:**

○		A±
○		
○		
○		
○		
○		
○		
○		
○		
○		
○		
○		
○		
○		
○		
○		
○		
○		
○		
○		

ARMOR CHECK: Ephesians 6:10-18

Belt of Truth	S ☐	M ☐	T ☐	W ☐	T ☐	F ☐	S ☐
Breastplate of Righteousness	S ☐	M ☐	T ☐	W ☐	T ☐	F ☐	S ☐
Shoes / Gospel of Peace	S ☐	M ☐	T ☐	W ☐	T ☐	F ☐	S ☐
Shield of Faith	S ☐	M ☐	T ☐	W ☐	T ☐	F ☐	S ☐
Helmet of Salvation	S ☐	M ☐	T ☐	W ☐	T ☐	F ☐	S ☐
Sword of the Spirit / Word of God	S ☐	M ☐	T ☐	W ☐	T ☐	F ☐	S ☐

No weapon formed against you will prosper. This is the heritage of the servants of ADONAI.
Is. 54:17

WEEK 39
DELIVERER IN DISGUISE
(GENESIS 42:7; LUKE 24:15-16)

Joseph recognized his brothers instantly, but he pretended to be a stranger and spoke harshly to them. (NLT)

As they talked and discussed these things, Jesus himself suddenly came and began walking with them. But God kept them from recognizing him. (NLT)

In last week's devotional, I mentioned that the main reason for Joseph's brothers' failure to recognize him as their Hebrew brother was the same reason Israel (Jews) fail to recognize *Jesus* as their long-awaited and promised Hebrew Messiah. We have Jesus all dressed up and disguised as an Egyptian, a Gentile...

When Joseph's brothers came before the Egyptian magistrate – the governor, no less – for food, they had no idea that they were bowing down before their Hebrew brother, and Joseph wasn't revealing his identity to them either. It's an amazing encounter found in Genesis 42.

Since Joseph was governor of all Egypt and in charge of selling grain to all the people, it was to him that his brothers came. When they arrived, they bowed before him with their faces to the ground.

Joseph recognized his brothers instantly, but he pretended to be a stranger and spoke harshly to them. "Where are you from?" he demanded. "From the land of Canaan," they replied. "We have come to buy food."

And he remembered the dreams he'd had about them many years before. He said to them, "You are spies! You have come to see how vulnerable our land has become."
Genesis 42:6-7, 9 (NLT)

Joseph was, for all intents and purposes, an Egyptian. Twenty years had passed, and he had been serving in the court of Pharaoh and in charge of the entire land of Egypt for at least seven years by the time his brothers showed up to buy food.

Pharaoh had taken the ring off of his own finger and given it to Joseph. It was the ring with which Pharaoh stamped all official documents, and it had been on Joseph's finger for quite some time now. Pharaoh had also dressed Joseph in robes made of fine linen, and he wore a gold chain around his neck. Joseph also rode with Pharaoh in a chariot and had been made second in command to Pharaoh himself.

Where have we discussed something like this before? On the issue of identity: the prodigal son and Jerusalem in Ezekiel 16, Week 31.

> *And Pharaoh said to him, "I am Pharaoh, but no one will lift a hand or foot in the entire land of Egypt without your approval."*
>
> *Then Pharaoh gave Joseph a new Egyptian name, Zaphenath-paneah. He also gave him a wife, whose name was Asenath. She was the daughter of Potiphera, the priest of On. So Joseph took charge of the entire land of Egypt.*
>
> *Genesis 41:44-45 (NLT)*

Joseph was in charge of all of Egypt. He wore Egyptian clothing, was clean shaven, did his hair in the latest Egyptian style and wore the makeup of Egyptian royalty. He spoke Egyptian... he was essentially a Gentile prince.

To a large extent, Gentile Christianity has inadvertently wrapped on additional layers to the disguise which conceals the identity of Yeshua [Jesus] from His brothers, the Jewish people. Christian artwork represents Jesus as a Gentile. Christian theology presents Him as an enemy to the Jewish people. Church tradition has removed Him from His Jewish context and made Him unrecognizable to His own brothers. Historically, the harder Christians have tried to convince Jews otherwise, the more that we have strengthened the Jewish people in their conviction that Jesus is not a Jew and that He is certainly not the Messiah.

The ten brothers did not recognize Joseph, but he recognized them. The Midrash Rabbah notes the irony of the situation between Joseph and his brothers: "Joseph had recognized his brothers" when they fell into his hand, "although they did not recognize him" when he fell into their hands. (Genesis Rabbah 91:7)

(Source: Torah Club Commentary Set: *Shadows of the Messiah*)

Joseph put his brothers through a series of tests to determine their heart of repentance:

Speaking among themselves, they said, "Clearly we are being punished because of what we did to Joseph long ago. We saw his anguish when he pleaded for his life, but we wouldn't listen. That's why we're in this trouble."

"Didn't I tell you not to sin against the boy?" Reuben asked. "But you wouldn't listen. And now we have to answer for his blood!"

Of course, they didn't know that Joseph understood them, for he had been speaking to them through an interpreter. Now he turned away from them and began to weep. When he regained his composure, he spoke to them again. Then he chose Simeon from among them and had him tied up right before their eyes.
Genesis 42:21-24 (NLT)

So heartbreaking! And it gets worse. They return to their father, Israel / Jacob, without one of their brothers and with a harsh story to tell of how they must bring their baby brother, Benjamin, back to Egypt with them!

The morning after the resurrection of Messiah, that Sunday morning (the resurrection had occurred the night before, Saturday night after the Sabbath ended, at the beginning of the Feast of Firstfruits), two of Jesus' followers were on their way to a village about seven miles from Jerusalem called Emmaus. They were reasoning together about everything that had just happened.

It was the week-long Feast of Unleavened Bread. Passover had been on Wednesday evening before sunset, but the night before, Jesus and the original twelve disciples had been accosted by temple guards in the garden in the middle of the night!

Jesus had been shuffled around all day long on Wednesday, the day of preparation, between Pilate, Herod and then *back* to Pilate, who by then had conceded to the pressures of the Sanhedrin, giving them what they wanted – a crucifixion!

Jesus had been crucified and was just barely buried in time for the High Sabbath of the first day of the Feast of Unleavened Bread, Wednesday night, right after sunset following Passover.

The Marys had purchased spices and burial accruements for the body but didn't get to the tomb until Saturday night after the Sabbath as the first day of the week was beginning. That's when they found the empty tomb.

As they talked about those things, Jesus himself came up and walked along with them. But God kept them from recognizing him.
Luke 24:15-16 (NIRV)

Jesus was in disguise. He asked them what they were talking about, so they stopped and looked at the stranger in sorrow, downcast. Verse 18:

One of them was named Cleopas. He said to Jesus, "You must be a visitor to Jerusalem..."

The disciples proceeded to tell "Messiah in disguise" all that had happened in Jerusalem the last four days, to which Jesus replied:

"Foolish people! So unwilling to put your trust in everything the prophets spoke!"
Verse 25 (CJB)

Jesus began to explain to them all that was said and written about Him in the Scriptures, starting with Moses and then going through all the Prophets. Like Joseph, Jesus wasn't revealing his identity to them either. Instead "he pretended to be a stranger and spoke harshly to them..."

We, the Romanized Western Church, have misrepresented Messiah to Israel for well over 1700 years. We believe in, preach and proselytize a Gentile messiah that opposes Moses, the Torah and everything God warns us scripturally about what a "false prophet" will look like in Deuteronomy 13. Is it any wonder they don't believe us or in Him?

Paul clearly taught that Gentiles are to provoke Israel, Jews, to salvation by making them jealous – jealous of their Messiah, not repulsed (Romans 11).

Joseph eventually revealed himself to his brothers, showing them that he was indeed their Hebrew brother. Jesus will also do the same:

Lest you be wise in your own sight, I want you to understand this mystery, brothers: a partial hardening has come upon Israel, until the fullness of the Gentiles has come in.

And in this way all Israel will be saved, as it is written, "The Deliverer will come from Zion, he will banish ungodliness from Jacob" [Is. 59:20-21]; "and this will be my covenant with them when I take away their sins."[Is. 27:9]
Romans 11:25-26

The Deliverer takes off His disguise…

Joseph's brothers did not "recognize" him in that they did not treat him like a brother. He recognized his brothers in that he treated them with mercy when they fell into his power. Though the Jewish nation has not yet recognized Him as a brother and as the Messiah, He recognizes His brothers.

(Source: Torah Club Commentary Set: *Shadows of the Messiah*)

○ FIELD NOTES

DATE: / / **TIME:** : AM/PM **PLACE:**

		A±
○		
○		
○		
○		
○		
○		
○		
○		
○		
○		
○		
○		
○		
○		
○		
○		
○		
○		
○		
○		

ARMOR CHECK: Ephesians 6:10-18

Belt of Truth	S ☐	M ☐	T ☐	W ☐	T ☐	F ☐	S ☐
Breastplate of Righteousness	S ☐	M ☐	T ☐	W ☐	T ☐	F ☐	S ☐
Shoes / Gospel of Peace	S ☐	M ☐	T ☐	W ☐	T ☐	F ☐	S ☐
Shield of Faith	S ☐	M ☐	T ☐	W ☐	T ☐	F ☐	S ☐
Helmet of Salvation	S ☐	M ☐	T ☐	W ☐	T ☐	F ☐	S ☐
Sword of the Spirit / Word of God	S ☐	M ☐	T ☐	W ☐	T ☐	F ☐	S ☐

No weapon formed against you will prosper. This is the heritage of the servants of ADONAI.
Is. 54:17

○ WEEK 40
BATTLE TACTICS
(PSALM 18:34)

He trains my hands for war, so that my arms can bend a bow of bronze.

The goal with the *E2iSeries* is to provide you with information designed to assist you in going ever forward and successfully making it over the Jordan and into your prophetic inheritance, your Promised Land, without getting "taken out" in the desert by either the enemy or yourself.

With that in mind, two of the themes we go through repeatedly in the *E2iSeries*, even if you haven't realized it, are the themes of "Battle Tactics" and "Spiritual Warfare." Think "Karate Kid" and the "wax on / wax off" concept: you think you're learning how to wax a car or paint a fence, but in all actuality, you're learning martial arts and how to defend yourself. Whatever it is you might *think* we're discussing, we're actually deliberating battle tactics for spiritual warfare.

Do you know how many times the New Testament mentions our needing to be vigilant in making sure that our position is secure; that our salvation is secure; that after doing everything that we can, to stand! Many. We're constantly being told this in Paul's letters and epistles alone.

It is our responsibility to make sure that not only are we still *in* the race, but that we're also *running* that race *as to win*; not fighting and beating the air. We are to remain constantly vigilant and have our abilities of situational awareness, in both the physical *and* spiritual realms, finely tuned. There are so many potential obstacles and variables vying for our affection and attention – demonic distractions designed to detour and derail – that we need to determine whether or not they are conducive to our succeeding and completing this amazing journey that we're on. Stay alert!

Romanized Mainstream Western Christianity has programmed us into thinking contrary to all New Testament teaching: "Oh, don't worry about it. We're saved. We're good to go. We literally don't have to do anything to keep that salvation."

We have to continue to fan that flame! We have to bear big, juicy, godly and eternal fruit. If your branch isn't bearing fruit, you're cut off and thrown into the fire. You don't want to "die on the vine!" (Jn 15:1-10) You've got to do everything you can, and everything that you're supposed to do, to keep that flame alive and to bear that godly fruit. That's where spiritual training comes in.

Israel left Egypt dressed for battle, but God avoided that battle by leading them the long way around. He knew Israel wouldn't be able to handle a fight (Ex. 13:17-18), because they weren't a warring people. Israel had no idea what God was about to do to them. He was going to start preparing them and transforming them into a warring people.

I don't think that we, as believers, fully grasp that same reality about ourselves. God is trying to prepare and train us into a warring people, even as we're not cooperating fully with that goal – *His* goal. The whole purpose of Christendom is to make us like Jesus, and one of those processes of being transformed into the likeness of His Son is to make us into a warring people. When Jesus was healing the sick and the demonically unclean; speaking words of knowledge into people (i.e., the Samaritan woman); arguing with the religious leaders; healing the blind, the deaf and the paralyzed; walking on water; multiplying fish and bread; transforming into light; casting out demons; raising the dead; He was doing spiritual warfare. Why? Because there's a spiritual war going on for your physical life and eternal soul, and we are commanded to imitate Jesus. (1 Pe. 2:21; 1 Jn. 2:6)

Spiritual warfare has been coming at us since before any of us were ever saved, and we need to learn how to fight that battle – that spiritual war. We either cooperate with His desire to make us into a warring people so as to be able to be victorious in that fight, or we'll lose the spiritual war.

And so, Israel – God knows Israel will more than likely not fight if the Philistines pick a fight. So to avoid that fight, He leads them the long way around. But regardless, He has them dressed for battle when they leave Egypt. Why?

He begins Israel's identity transformation process from the very beginning!

He has already begun their training. It even says in Judges 2, "I'm training you to be a warring people; that's what I did in the desert. I was training you to be a warring people, because if I hadn't, you would have died a long time ago. You have to learn to defend yourself and to protect yourself."

God's long game is (not "was") to create a warring people out of Israel. They don't know this, so they freak out when the 12 spies return with the report that not all of the inhabitants of Canaan are entirely human, that there are indeed, Nephilim in the land.

"What are You talking about, we have to go up and war with Giants? We can't beat the Nephilim!"

Nevertheless, they were going to have to, because the Nephilim possessed and inhabited their land; the Nephilim were in possession of Israel's prophetic destiny, and Israel was going to have to dispossess them to acquire it – obtain it – possess it.

That's entirely the same transcript of our battles. Yet the majority of us have never been taught that God's desire is for us to be a warring people so that we ourselves can fight the same spiritual war *and win* in order to possess our land, our territory and our prophetic destiny. That victory requires our dispossessing of demonic strongholds – giants – in our physical and spiritual lives and territory. In the same manner, many of us have never been taught how to be a warring people that can successfully prepare, train, strategize, fight and win a war outside our physical realm – a war in the spiritual realm.

INSTRUCTIONS CONCERNING WARFARE

We find "Instructions Concerning Warfare" in Deuteronomy 20. In that teaching, we're taught that we are not to fear our enemy regardless of weaponry or size, for ADONAI our God is with us. It reminds you that, "After all, He brought you out of Egypt."

Before battle, your spiritual authority is to encourage you saying, "Don't be afraid. Don't be scared. Don't panic. Don't be terrified. ADONAI your God is going with and before you. He will fight for and help you and triumph in battle on your behalf against your enemies."

Israel was instructed to destroy all the inhabitants of Canaan, because they were not entirely human. If they weren't destroyed, the inhabitants of Canaan would teach Israel to follow everything ADONAI hates – not *hated*, past tense, but, *hates*, present tense. God *hates* the way they worship their gods. The ruling still stands that if you do those things, you'll be sinning against the LORD your God. Israel didn't carry out those orders of total destruction, and they fell into every form of pagan worship the land of Canaan had to offer, sadly including child sacrifice.

"Instructions Concerning Warfare" even considered the trees (verses 19-20):

"When you besiege a city for a long time, making war against it in order to take it, you shall not destroy its trees by wielding an axe against them. You may eat from them, but you shall not cut them down. Are the trees in the field human, that they should be besieged by you?

Only the trees that you know are not trees for food you may destroy and cut down, that you may build siegeworks against the city that makes war with you, until it falls.
Deuteronomy 20:19-20

Consider the following:
God leads Israel out of Egypt dressed for battle but avoids one:
Exodus 13:17-18

Israel doesn't know it yet, but they will have to become a warring people to possess their prophetic inheritance. They begin to train:
Exodus 17:8-13
Numbers 21:23-30

God had already established Israel's triumph over the Nephilim. Joshua and Caleb believed in what the Spirit of God was saying, but 80% of the spies didn't, and so put fear, doubt and unbelief into the people:
Numbers 13:25 - 14:39

Do not do battle in your own strength and/or out of disobedience:
Numbers 14:40-45

Moses petitions for a warring leader to succeed him after his death:
Numbers 27:15-23

The tactic of priestly, prophetic worship in obedience defeats all the ruling enemies in your territory:
Numbers 31

Circumcision before battle allows for purification, alignment, identity:
Joshua 5

Judah (praise, worship) goes first.
Judges 1:1-2, 20:18

Failure to complete the conquest (Jg. 1:27-36) caused more problems for Israel. They had once again disobeyed. Because of that disobedience (Jg. 2:1-5) and their unfaithfulness (Jg. 2:11-13) Israel's protection in battle was lifted (verse 15).
Judges 2:20 - 3:6

God's battle tactic for Gideon: Less men:
Judges 6 - 8

Jephthah – a warring Judge of Israel:
Judges 11 - 12:7

The Ark of the Covenant used in battle:
1 Samuel 4 - 7

The battle is the Lords:
1 Samuel 14:1-23
2 Chronicles 20:1-22

David and Goliath:
1 Samuel 17

Sometimes in battle you come across giants:
2 Samuel 21:15-22

"He trains my hands for battle…"
2 Samuel 22:35-51; Psalm 18:34-42

Do you go into battle when 400 prophets unanimously prophesy for it?
1 Kings 22 / 2 Chronicles 18

Boldness – an attribute for battle:
Acts 4:23-31

The full armor of God:
Ephesians 6:10-18a

Testimonies about warriors:
Hebrews 11:32-34

You have won your battle with the evil one:
1 John 2:13-14

The battle is won by the blood of the Lamb and the word of their testimony:
Revelation 12:7-12

Armageddon:
Revelation 16:13-16

> *When the thousand years come to an end, Satan will be let out of his prison. He will go out to deceive the nations— called Gog and Magog— in every corner of the earth. He will gather them together for battle— a mighty army, as numberless as sand along the seashore.*
>
> *And I saw them as they went up on the broad plain of the earth and surrounded God's people and the beloved city. But fire from heaven came down on the attacking armies and consumed them.*
>
> *Then the devil, who had deceived them, was thrown into the fiery lake of burning sulfur, joining the beast and the false prophet. There they will be tormented day and night forever and ever.*
> *Revelation 20:7-10 (NLT)*

When you finish this resource, go back and re-read, re-study all of this again from the beginning, with all of this "battle" stuff in mind. Track the changes, the new way you process this information. That's because of the training. That's called "discipleship".

And remember how we win this war: "little by little".

○ FIELD NOTES

DATE: / / TIME: : AM/PM PLACE:

○		A±
○		
○		
○		
○		
○		
○		
○		
○		
○		
○		
○		
○		
○		
○		
○		
○		
○		
○		
○		

ARMOR CHECK: Ephesians 6:10-18

Belt of Truth	S ☐ M ☐ T ☐ W ☐ T ☐ F ☐ S ☐
Breastplate of Righteousness	S ☐ M ☐ T ☐ W ☐ T ☐ F ☐ S ☐
Shoes / Gospel of Peace	S ☐ M ☐ T ☐ W ☐ T ☐ F ☐ S ☐
Shield of Faith	S ☐ M ☐ T ☐ W ☐ T ☐ F ☐ S ☐
Helmet of Salvation	S ☐ M ☐ T ☐ W ☐ T ☐ F ☐ S ☐
Sword of the Spirit / Word of God	S ☐ M ☐ T ☐ W ☐ T ☐ F ☐ S ☐

No weapon formed against you will prosper. This is the heritage of the servants of ADONAI.
Is. 54:17

WEEK 41
LOVE IS A BATTLEFIELD
(1 JOHN 4:7)

Beloved, let us love one another, for love is from God, and whoever loves has been born of God and knows God.

Last week, we talked about "Battle Tactics" and "Spiritual Warfare." Want to know one of the most powerful battle tactics there is in the physical realm that transcends into the spiritual?

It was now the day before the Passover Festival. Jesus knew that the hour had come for him to leave this world and go to the Father. Jesus and his disciples were at supper (the "Last Supper"). So he rose from the table, took off his outer garment, and tied a towel around his waist. Then he poured some water into a washbasin and began to wash the disciples' feet and dry them with the towel around his waist.

He came to Simon Peter, who said to him, "Are you going to wash my feet, Lord?" Jesus answered him, "You do not understand now what I am doing, but you will understand later." Peter declared, "Never at any time will you wash my feet!" "If I do not wash your feet," Jesus answered, "you will no longer be my disciple."
John 13:1a-2a, 4-8 (GNT)

Washing the feet of another human being is one of the most powerful weapons in your arsenal – a physical, strategic battle tactic for and in a spiritual war. I say that, because washing another's feet is serving that individual, and it requires humility and love to serve in that capacity.

Love. Love needs to be our weapon of choice. Now, what can I tell you about love that you don't already know? Well, how about some practical, real-world, everyday type examples of love, like:

- Carry some nondescript backpacks or small duffel bags or any sort of bag in your car. Fill the bag with basic toiletries, toilet paper, water bottles, socks, granola bars, a gift card to a fast food restaurant, a sweatshirt and/or blanket, etc. You can distribute them every time you see a person in need.

- Take a single-parent family out to lunch after church.
- Be a "big brother" or "big sister" to a child in that single-parent home.
- Bring back coffee for your co-workers in the office.
- Tip generously.

There's that saying that circulates social media every so often: *"Preach the Gospel at all times. Use words if necessary."*

You can do everything above and more with a simple smile. You don't have to be that creepy Christian that qualifies acts of kindness with some uncomfortable attempt at evangelizing. Please don't do that. Make friends with that individual first. Or better yet, let them ask you what prompts your generosity. "Jesus and His love for you" is all you ever need say. And leave it at that.

> *So then, as we have opportunity, let us do good to everyone, and especially to those who are of the household of faith.*
> *Galatians 6:10*

Have you ever gone "treasure hunting?" That's when you ask the Holy Spirit to reveal the individual(s) He would have you encounter that day – the person or persons for whom you need to be on the lookout. You also ask the Holy Spirit what it is that He would have you say or do for those "treasures."

Ask for a word of knowledge to give them or the physical acts of charity with which you're to bless them or the spiritual gift you're to impart like healing, deliverance, or simply a kind word or gesture. This is being proactive and vigilant out in the field. Don't wait for needs to come to you. Go looking for them.

> *"'[...] for I was hungry and you gave Me food; I was thirsty and you gave Me drink; I was a stranger and you took Me in; I was naked and you clothed Me; I was sick and you visited Me; I was in prison and you came to Me. Assuredly, I say to you, inasmuch as you did it to one of the least of these My brethren, you did it to Me.'"*
> *Matthew 25:35-36, 40 (NKJV)*

Jesus is paraphrasing the prophets Isaiah and Ezekiel from the Old Testament: Isaiah 59:7-9 and Ezekiel 18:7-9. He's also referencing Job 31:32 and Proverbs 14:31. Don't you just love the whole counsel of scripture?

Proverbs 19:17 says,

Whoever is generous to the poor lends to the Lord, and he will repay him for his deed. [See also Proverbs 22:9, 28:27]

One of the blessings that comes with keeping God's commandments – His Torah, is the absence of poverty in your life (among other things) and the lives of those around you:

"And because you listen to these rules and keep and do them, the Lord your God will keep with you the covenant and the steadfast love that he swore to your fathers.

He will love you, bless you, and multiply you. He will also bless the fruit of your womb and the fruit of your ground, your grain and your wine and your oil, the increase of your herds and the young of your flock, in the land that he swore to your fathers to give you."
Deuteronomy 7:12-13 [See also Exodus 23:25-26]

Even though poverty is scripturally a result of disobedience, regardless, God has always championed the less fortunate. For example, every seven years debt is to be erased, fields are not to be harvested to their boundary lines specifically so that the poor can glean from them. What *is* harvested but is left on the ground, is to be left for the poor. Any unfair or ill treatment of the poor is to be severely punished by the hand of God and man alike (Lev. 19:10, 15; 23:22; 25:25, 35, 39).

"For there will never cease to be poor in the land. Therefore I command you, 'You shall open wide your hand to your brother, to the needy and to the poor, in your land.'"
Deuteronomy 15:11

"Therefore I command you…" Our caring for the poor is serious stuff.

Serving and caring for those less fortunate than yourself is God's heart, and it's an easy way for us to *represent* His heart to and in the world around us. It's that "love" thing, our weapon of choice. Love: the most powerful battle tactic there is in the physical realm that transcends into the spiritual. Besides… it's just civil of us and is the right thing to do for our fellow man.

The love of God in our lives is always backed with action. We're being watched: how we treat people – our compassion, our generosity and simply being good to people. Everything about us is either a good representation or a bad representation of our God. It is our witness.

I recently was having issues with my internet service. I'd had a couple reps and a supervisor over multiple times, and a couple trucks were dispatched to repair an issue that was found in the main neighborhood line. Even then, my service wasn't working correctly. They decided to concentrate on the unstable and unacceptable wireless signal, so they sent a rep out for the fourth time. Instead of sending out the rep that was familiar with my situation (I was on month two of having less-than-adequate service), they sent out a kid... literally.

I called and complained to the supervising manager that I had been working with and explained to him the inconvenience of sending someone that wasn't familiar with my situation – my having to start from the beginning, explaining / repeating myself for the umpteenth time and how I didn't have the time or the patience for this after two long months... I was rude and, well, not very "Christlike" with my condescending and frustrated attitude.

Long story short, the kid fixed it and was able to determine the issue... *after* I had kicked him out. Yes, it's a longer story, but I asked him to leave – rudely, I might add – and when I backtracked and had him return, he had resolved it, and I had one of the biggest portions of crow that I remember having to eat in a very long time.

I apologized, we made up, and I even called back the supervisor and apologized to him and confessed that I had apologized to his young rep as he had fixed the other older and more experienced rep's error. Le sigh.

> *By this it is evident who are the children of God, and who are the children of the devil: whoever does not practice righteousness is not of God, nor is the one who does not love his brother.*
> *1 John 3:10*

Ouch.

The Apostle John, the "beloved disciple," continues by explaining that we should love one another, that loving the brethren passed us out of death and into life and that "whoever doesn't love abides in death" (1 Jn 3:14b ESV).

> *By this we know love, that he laid down his life for us, and we ought to lay down our lives for the brothers.*
>
> *But if anyone has the world's goods and sees his brother in need, yet closes his heart against him, how does God's love abide in him? Little children, let us not love in word or talk but in deed and in truth.*
> *I John 3:16-18*

The world will notice how well we love, how well we help, and how well we meet the needs of others. They'll notice, because they're already watching us...

○ FIELD NOTES

DATE: / / TIME: : AM/PM PLACE:

○		A±
○		
○		
○		
○		
○		
○		
○		
○		
○		
○		
○		
○		
○		
○		
○		
○		
○		
○		
○		

ARMOR CHECK: Ephesians 6:10-18

Belt of Truth	S ☐ M ☐ T ☐ W ☐ T ☐ F ☐ S ☐
Breastplate of Righteousness	S ☐ M ☐ T ☐ W ☐ T ☐ F ☐ S ☐
Shoes / Gospel of Peace	S ☐ M ☐ T ☐ W ☐ T ☐ F ☐ S ☐
Shield of Faith	S ☐ M ☐ T ☐ W ☐ T ☐ F ☐ S ☐
Helmet of Salvation	S ☐ M ☐ T ☐ W ☐ T ☐ F ☐ S ☐
Sword of the Spirit / Word of God	S ☐ M ☐ T ☐ W ☐ T ☐ F ☐ S ☐

No weapon formed against you will prosper. This is the heritage of the servants of ADONAI.
Is. 54:17

○ WEEK 42 MOSES (EXODUS 2:24)

And God heard their groaning, and God remembered his covenant with Abraham, with Isaac, and with Jacob.

I figured that since this week's Torah portion introduces us to Moses, and since Moses is our leader through this journey from exodus to ngathering, we would do a brief profile on the man taken from *The Feasts Unlocked.*

"Israel has been living in Egypt for approximately 200 years. There's a new Pharaoh in town, and he doesn't know, respect or honor Joseph. It seems that this new Pharaoh also doesn't recognize Joseph's contribution to the Egyptian empire and is more concerned with the size of Israel's population; that their numbers may be more than Egypt can manage or control. What if war broke out, and Israel decided to join Egypt's enemies, fight against them and leave? So, Pharaoh decides to deal with Israel shrewdly by distressing, oppressing and tasking them with Egypt's heavy lifting, such as building Pharaoh's store cities (If you recall from Week One, this was prophesied to Abram about his descendants.) In spite of this, Israel continues to multiply and spread across Egypt.

"This only increased Egypt's anxiety and fear towards Israel, so they enslaved them and were ruthless towards them. The Hebrew midwives were instructed to kill all newborn Israeli males, but out of their fear of God, they disobeyed the Pharaoh's instructions so that Israel continued to multiply and strengthen. Pharaoh then instructs Egyptians to carry out the task of murder by throwing all Israeli newborn boys into the Nile.

Now a man from the house of Levi went and took as his wife a Levite woman. The woman conceived and bore a son, and when she saw that he was a fine child, she hid him three months. Exodus 2:1-2

"Did you notice that Moses was a Levite, of a pure Levitical line (Ex. 6:19-20)? But of course he was! The Hebrew midwives have been instructed to murder males at birth. They fear God over Pharaoh and disobey the Egyptian's edict. Pharaoh then instructs all male Israelites to be thrown into the Nile. This is the climate into which this little Levite boy was born. Moses is put into a basket and into the Nile to hide him:

> *Now the daughter of Pharaoh came down to bathe at the river, while her young women walked beside the river. She saw the basket among the reeds and sent her servant woman, and she took it. When she opened it, she saw the child, and behold, the baby was crying. She took pity on him and said, "This is one of the Hebrews' children."*
> *Exodus 2:5-6*

"Moses' sister, Miriam, had been watching the basket, and when she saw Pharaoh's daughter take the basket with the crying baby, she asked if she should go and call on a Hebrew nurse to nurse the child for her. With the Egyptian Princess' permission, Miriam goes and gets her mother. They were instructed to take the child and nurse it and were paid to do so. Verse 10:

> *When the child grew up, she brought him to Pharaoh's daughter, and he became her son. She named him Moses, "Because," she said, "I drew him out of the water."*

"Moses will be raised in Pharaoh's family and in Egypt's court. He will have the best education the world has to offer and will lack nothing. He will also have power as a favored Son of Egypt. 1500 years later, a disciple of Jesus, Stephen, will say this about Moses:

> *And Moses was instructed in all the wisdom of the Egyptians, and he was mighty in his words and deeds.*
> *Acts 7:22*

It is said that Moses was raised up as a general of Egypt's armies at the suggestion of Egypt's oracles and prophets to counter the strained relations with Ethiopia. Moses is victorious against Ethiopia and becomes a celebrated war hero, turning Egyptian leaders against him out of fear:

- *Moses is a foreigner, a Hebrew*
- *Moses represents Israel, who are numerous*
- *Moses has become very powerful*
- *Moses has shown military innovation that might introduce new customs*
- *Envy and fear turns Egypt against Moses*

(Source: Josephus: Antiquities of the Jews 2/9:7-10:2)

"Then Moses makes a mistake; he kills an Egyptian. If the account of Josephus is true, Pharaoh now has his reason to get rid of Moses. When Pharaoh hears that Moses has murdered a fellow Egyptian, Pharaoh wants Moses dead.

"Moses flees Egypt through the desert to Midian, where he immediately makes a name for himself by stopping some shepherds that were bullying the seven daughters of the Midian priest:

> *When they [the seven daughters] came home to their father Reuel, he said, "How is it that you have come home so soon today?" They said, "An Egyptian delivered us out of the hand of the shepherds and even drew water for us and watered the flock." He said to his daughters, "Then where is he? Why have you left the man? Call him, that he may eat bread."*
> *Exodus 2:18-20*

"Two verses later, Moses is married to Reuel's daughter, Zipporah, and they have a son named Gershom.

"There's an hypothesis that Moses lived in the 18th Dynasty when two to three Pharaohs ruled regionally at the same time. It suggests that a people called the Hyksos lived in the northern delta region and are described as "shepherd kings" whom the Egyptians considered foreigners. This hypothesis suggests that these are the descendants of Joseph who lived there with royal status because of Joseph's good standing in Egypt during the seven-year famine.

"An inscription of Queen Hatshepsut, Pharaoh's daughter, refers to the Hyksos people being driven out of this northern delta. Egyptian records suggest a warrior people (barbarians) that lived in the Northland among these shepherd kings were driven out by Egypt due to a situation that threatened what could be the Hebrews. Because they were shepherds, they were unable to defend themselves. This weakness, though their number was great, was the ideal combination for an Egyptian workforce, thus the slavery of Israel and Egypt's protection of them.

"In this 18th Dynasty hypothesis, Pharaoh's daughter is possibly the daughter of Pharaoh Thutmosis I, who had no male heir. Her name was Nefure / Hatshepsut. There are several statutes of Nefure holding a male child who is wearing ornaments indicating royalty and/or the heir to the Egyptian throne. Is the child she's holding, named Senmut, the Hebrew Levite, Moses? Did she adopt this Israeli boy, born into slavery, because her father had no heir, positioning herself for future rule? The name Senmut means "mother's brother" meaning that through her, Senmut had the right to inherit the throne, since Nefure bore the right but couldn't become Pharaoh herself. History tells us that she would eventually become Queen. If this Senmut is indeed Moses, what happens to him in Egyptology?

It is probably that Senmut abused his power and that at a particular point in the reign of Hatshepsut he fell into disgrace, as demonstrated by the damage done to most of his monuments.

(Source: F. Tiradritti (1999) The Cairo Museum Master Pieces of Egyptian Art, Thames and Hudson, London, England)

"This is exactly what happened to Moses:

"As heir to the throne, murdering a fellow Egyptian, then escaping Egypt; this would have been a disgrace from an Egyptian perspective. According to Egyptian tradition, everything – monuments, statues, scrolls etc. – would have been destroyed. You would have been erased from history.

"Here's a very interesting fact that I never stopped to consider before: History tells us that Thutmosis IV (also known as Amenhotep III), the Pharaoh that succeeded Thutmosis I, was not a firstborn son. Whoever the Pharaoh of the Exodus account was, he survives the Angel of Death during the first Passover. This could be because of the fact that he was not a firstborn son or because the Exodus account states that The Destroyer would begin with Pharaoh's first born. Or does the Exodus account state that The Destroyer would begin with Pharaoh's first born, because Pharaoh himself wasn't a firstborn son?

"Regardless, here are some interesting facts about Thutmosis IV / Amenhotep III, the Pharaoh from the 18th Dynasty that could parallel the Pharaoh that Moses was sent to in the Exodus account:

- Thutmosis IV was the second born son of Amenhotep II.
- Thutmosis IV killed his firstborn brother to take the crown
- The Dream Stela of Thutmosis IV, found between the front paws of the Sphinx, was used to legitimize the murder by claiming it was directed by the Sphinx in a dream
- King Tutankamun (yes, that King Tut): An inscription on a statue of a lion dedicated by King Tutankhamen to the temple of Soleb, claims Amenhotep III as his father
- King Tutankhamen supposedly reigned from the age of 9 until his mysterious death at 18. He was the only heir apparent to the throne (Crowned Prince) that may have co-reigned with his father in his later years (Exod. 11:5: ...from the firstborn of Pharaoh who sits on his throne...)
- King Tut's tomb, found in the Valley of the Kings by Howard

Carter in 1922, was said to be a "cursed" tomb. His burial looks rushed and in a tomb generally too small and not designed for a reigning pharaoh's burial

(Source: "The Hidden Moses." http://www.aloha.net/~mikesch/moses.htm)

"Is Thutmosis IV the Pharaoh that perished with his armies while pursuing Moses into the Sea?

"Is King Tutankamun, the firstborn son of Pharaoh Thutmosis IV, the firstborn son of Pharaoh struck dead by the Angel of Death in Exodus 12:29?

> *And the LORD said to Moses in Midian, "Go back to Egypt, for all the men who were seeking your life are dead."*
> *Exodus 4:19*

"Thutmosis III died ca. 1450, and his son, Amenhotep II, ascended the throne. If the chronology proposed in this hypothesis is correct, Moses returned to Egypt around 1446 BC, roughly four years into the reign of Amenhotep II. Again, if this hypothesis has any merit, how were Moses and Aaron able to gain an audience with this new Pharaoh? Moses - Senmut / Thutmosis II, the adopted son of Hatshepsut and living heir to the throne, was Pharaoh Amenhotep II's step-uncle.

> *Moreover, the man Moses was very great in the land of Egypt, in the sight of Pharaoh's servants and in the sight of the people.*
> *Exodus 11:3b*

> *By faith Moses, when he was born, was hidden for three months by his parents, because they saw that the child was beautiful, and they were not afraid of the king's edict. By faith Moses, when he was grown up,* ***refused to be called the son of Pharaoh's daughter****, choosing rather to be mistreated with the people of God than to enjoy the fleeting pleasures of sin. He considered abuse suffered on behalf of the Messiah greater wealth than the treasures of Egypt, for he was looking to the reward. By faith he left Egypt,* ***not being afraid of the anger of the king*** *[Pharaoh], for he endured as seeing him who is invisible. By faith he kept the Passover and sprinkled the blood, so that the Destroyer of the firstborn might not touch them [Israel].*
> *Hebrews 11:23-28 [Emphasis mine]*

"I included this information, because I want to paint a picture of this man, this Levite, this Prophet that precedes the Messiah Jesus; this Egyptian noble, this warrior, this Nephilim killer... This is the man that delivers Israel from Egypt, that has been given the task to fashion Israel from a people into a nation – a nation of Kings and Priests unto ADONAI. This is who God calls the humblest man that ever walked the face of the earth; the man that God chose to speak to face to face – like you speak to a man; the man that God showed His physical manifestation to and lived to tell about it! The man whose body Lucifer argued over... This is the man, the Levitical priest, who was personally given God's instruction on how you and I are to live – here on this earth – in the Way that proves to everyone that we are truly His."

(Source: Aguirre, Allan R. "Passover (Pesach) and the Feast of Unleavened Bread," In *The Feasts Unlocked*, 89-95. Park City, Utah: Planet Blue Media, 2018. http://planetblue-media.com)

○ FIELD NOTES

DATE: / / TIME: : AM/PM PLACE:

○		A±
○		
○		
○		
○		
○		
○		
○		
○		
○		
○		
○		
○		
○		
○		
○		
○		
○		
○		
○		

ARMOR CHECK: Ephesians 6:10-18

Belt of Truth	S ☐ M ☐ T ☐ W ☐ T ☐ F ☐ S ☐
Breastplate of Righteousness	S ☐ M ☐ T ☐ W ☐ T ☐ F ☐ S ☐
Shoes / Gospel of Peace	S ☐ M ☐ T ☐ W ☐ T ☐ F ☐ S ☐
Shield of Faith	S ☐ M ☐ T ☐ W ☐ T ☐ F ☐ S ☐
Helmet of Salvation	S ☐ M ☐ T ☐ W ☐ T ☐ F ☐ S ☐
Sword of the Spirit / Word of God	S ☐ M ☐ T ☐ W ☐ T ☐ F ☐ S ☐

No weapon formed against you will prosper. This is the heritage of the servants of ADONAI.
Is. 54:17

WEEK 43
HOLY SPIRIT OR BEELZEBUL
(LUKE 11:15B)

"He casts out demons by Beelzebul, the prince of demons"

Keeping with the themes of "Battle Tactics" and "Spiritual Warfare," it is vital to be equipped in and with discernment in order to know and understand the spirit(s) behind things (1 Jn. 4:1-6).

The Pharisees had very little to no discernment. And for the record, I will not make a blanket remark about them not having *any* discernment, because I don't believe that all of them were unaware that Jesus was actually Messiah. We know from the Gospel accounts and Acts that many believed in Jesus from the sect of the Pharisees, but I'm not convinced that all of those that *didn't* believe did so because they didn't know He was who He said He was (and who He still is).

I think many of the unbelievers among the Pharisees didn't believe because they knew that there wasn't a seat for them at His table – not the seat that *they* wanted – nor were they going to submit to what they would have to submit to in order to *get* that seat.

I think they loved their positions with Rome and the people and the life that afforded them, and following Jesus might have conflicted with that – at least, they thought it would. Whereas, Jesus' heart was for them, as leaders, to lead the people:

> *"The scribes and the Pharisees sit on Moses' seat, so practice and observe whatever they tell you--but not what they do. For they preach, but do not practice."*
> *Matthew 23:2-3*

I don't think they believed that about Jesus because they didn't trust Him (calling them out as hypocrites all the time didn't help either, I'm sure). So, as people do, they projected themselves onto Him. I think the majority of them knew who He was, and they didn't like it.

The mainstream media agenda to discredit Jesus consisted of fake news, slander, lies, false witnesses, character assassination, fear mongering and rumors. If they could convince the public at large that the supernatural signs and wonders and miracles that Jesus was doing were done with the demonic powers and forces of the greatest spiritual nemesis of Israel, Baal, aka Beelzebul, then Jesus was discredited.

Beelzebul, also Beelzebub: A name derived from a Philistine god, formerly worshipped in Ekron, and later adopted by some Abrahamic religions as a major demon. The name Beelzebub is associated with the Canaanite god Baal.

(Source: Wikipedia)

We have discussed a bit about how absolutely contrary to the essence of God are witchcraft, paganism, the occult in general, spells, etc. So, to say that the Man that's claiming to be the Son of God, Messiah, is functioning from the power of one of the most popular Canaanite deities – one of the biggest spiritual foes of Israel… to say that Messiah Himself was guilty of syncretism (the mixture of the holy and the profane), an act strictly forbidden by God Himself (Dt. 12:1-4, 28-32)… well, you get the idea.

Discernment is the tool / gift used to determine these things, and it requires the spiritual gift of the discerning of spirits to discern, decipher and determine whether or not spirits are angels of light or angels of darkness (1 Co. 12:10) – or, in this case, if Jesus is actually a covert agent of Baal.

It requires the spiritual gift of casting out demons, should you determine that the spirit talking to you or manifesting itself physically is actually demonic, in order to get rid of it (Mk 3:14-15, 16:17; Lk 10:17), and since walking in all of this requires you to walk in the gifts of the Spirit (charismatica) in order to be able to do any of the above, not believing in the manifest giftings of the Holy Spirit isn't going to help in any of this at all (1 Co. 12:8-11; Ga. 5:25).

There is a reason why the New Testament church model is structured the way that it is. Any deviant version of that model will not function as God intended:

"Some people have discernment. Others don't. Discernment can be taught and learned, and it is an indispensable and foundational characteristic that needs to be present in our ever-growing arsenal:

> *About this we have much to say, and **it is hard to explain,** since you have become dull of hearing.*
>
> *For though by this time you ought to be teachers, **you need someone to teach you again the basic principles of the oracles of***

God*. You need milk, not solid food, for everyone who lives on milk is* ***unskilled in the word of righteousness****, since he is a child.*

But solid food is for the mature, for those who have their powers of discernment trained by constant practice to distinguish good from evil.

Hebrews 5:11-14 [Emphasis mine]

"The lack of discernment, physical and/or spiritual, is synonymous with being dull of hearing, unskilled, childish and immature; just in the above passage from Hebrews alone.

"The disciples' inability to grasp the teachings of Jesus was attributed to their lack of understanding. For example, in Matthew 15:16, where the Greek word for "understanding" is "*asunetos*" (Strongs #G801), meaning:

- Unintelligent
- Stupid
- Foolish

"One of the spiritual gifts that we'll look into later is the discernment of spirits, a gift that Jesus functioned in and bestowed on the disciples. This is a very important gift, and the lack of it leads to unsound spiritual conclusions, situations and belief systems. We must have our "powers of discernment trained by constant practice to distinguish good from evil"!"

(Source: Aguirre, Allan R. "The Power of Discernment," In *This Thing Is Spiritual*, 44-45. Park City, Utah: Planet Blue Media, 2018. http://planetbluemedia.com)

And this is my prayer: that your love may abound more and more in knowledge and depth of insight [discernment], so that you may be able to discern what is best and may be pure and blameless for the day of Christ, filled with the fruit of righteousness that comes through Jesus Christ— to the glory and praise of God.

Philippians 1:9-11 (NIV)

"Discernment is honed in the same way that all of the spiritual gifts were honed in the New Testament: Jesus taught, modeled, exemplified and raised up His disciples in these attributes and abilities and, in turn, His disciples taught, modeled, exemplified and raised up their disciples in these attributes and abilities. This wasn't done in seclusion nor was it done alone. This was done through interactive human relationships requiring and consisting of discipline and correction from the established leadership as all training does!

"Have we forgotten the words of Jesus in regards to this matter? Jesus' miracles and acts of charismatica by and through the demonstrative gifts and power of the Holy Spirit were also rejected and called demonic. Jesus made it very clear that it was impossible that his spiritual acts were "of the devil." Furthermore, it is blasphemy to state that the manifest power of Holy Spirit is demonic:

> *"And the scribes who came down from Jerusalem were saying, "He [Jesus] is possessed by Beelzebul," and "by the prince of demons he casts out the demons."*
>
> *"And he called them to him and said to them in parables, "How can Satan cast out Satan? If a kingdom is divided against itself, that kingdom cannot stand. And if a house is divided against itself, that house will not be able to stand. And if Satan has risen up against himself and is divided, he cannot stand, but is coming to an end.*
>
> *Truly, I say to you, all sins will be forgiven the children of man, and whatever blasphemies they utter, but whoever blasphemes against the Holy Spirit never has forgiveness, but is guilty of an eternal sin"- - for they were saying, "He has an unclean spirit."*
>
> *Mark 3:22-26, 28-30*

"This thing is spiritual. It requires an extremely interactive relationship with Holy Spirit and the manifestation of that Spirit in your life through His gifts, power and abilities – correctly, maturely and soundly. It's modeled, trained and designed to be a part of your basic discipleship [...]"

(Source: Aguirre, Allan R. "The Power of Discernment," In *This Thing Is Spiritual*, 54-55. Park City, Utah: Planet Blue Media, 2018. http://planetbluemedia.com)

Because they said that Jesus has an unclean spirit, it was written that whoever blasphemes against the Holy Spirit never has forgiveness but is guilty of an eternal sin. Yikes...

As part of our Spiritual Warfare training and Battle Tactics situational report, it is absolutely crucial that we know and understand when a supernatural act

- Is of God,
- Is God testing us through falsehood or adversaries (I discuss and explain that in my book *This Thing Is Spiritual*) and/or
- Is demonic.

It is absolutely crucial that we know and understand if the spirit behind the supernatural act

- Is of God,
- Is sent by God to test us and/or
- Is a demonic agent.

It is absolutely crucial that we know and understand if and when the human behind the supernatural act

- Is of God,
- Is testing us on God's behalf,
- Is entirely human or not and/or
- Is a demonic agent.

It requires a spiritual gift to hear the voice of God, and that gift comes from constant, tenacious and faithful training. So, be encouraged and pursue those greater gifts of speaking in tongues and prophecy (1 Co. 14) in order to hear more clearly.

As each has received a gift, use it to serve one another, as good stewards of God's varied grace: whoever speaks, as one who speaks oracles of God; whoever serves, as one who serves by the strength that God supplies--in order that in everything God may be glorified through Jesus Christ. To him belong glory and dominion forever and ever. Amen.

1 Peter 4:10-11

○ FIELD NOTES

DATE: / / TIME: : AM/PM PLACE:

○		A±
○		
○		
○		
○		
○		
○		
○		
○		
○		
○		
○		
○		
○		
○		
○		
○		
○		
○		
○		

ARMOR CHECK: Ephesians 6:10-18

Belt of Truth	S ☐ M ☐ T ☐ W ☐ T ☐ F ☐ S ☐
Breastplate of Righteousness	S ☐ M ☐ T ☐ W ☐ T ☐ F ☐ S ☐
Shoes / Gospel of Peace	S ☐ M ☐ T ☐ W ☐ T ☐ F ☐ S ☐
Shield of Faith	S ☐ M ☐ T ☐ W ☐ T ☐ F ☐ S ☐
Helmet of Salvation	S ☐ M ☐ T ☐ W ☐ T ☐ F ☐ S ☐
Sword of the Spirit / Word of God	S ☐ M ☐ T ☐ W ☐ T ☐ F ☐ S ☐

No weapon formed against you will prosper. This is the heritage of the servants of ADONAI.
Is. 54:17

○ WEEK 44
THE EXODUS
(EXODUS 10:1-2)

Then the LORD said to Moses, "Go in to Pharaoh, for I have hardened his heart and the heart of his servants, that I may show these signs of mine among them, 2 and that you may tell in the hearing of your son and of your grandson how I have dealt harshly with the Egyptians and what signs I have done among them, that you may know that I am the LORD."

God showed Egypt nine separate plagues that should have been enough to make them concede and let Israel go. A lot is happening on the eve of their anniversary of entering Egypt 430 years ago, which will also be the eve of their departure from Egypt (Ex. 12:40-41). Let's take look at that busy last night in Egypt.

Israel is going to ask their Egyptian neighbors for silver and gold in currency and/or property. God is going to cause the Egyptians to show kindness and favor to them before their departure.

At midnight, God is going to go throughout Egypt, and every firstborn human and animal will die – from the oldest son of Pharaoh to the oldest son of the slave woman – because Egypt wouldn't let Israel go free when they had the chance. It would be the worst tragedy to ever hit Egypt.

But among Israel, not even a dog would bark at an Israeli human or animal to show that God made a distinction between the two and to show that God treated Egyptians differently than Israelis. God was about to turn the tables, even causing Egyptian royalty and magistrates to bow down before Moses.

God institutes that month to be the first month of the year – *His* calendar year – the month of Abib. On the tenth day of that month, each head of household is to take a male lamb from his flock, a male lamb a year old for each family and home. The one-year-old male lamb cannot have any flaws or blemishes, and it can be a sheep or goat. This lamb is to be cared for for four days, until the 14th day of the month.

At that time, the entire Israeli community will kill the lambs at sunset, taking some of the blood and smearing it on the tops and sides of the door-frames of the homes where the lambs are being eaten.

The lamb meat is to be cooked over a fire, not eaten raw or boiled, and eaten with bitter herbs and bread made without yeast.

> *"In this manner you shall eat it: with your belt fastened, your sandals on your feet, and your staff in your hand. And you shall eat it in haste. It is the LORD's Passover."*
> *Exodus 12:11*

God was going to pass through Egypt that night, striking down every firstborn male, human and animal alike. By doing so, God was also judging all the gods of Egypt as well.

> *The blood shall be a sign for you, on the houses where you are. And when I see the blood, I will pass over you, and no plague will befall you to destroy you, when I strike the land of Egypt.*
>
> *"This day shall be for you a memorial day, and you shall keep it as a feast to the LORD; throughout your generations, as a statute forever, you shall keep it as a feast.*
> *Exodus 12:13-14*

For the following week, they were only to eat bread made without yeast (leaven), and on the first day of that week, they were to remove all yeast / leaven from their homes. Anyone caught eating bread made with yeast (leavened bread) was to be cut off. The first and seventh days of this week were to be High Sabbaths, and they were to gather to feast and to hold a holy convocation.

Because the first and seventh days were High Sabbaths, they were not to do any of their ordinary work. The only work allowed was to prepare the food that was to be eaten on those two feast days. These instructions applied to both Israelis and Gentiles alike (Ex. 12:19).

> *"You shall observe this rite as a statute for you and for your sons forever. And when you come to the land that the LORD will give you, as he has promised, you shall keep this service.*
>
> *And when your children say to you, 'What do you mean by this service?' you shall say, 'It is the sacrifice of the LORD's Passover, for he passed over the houses of the people of Israel in Egypt, when he struck the Egyptians but spared our houses.'" And the people bowed their heads and worshiped.*
> *Exodus 12:24-27*

They did *exactly* what Moses had been instructed by ADONAI for them to do. As we come to find out, it was also one of the few times they actually listened and obeyed without question or deviation. At midnight, God went throughout Egypt as He promised.

They traveled from Rameses to Succoth, 600,000 men old enough for battle (approximately 20-40 years of age), not including women and children. Verse 38 of Exodus 12 states that:

- A mixed multitude,
- Many other people,
- Non-Hebrew peoples and
- Egyptians and Gentiles of various nationalities

also left Egypt under Moses. The New Living Translation says:

"A rabble of non-Israelites went with them."

I make a point of this so that you'll understand that everything that happened to the Children of Israel under Moses in the desert – the manna, the pillar of fire by night, the cloud of smoke by day, the water from rocks, the commandments, the Torah, the punishments, the plagues, death and disobedience, the obligation to obey God at all costs – happened also to the Gentiles who left Egypt with them. They ate the manna, drank water from the rock and had to make the same choice as Israel on whether they were going to obey God or not, whether they were going to keep His commandments or not.

> *For I would not, brethren, have you ignorant, that our fathers were all under the cloud, and all passed through the sea; and were all baptized unto Moses in the cloud and in the sea; and did all eat the same spiritual food; and did all drink the same spiritual drink: for they drank of a spiritual rock that followed them: and the rock was Christ.*
> *1 Corinthians 10:1-4 (ASV)*

This is why there are instructions including and regarding the Gentiles all throughout this journey. It's Christianity, not our Bibles, that tells us that Gentiles are immune from having to obey or keep "the law". Again, this is why the Apostle Paul, the apostle to the Gentiles, is warning his predominantly-Gentile church in Corinth regarding all of this in our premise, 1 Corinthians 10:1-12. It *absolutely* includes and involves you.

For example: here are some of the rules regarding Passover from

Exodus 12:43-49 based on what we are discussing:

- No non-Israeli (non-Jew) is allowed to eat the Passover meal unless they are circumcised.
- A slave may partake if they are circumcised.
- It is eaten indoors only.
- No bones are to be broken.

> *"The law is the same for him who is an Israelite by birth and for the man from a strange country who is living with you."*
> *Exodus 12:49 (The Bible in Basic English)*

That's a basic breakdown of the exodus from Egypt and the beginning of this amazing journey to His ingathering.

We are to remember the day that Israel was delivered from out of the house of Egyptian slavery. We are to remember that it was with a "strong hand" that God delivered Israel. We are to remember this day because it also speaks of *our* deliverance from out of the house of Egyptian slavery, and it was with a "strong hand" that God delivered us as well.

In the same way that Israel is to remember all of this and keep this ordinance – this memorial – when they finally enter the Promised Land that was riddled with godlessness, we too are to remember all of this and keep the ordinance – this memorial that speaks of Messiah – in our real world scenarios as well.

Be encouraged. His commandments aren't burdensome (1 Jn. 5:3).

> *"You shall tell your son on that day, 'It is because of what the LORD did for me when I came out of Egypt.' And it shall be to you as a sign on your hand and as a memorial between your eyes, that the law of the LORD may be in your mouth. For with a strong hand the LORD has brought you out of Egypt. You shall therefore keep this statute at its appointed time from year to year."*
> *Exodus 13:8-10*

○ FIELD NOTES

DATE: / / TIME: : AM/PM PLACE:

○		A±
○		
○		
○		
○		
○		
○		
○		
○		
○		
○		
○		
○		
○		
○		
○		
○		
○		
○		
○		

ARMOR CHECK: Ephesians 6:10-18

Belt of Truth	S ☐ M ☐ T ☐ W ☐ T ☐ F ☐ S ☐
Breastplate of Righteousness	S ☐ M ☐ T ☐ W ☐ T ☐ F ☐ S ☐
Shoes / Gospel of Peace	S ☐ M ☐ T ☐ W ☐ T ☐ F ☐ S ☐
Shield of Faith	S ☐ M ☐ T ☐ W ☐ T ☐ F ☐ S ☐
Helmet of Salvation	S ☐ M ☐ T ☐ W ☐ T ☐ F ☐ S ☐
Sword of the Spirit / Word of God	S ☐ M ☐ T ☐ W ☐ T ☐ F ☐ S ☐

No weapon formed against you will prosper. This is the heritage of the servants of ADONAI.
Is. 54:17

WEEK 45
THE LONG WAY AROUND
(EXODUS 13:17-18)

When Pharaoh finally let the people go, God did not lead them along the main road that runs through Philistine territory, even though that was the shortest route to the Promised Land. God said, "If the people are faced with a battle, they might change their minds and return to Egypt." So God led them in a roundabout way through the wilderness toward the Red Sea. Thus the Israelites left Egypt like an army ready for battle. (NLT)

"You know, Israel left Egypt dressed for battle, but God avoided a battle by going the long way, because He knew they wouldn't be able to handle it. Israel has no idea that what God is about to do to them is to prepare them to become a warring people. We, as believers, don't understand who God is. The whole purpose of Christendom is to make us like Jesus and [one of] the process[es] of being transformed into the likeness of His Son is to make us into a warring battle people. Why? Because there's spiritual warfare that's been coming at you since before you even got saved, and you need to learn how to fight that battle, that spiritual war. He has to make us a warring people, or we'll lose the spiritual war.

"And so, [God] knows Israel will not fight if the Philistines pick a fight. So, to avoid that, He takes them the long way, but He has them dressed for battle. Why? He begins the identity transformation process from the very beginning. He's training them, and it even says in Judges 2, "I'm training you to be a warring people... that's what I did in the desert – it was to train you to be a warning people because if I didn't, you would have died a long time ago." You have to learn to defend yourself and to protect yourself.

"God's long game is to create a warring people out of [Israel]. They don't know this, so when they get to the 12 spies, that's why they freaked out. "What are You talking about, we have to go [up] there and beat up the Giants? We can't take on the Nephilim." "Well, you're going to have to, because they're in possession of the land. You have to dispossess them."

"We have never been taught that God's desire is for us to be a warring people so that we can fight a spiritual war and win and to possess a land. That is going to require our dispossessing of demonic strongholds."

(Source: Allan Aguirre on *The Chameleon Church Show.* The Messianic Lamb Network. Feb. 11, 2020. https://youtu.be/TFuvwVp2jr0)

As believers, the majority of us have been robbed from the teaching – the training, really – that we are expected to be a warring people, prepared for battle. A warring people prepared for spiritual warfare – a war we *have* to win. A people prepared to win in battle in order to dispossess the giants that live and rule, that have perverted our prophetic inheritance – our Promised Land, our territory, our spiritual destiny, our "on earth as it is in heaven."

Does New Testament teaching support this idea?

> *Indeed, we live as human beings, but we do not wage war according to human standards; for* ***the weapons of our warfare*** *are not merely human, but they* ***have divine power to destroy strongholds****. We destroy arguments and every proud obstacle raised up against the knowledge of God, and we take every thought captive to obey Christ.*
> *2 Corinthians 10:3-5 (NRS) [Emphasis mine]*

And then, of course, there's Ephesians 6:

> *Finally, be strong in the Lord and in his great power. Put on the full armor of God so that you can fight against the devil's evil tricks. Our fight is not against people on earth but against the rulers and authorities and the powers of this world's darkness, against the spiritual powers of evil in the heavenly world.*
>
> *That is why you need to put on God's full armor. Then on the day of evil you will be able to stand strong. And when you have finished the whole fight, you will still be standing.*
> *Verses 10-13 (NCV)*

How well-versed / armed, trained and equipped do you suppose someone needs to be to be able to fight against the world-rulers of this earth's darkness? How about the forces of cosmic darkness, the cosmic powers *governing* this darkness? Or to do battle against the universal lords of this darkness? To be able to fight, do battle against, spiritual powers in the heavenly world; the supernatural, spiritual realm – to war against spiritual wickedness in high places?

I'm trying to get you to see, both physically and spiritually, what Ephesians 6:12 is actually talking about. You / we need to understand that Paul isn't just being dramatic. Paul is literally telling us what it is we're up against, and you have to be victorious against it!

So, instead of training us for this (remember, our leaders can't teach us what they don't actually know themselves), we've been told that *Jesus* does the fighting for us, and we've been taught this because of standalone verses like 2 Chronicles 20:15 and 1 Samuel 17:47, when Israel was told "for the battle is not yours but God's" and "'not by might nor by power, but by my Spirit,' says the LORD" (Zc. 4:6).

Yes, God absolutely does say that in the Bible. But, contextually, in 2 Chronicles 20, here's what we actually find:

King Jehoshaphat calls a fast for all of Judah and leads the people in prayer to inquire of ADONAI regarding the attack that was mounting against him. The recipe for spiritual success is in motion now, because all the proper ingredients are in place:

- The nation's leader has called a national fast.
- The nation's leader has assembled the people to
- inquire of the Lord.
- The people "come together" as one, under the king, to inquire of ADONAI (see Ne. 8).
- They humble themselves as one man and wait in anticipation upon ADONAI to answer.

It was only after that that the Spirit of the LORD came on Jahaziel, a Levite and descendant of Asaph, with the word: "Do not be afraid or discouraged because of this vast army. For the battle is not yours, but God's" (verses 13-15). But wait, there's more: Jahaziel continues with his prophecy that includes strategies on when to go against the enemy and where to find the enemy.

See, they just didn't sit around and "wait for Jesus" to do the fighting for them. They were proactive in fasting, praying and waiting. Then they received the battle tactics / strategies on when and where to encounter the enemy. They still had to go and fight, even though the battle wasn't theirs but God's.

And how did they go into battle?

> *After consulting the people, Jehoshaphat appointed men to sing to the LORD and to praise him for the splendor of his holiness as they went out at the head of the army, saying: "Give thanks to the LORD, for his love endures forever."*
>
> *As they began to sing and praise, the LORD set ambushes against the men of Ammon and Moab and Mount Seir who were invading Judah, and they were defeated.*
>
> *2 Chronicles 20:20-22 (NIV)*

Notice also how the singers went before the army. Psalm 68 describes the procession:

> *Your procession, God, has come into view, the procession of my God and King into the sanctuary. In front are the singers, after them the musicians; with them are the young women playing the timbrels.*
> *Psalm 68:24-25 (NIV)*

The verse in 1 Samuel 17:47 is even more out of context. Here's what verse 47 actually says:

> *and that all this assembly may know that the LORD saves not with sword and spear. For the battle is the LORD's, and he will give you into our hand."*

It's a verse containing 30 words in the middle of a sentence, and we're only quoting six of those words, horribly out of context, to establish the pretense that God is going to do all our fighting / battles for us, and we don't have to be engaged at all. Le sigh… Let's see what 1 Samuel 17:47 is really talking about.

Oh! It's David talking smack to Goliath, on the battlefield, sling in hand:

> *David said to the Philistine, "You come against me with sword and spear and javelin, but I come against you in the name of the LORD Almighty, the God of the armies of Israel, whom you have defied.*
>
> *This day the LORD will deliver you into my hands, and I'll strike you down and cut off your head. This very day I will give the carcasses of the Philistine army to the birds and the wild animals, and the whole world will know that there is a God in Israel.*
>
> *All those gathered here will know that it is not by sword or spear that the LORD saves; for the battle is the LORD's, and he will give all of you into our hands."*
> *1 Samuel 17:45-47 [In context]*

David is literally on the battlefield, armed, with sling in hand. Goliath's spear and javelin are contextually in the picture. There is nothing "passive" or disengaged about any of this. David says he's going to "strike you down" and "cut off your head" – extreme action words – and he literally does.

I love it when we read the bible in context. You remove all the "fake news" out of it!

In Ephesians 6, Paul says "be strong," not, "Jesus will be strong." He says, "put on," not, "Jesus will put on." He says, "that *you* may," not, "that Jesus may." He says, "for *we* do not wrestle," not, "Jesus does not wrestle." See how silly we are? Besides, it clearly states the following in verse 13:

> *Therefore take up the whole armor of God, that you may be able to withstand in the evil day, and having done all, to stand firm.*

Yes, dear reader, you and I are both expected and required to be more than well-versed, armed, trained and equipped to be able to fight against the world-rulers of this earth's darkness and against the forces of cosmic darkness – but not only them, but also against the cosmic powers *governing* this darkness.

We are to do battle against the universal lords of this darkness and to fight, do battle against, spiritual powers *in the heavenly world – the supernatural, spiritual realm. We are to war against spiritual wickedness in high places!*

Now, how are we going to do that?!?

Ephesians 6:13-18, silly...

> *And the LORD went before them by day in a pillar of cloud to lead them along the way, and by night in a pillar of fire to give them light, that they might travel by day and by night. The pillar of cloud by day and the pillar of fire by night did not depart from before the people.*
> *Exodus 13:21-22*

> *The night is far gone; the day is at hand. So then let us cast off the works of darkness and put on the armor of light.*
> *Romans 13:12*

Put on the Armor of Light, and let Him guide you with the Pillars of His Holy Spirit.

○ FIELD NOTES

DATE: / / TIME: : AM/PM PLACE:

		A±
○		
○		
○		
○		
○		
○		
○		
○		
○		
○		
○		
○		
○		
○		
○		
○		
○		
○		
○		
○		

ARMOR CHECK: Ephesians 6:10-18

Belt of Truth	S ☐ M ☐ T ☐ W ☐ T ☐ F ☐ S ☐
Breastplate of Righteousness	S ☐ M ☐ T ☐ W ☐ T ☐ F ☐ S ☐
Shoes / Gospel of Peace	S ☐ M ☐ T ☐ W ☐ T ☐ F ☐ S ☐
Shield of Faith	S ☐ M ☐ T ☐ W ☐ T ☐ F ☐ S ☐
Helmet of Salvation	S ☐ M ☐ T ☐ W ☐ T ☐ F ☐ S ☐
Sword of the Spirit / Word of God	S ☐ M ☐ T ☐ W ☐ T ☐ F ☐ S ☐

No weapon formed against you will prosper. This is the heritage of the servants of ADONAI.
Is. 54:17

WEEK 46
AT THE BASE OF MOUNT SINAI
(EXODUS 19:5-6A)

"Now therefore, if you will indeed obey my voice and keep my covenant, you shall be my treasured possession among all peoples, for all the earth is mine; and you shall be to me a kingdom of priests and a holy nation."

"Since this week's Torah Portion includes the account of Mount Sinai, I figured we'd do a quick refresher. Shall we?

"In Exodus 19, we see that Moses and all of Israel have assembled before the Living God, per His instructions, at the base of Mount Sinai. This is when and where God established His instructions in written form for those that would call upon His name; His instructions for mankind, for those that make the voluntary decision to serve Him; His covenant instructions for those who call themselves "Believers." In essence, these instructions are the keys of blessing for you, as a Christian / a Believer; the wedding vows, if you will, between the Bridegroom and His Bride – the vows His Bride voluntarily makes covenant with to be known as His. These are the instructions that "set you apart" from the rest. The covenant instructions, the "good works" we were created for in Messiah to do, the works prepared for us in advance (Eph. 2:10). The covenants that make Him your God and you His people, a nation of Kings and Priests (Ex. 24).

"This was the reason they had traveled these difficult and end- less 40-some-odd days from Egypt to Sinai. Three days later, there was a blast from a shofar summoning Israel to Mount Sinai where there was smoke, fire and earthquakes while the Shofar's blast grew louder and louder. When God finally spoke, it sounded like thunder. They were terrified and stood a long way off.

"Moses, you speak to us and we'll listen. But not God; don't let Him speak to us or we'll die."

"That long-standing, identifiable fear as a people was now keeping them from the very reason God delivered them from Egypt: Covenant Relationship:

"Instead of desiring that personal relationship with ADONAI, the relationship He also desired for them, a relationship that required / re- quires "obeying His voice" and "keeping His covenants," they balked out of fear and opted for Moses to be their mediator.

"This gripping and debilitating fear, their identity, was keeping Israel from wanting to hear His voice, "...lest we die," and it would continue to stand in the way of their relational obedience to God. In addition, this same fear and stubbornness would cause them to reject His prophets as well and, consequently, Messiah.

"As God set out the parameters of the Covenant and His promises of their eventual and successful possession of the Land of Canaan, Moses drew near to the thick darkness where God was manifest.

"In Exodus 24, Moses tells Israel everything ADONAI spoke, including His rules, and to that the entire assembly responded with a resounding, "*Na'aseh v'nishma*" – "All these words and rulings that ADO- NAI has spoken '*we will do and we will hear / understand.*'" Then Moses wrote down all that ADONAI had spoken. An altar was built, and twelve pillars representing the twelve tribes were erected. Burnt offerings and peace offerings were made."

(Taken from "Shavuot (Weeks) / Pentecost," In *The Feasts Unlocked*, 165-169. Park City, Utah: Planet Blue Media, 2018. http://planetbluemedia.com)

In Exodus 32, after Moses was up on Mount Sinai with God 40 days, Israel went to Aaron saying, "We don't know what has become of this man Moses. Make us a god that will lead us."

Aaron had all of Israel bring him the gold earrings worn by their wives, sons and daughters that he then took and fashioned it into a golden statue of a god that resembled a calf.

Israel shouted, "Israel! Here is your god who brought you out of Egypt!"

Aaron then built an altar and proclaimed a feast day in God's honor for the following day. (What's wrong with that? We do that as Christians at least twice a year) ...

The next day, the assembly rose early and sacrificed burnt offerings and also brought along friendship offerings. They ate and drank and then danced wildly in front of their new golden god.

Meanwhile, at some higher altitude, the LORD says to Moses, "Go. Your people that you brought out of Egypt "have corrupted themselves." That's the common way most translations put it. "Have perverted themselves" is a close second. Apparently, you just can't decide to make up your own articles of celebration, choose your own dates and times, and stamp, "In God's Honor," for it to be okay with Him... go figure... (I'll just stop now before I say something blatantly obvious.)

They have turned aside quickly out of the way that I commanded them. They have made for themselves a golden calf and have worshiped it and sacrificed to it and said, 'These are your gods, O Israel, who brought you up out of the land of Egypt!'"

And the LORD said to Moses, "I have seen this people, and behold, it is a stiff-necked people. Now therefore let me alone, that my wrath may burn hot against them and I may consume them, in order that I may make a great nation of you."

Exodus 32:8-10

Oh wow. He's not kidding. He's serious. He's using words like, "burning hot wrath" and talking about "consuming them" and starting over with Moses, *just* Moses, and making a great nation out of *him*!

In true form, Moses intercedes, asking God to forgive Israel. But it's *how* he intercedes that's amazing. Moses brings up Egypt and how God used power and a "mighty hand" to deliver them; why should He be so angry with Israel? Why give the Egyptians a reason to ridicule Him by saying that He *did* bring them out to the desert to kill them?

As Moses and Joshua came down the mountain and approached the camp, they saw the golden calf and the people dancing. Moses was burning with so much anger that he threw the two tablets with the Ten Commandments that had been written with the Finger of God; breaking them into pieces at the base of Mount Sinai.

Moses takes down the golden calf, burns it in the fire, grinds it into powder, pours it into water, and makes every Israeli drink it. The discourse that follows between Moses and Aaron, sadly, is classic denial:

"What did these people do to you, that you led them into such great sin?" "Do not be angry, my lord," Aaron answered. "You know how prone these people are to evil. They said to me, 'Make us gods who will go before us. As for this fellow Moses who brought us up out of Egypt, we don't know what has happened to him.' So I told them, 'Whoever has any gold jewelry, take it off.' Then they gave me the gold, and I threw it into the fire, and out came this calf!"

Moses saw that the people were running wild and that Aaron had let them get out of control and so become a laughingstock to their enemies.

Verses 21-25 (NIV)

Don't be a laughingstock to your enemies and misrepresent God because of godless acts. Verse 26:

> *[...] then Moses stood in the gate of the camp and said, "Who is on the LORD's side? Come to me." And all the sons of Levi gathered around him.*

All the Levites answered the call. The same Levites that will turn on him in the not so distant future under Korah. Moses instructs the Levites that God would have them go throughout the camp, killing their brother, friend and neighbor with the sword, and 3,000 people died that day. Also on that day, the Levites were set apart for ADONAI, for standing against their own sons and brothers. But it wasn't over. Because of what they did with the calf that Aaron made, God struck the people with a plague.

Takeaways:

- Mount Sinai is the game changer. By this time Israel should have understood and been in alignment.
- Do not mess with God (Ga. 6:7).
- Know who you are and who you are in Him.
- Stand firm! No matter what – Stand Firm!
- Do not participate with unsanctioned and manmade "holy days" – times, dates or seasons – they're not godly (let's discuss Co. 2:16 this week over at Exodus Expedition).
- Do not subject yourself to idolatry – false and/or pagan worship – spiritual adultery.
- Keep your earrings! Don't give them away! (Just kidding – lol).
- Guard closely your testimony and witness so as not to become a laughingstock due to disobedience.
- Be a Levite and on the side of God by taking the Sword of the Spirit / the Word of God to your brothers, sons, friends and neighbors. Love them into a right relationship with Jesus.

Did I miss anything?

○ FIELD NOTES

DATE: / / TIME: : AM/PM PLACE:

○		A±
○		
○		
○		
○		
○		
○		
○		
○		
○		
○		
○		
○		
○		
○		
○		
○		
○		
○		
○		

ARMOR CHECK: Ephesians 6:10-18

Belt of Truth	S ☐	M ☐	T ☐	W ☐	T ☐	F ☐	S ☐
Breastplate of Righteousness	S ☐	M ☐	T ☐	W ☐	T ☐	F ☐	S ☐
Shoes / Gospel of Peace	S ☐	M ☐	T ☐	W ☐	T ☐	F ☐	S ☐
Shield of Faith	S ☐	M ☐	T ☐	W ☐	T ☐	F ☐	S ☐
Helmet of Salvation	S ☐	M ☐	T ☐	W ☐	T ☐	F ☐	S ☐
Sword of the Spirit / Word of God	S ☐	M ☐	T ☐	W ☐	T ☐	F ☐	S ☐

No weapon formed against you will prosper. This is the heritage of the servants of ADONAI.
Is. 54:17

○ WEEK 47
LITTLE BY LITTLE
(EXODUS 23:20)

"Behold, I send an angel before you to guard you on the way and to bring you to the place that I have prepared."

I remember the first time I heard about the angel that was sent before Israel in the Wilderness Campaign under Moses, and how, if Israel didn't obey this angel, there would be no forgiveness for Israel; this angel would not be forgiving them the sin of rebellion should they sin against him.

It came up in conversation decades ago when the point was being made of what kind of God would do that? What sort of benevolent God would send an angel with Israel that if Israel rebelled against Him there would be no forgiveness?

I thought it interesting that this person, who I already knew had authority issues with church leadership, was focused on that aspect of this part of the exodus to ingathering narrative, the "no forgiveness for their rebellion" piece.

Maybe it was because I'm an old punk rocker and punk rock is based on rebellion, anarchy, being anti-establishment and usurping that established authority. Maybe it was because when I came to Jesus, I found out that rebellion was like witchcraft to God. Maybe that's why I focused on the warning against Israel's rebellion and what would happen to Israel if they rebelled against this angel versus the fact that there was no repentance in this angel should Israel rebel against him.

Perspective: This individual was more concerned about how "unfair" God was for sending an angel that wouldn't forgive than the need for obedience – than the call to obey. They knew that they were rebellious and it was their right – their "Sinner's Privilege" – to be forgiven. That's twisted. That's demonic.

Perspective: I see a benevolent God that forewarns me *not* to sin and what will happen if I *do* rebel and disobey:

Pay careful attention to him and obey his voice; do not rebel against him, for he will not pardon your transgression, for my name is in him.
Exodus 23:21

Humans project themselves in life situations. They project themselves based on their practical reasoning and reference experiences. Consciously and subconsciously, they project on other humans what they would do and how they would react.

If it's in your nature to lie, you're going to assume that the other person is also lying. If it's in your nature to manipulate, you're going to be convinced you're being manipulated. That's what you would do, why wouldn't they? And so on.

I see this among people of faith all the time. They make the other individual a victim of *their* own insecurities and then add "spirituality" on top of it. That's also demonic. This person who was focused on the lack of mercy and forgiveness by God's angel was coming from the perspective of their own human nature to rebel and their belief that God needed to be fair towards them. This individual wanted to force God into their human level of play. It doesn't work like that.

So many bitter, resentful and broken people in the church or disenfranchised from the church, mostly by their own doing, are self-imposed victims due to what we're talking about (of course I know that there are people out there that have been hurt by church, pastors, leaders, etc. I'm not addressing that right now).

They have a chip on their shoulder toward God, church, Christians, or some tele-evangelist they've never met, their own shadow – who knows? – for some self-induced reason. It's like that meme of the individual that jams a stick into the front rim of their own bicycle while riding it and then feels sorry for themselves because they've crashed or blames someone or something for making them crash. It's a form of the always-fun-to-deal-with "spiritual Munchausen Syndrome."

Think of what we've learned thus far about Israel in the desert. Think of all the times Israel rebelled, disobeyed, lacked faith, functioned from fear, doubt or unbelief. Think of their grumbling and complaining, and how many times they wanted to go back to Egypt – to slavery. Think of the drama and how they would rather die than do what was asked or expected of them.

Now, think of how they dealt with and/or processed being confronted with their choices and decisions, or the lack thereof – from extreme contempt and arrogance to woe is me, here we are to obey now that God has punished us. Do you know anyone like that? Maybe you're like that? As we have seen, that / those personality traits are not Kingdom traits. They're not godly or from His Spirit and we need to allow Holy Spirit to change those areas in us.

> *"But if you carefully obey his voice and do all that I say, then I will be an enemy to your enemies and an adversary to your adversaries."*
> *Exodus 23:22*

Sometimes we are our biggest adversary.

This angel from our study verse this week would go ahead of Israel, before them, and bring them into the land, wiping out the seven "Ites" ahead of them. Israel was not to do what the people in the land did of bowing down to their false gods and worshipping them. Instead, Israel was to destroy these false gods and their erected statues, pillars, monuments, etc.

> *"You shall worship the Lord your God, and I will bless your bread and your water; and I will take sickness away from among you. No one shall miscarry or be barren in your land; I will fulfill the number of your days. "*
> *Exodus 23:25-26 (NRS)*

God promises to go before Israel and to "send my terror ahead of you." He would throw the nations into a panic and Israel's enemies would run from them.

> *"Little by little I will drive them out before you, until you have increased enough to take possession of the land. Do not make a covenant with them or with their gods. Do not let them live in your land or they will cause you to sin against me, because the worship of their gods will certainly be a snare to you."*
> *Exodus 23:30, 32-33 (NIV)*

We have discussed possessing our territory and driving out the giants and the demonic local inhabitants *from* that territory. We have discussed not bowing down to the gods of this world, the gods in our territory, but instead destroying their places of false worship in our lives and erecting new and true ones.

Look at how God *always* has our best interests in mind:

"Little by little I will drive them out before you, until you have increased enough to take possession of the land."

I know how daunting a lot of this can seem:

- The sea is before us and Pharaoh and his armies are charging from behind – how is this water going to part before us?!
- The Nephilim are not only 'in the land,' they inhabit the land! They possess it – it's theirs – how am I going to make them my bread?!?
- The amount of witchcraft or the demonic in my real-world scenario is more than I can bear or manage!

The answer?

"*Little by little* I will drive them out before you, *until you have increased* enough *to take possession* of the land."

○ FIELD NOTES

DATE: / / TIME: : AM/PM PLACE:

		A±
○		
○		
○		
○		
○		
○		
○		
○		
○		
○		
○		
○		
○		
○		
○		
○		
○		
○		
○		
○		

ARMOR CHECK: Ephesians 6:10-18

Belt of Truth	S ☐	M ☐	T ☐	W ☐	T ☐	F ☐	S ☐
Breastplate of Righteousness	S ☐	M ☐	T ☐	W ☐	T ☐	F ☐	S ☐
Shoes / Gospel of Peace	S ☐	M ☐	T ☐	W ☐	T ☐	F ☐	S ☐
Shield of Faith	S ☐	M ☐	T ☐	W ☐	T ☐	F ☐	S ☐
Helmet of Salvation	S ☐	M ☐	T ☐	W ☐	T ☐	F ☐	S ☐
Sword of the Spirit / Word of God	S ☐	M ☐	T ☐	W ☐	T ☐	F ☐	S ☐

No weapon formed against you will prosper. This is the heritage of the servants of ADONAI.
Is. 54:17

○ WEEK 48
IN THE BEAUTY OF HOLINESS
(MARK 12:35-37)

As Yeshua (Jesus) was teaching in the Temple, he asked, "How is it that the Torah teachers say the Messiah is the Son of David? David himself, inspired by the Ruach HaKodesh, (the Holy Spirit) said, `ADONAI said to my Lord, "Sit here at my right hand until I put your enemies under your feet."' David himself calls him `Lord'; so how is he his son?" The great crowd listened eagerly to him. (CJB)

There's that "aggressive" Jesus again, throwing curve balls at the people and questioning the teaching of the ruling religious authorities. "Test everything."

Jesus is quoting Psalm 110:1. This is the last time Jesus would teach in the Temple, because He would be executed, buried and then would rise again within the week. It's between the 10th and 14th days of the month, when all Passover lambs are to be examined, and, for the last little bit, Jesus has been "inspected" by the Pharisees, the Herodians, the Sadducees and the Scribes (Mk. 12:13-34). Now, Jesus is inspecting them.

Jesus is quoting a prophecy by the prophet, King David, regarding Messiah and His being from the Line of David / Judah and also an eternal priest in / from the order of Melchizedek. The question to the Pharisees is about how the teachers of Torah say that Messiah can be both "Son of David" and "Adonai" / God.

Essentially, there's a word play happening that was confusing to them:

"Adonai" in verse one is first person, singular, masculine, possessive. It references both divinity and man. The issue is "ADONAI" in verse five: proper noun, no gender.

"David went from "ADONAI saying to Adonai (my Lord) sit at my right hand" to "Adonai sitting at the right hand of ADONAI." It is obvious that the Son is not the Father, but the Father gave the Son his title."

(Source: Rood, Michael John "Yeshua: the Passover Lamb of the First Year," In *The*

Chronological Gospels, 206-207. Fort Mill, SC: Aviv Moon Publishing, 2012)

> *Remember Jesus Christ, raised from the dead, descended from David. This is my gospel [...]*
> *2 Timothy 2:8 (NIV)*

> *The LORD swore to David a sure oath from which he will not turn back: "One of the sons of your body I will set on your throne."*
> *Psalm 132:11 [See also Is. 16:5; Lk. l:32-33]*

Isn't it amazing how we can read the Word of God and what didn't make sense to the players involved makes sense to us because of the Holy Spirit?

Like Israel in the desert: how many times do we read their account and think, "Oh man, if God revealed Himself to me like He did to them (the plagues of Egypt, parting the sea, manna, water out of rocks), I wouldn't have doubted!"

Jesus told the Pharisees, as they were currently planning how to trap and kill Him, that they were descendants of the prophet killers to which they took a massive offense. When you're deceived, you don't know that you're deceived. And, in all actuality, as "players" in our *own* narrative, we're exactly like Israel.

This is the importance of being under godly leadership, being in healthy spiritual fellowship and having real and meaningful relationships with other tangible, real-life believers and not just "cyber buddies." How else are we going to keep in check and make sure we haven't gone off on some crazy, esoteric and iconoclastic belief system that is sabotaging us, because we're not being accountable or walking alongside others?

Years ago, I established a group of godly men to whom I'm accountable. These men fulfill all the criteria for a leader (1 Ti. 3:3-10):

- Above reproach
- Faithful to his wife
- Temperate
- Self-controlled
- Respectable
- Hospitable
- Able to teach
- Not given to drunkenness or indulging in much wine
- Not violent but gentle
- Not quarrelsome
- Not a lover of money

- Manages his own family well
- Not a recent convert
- Has a good reputation with outsiders
- Worthy of respect
- Sincere
- Not pursuing dishonest gain
- Keeping hold of the deep truths of the faith with a clear conscience

While I do believe that leaders can have tattoos and piercings, the group of men that I have surrounded myself with to speak into my life are not pierced and tattooed. In fact, they know very little about the rock-and-roll lifestyle from which I came. They're very conservative. I did this deliberately so that any and all council, advice, etc. would be unbiased. In fact, more times than not, they should look at me, shake their collective heads and tell me I'm crazy!

I share this only to stress the importance of having your back covered, walking in submission to leadership and being accountable to people that can look you in the eye and speak truth, encouragement and/or correction if and when it is needed. I wouldn't have it any other way.

You can't fix something you don't know is broken...

Looking back on your notes, your journaling and prayer modules, if you examine the various outbreaks of disobedience and rebellion among Israel in the desert that we have studied, you should notice some commonalities that transcend time and culture. We should be able to recognize some of the same traits in ourselves and others that we know.

Since the premises of our exercises have been focused on our personal betterment, growth and understanding and not on how we can "change others," we'll continue examining ourselves.

Read through and note the wording in Psalm 110. This Messianic prophecy describes Messiah's return and establishment of His earthly kingdom as ruler, priest and judge. David uses some familiar battle / warfare lingo:

- Your enemies as your footstool / under your control
- Rule over your enemies that surround you.
- Your troops are willing to fight for you / volunteer on the day of battle / warfare.

It continues with killing / crushing kings and piling up bodies. Moving on from there:

Volunteers and drinking from the brook in verses three and seven sounds very reminiscent of Gideon's victory over the Midianites. Gideon's army of 300 (how many did Abram take with him?) were a volunteer force that were narrowed down based on how they drank from the brook.

I have very fond memories from when I visited the traditional religious site of Gideon's Brook some years ago. I left our tour group and started chatting with some local college-aged Arabs who were enjoying the beautiful May day. They shared their beverages and watermelon with me, and I had a great time just hanging with these locals. I'll try to find a pic and post it.

Let's conclude with verse three, and meditate, ponder and pray into this section, and then let's discuss it over on Facebook:

> *Your people stand ready on Your day of battle; in the beauty of holiness...*

○ FIELD NOTES

DATE: / / TIME: : AM/PM PLACE:

○		A±
○		
○		
○		
○		
○		
○		
○		
○		
○		
○		
○		
○		
○		
○		
○		
○		
○		
○		
○		

ARMOR CHECK: Ephesians 6:10-18

Belt of Truth	S ☐	M ☐	T ☐	W ☐	T ☐	F ☐	S ☐
Breastplate of Righteousness	S ☐	M ☐	T ☐	W ☐	T ☐	F ☐	S ☐
Shoes / Gospel of Peace	S ☐	M ☐	T ☐	W ☐	T ☐	F ☐	S ☐
Shield of Faith	S ☐	M ☐	T ☐	W ☐	T ☐	F ☐	S ☐
Helmet of Salvation	S ☐	M ☐	T ☐	W ☐	T ☐	F ☐	S ☐
Sword of the Spirit / Word of God	S ☐	M ☐	T ☐	W ☐	T ☐	F ☐	S ☐

No weapon formed against you will prosper. This is the heritage of the servants of ADONAI.
Is. 54:17

WEEK 49
LOOK HOW THEY SHINE FOR YOU (MATTHEW 5:16)

> *"[…] let your light shine before others, so that they may see your good works and give glory to your Father who is in heaven."*

The Weymouth New Testament translation says to let your light shine before all men, *in order that they may see your holy lives…* I like that.

Before we get started, we need to look at the "good works" portion of this encouraging word from Jesus, because the entire concept of "works" is completely distorted, perverted, misunderstood and erroneously taught by the majority of the mainstream, Romanized Western church.

Let me make it perfectly clear: we are not "saved" by works – any works – Torah or otherwise. The "proof" of our salvation, though, is *absolutely* based on whether you have any works in your life, good or bad, which sound New Testament teaching shows us generates and determines *fruit*. Furthermore, the *evidence* of fruit, good or bad, also establishes the quality and *maturity* of your salvation. Clear as mud?

This is 1,000% supported by Jesus, John, Paul, George and Ringo (just kidding). Jesus (in the Gospels and in the Revelation of John), John, Peter, James and Paul (in at least nine of his epistles).

> *"We must work the works of him who sent me while it is day; night is coming, when no one can work. As long as I am in the world, I am the light of the world."*
> *John 9:4-5*

Jesus said "we." And we're back to "light."

A time is coming, "nighttime" / darkness, when we will no longer be able to do works. Remember, these works are for the witness and testimony of others – your light shining before men – so that *they* can see the Father, *through* and *in* your works, and glorify Him.

*"That they may see **your** holy lives".*

I'm not going to go through all the New Testament verses in support of our absolute need to be doing works (I only technically need three) – you know, the "good works" Paul says you were created to do "in Christ"? But I do want to remind us of what James, the brother of Jesus and leader of the church, said about the matter:

> *What does it profit, my brethren, if someone says he has faith but does not have works? Can faith save him?*
> *James 2:14 (NKJV)*

James' conclusion and answer to what should be a rhetorical question is this:

> *Thus also faith by itself, if it does not have works, is dead. But someone will say, "You have faith, and I have works." Show me your faith without your works, and I will show you my faith by my works. But do you want to know, O foolish man, that faith without works is dead?*
>
> *You see then that a man is justified by works, and not by faith only. For as the body without the spirit is dead, so faith without works is dead also.*
> *James 2:17-18, 20, 24, 26 [Emphasis mine] (NKJV)*

Your light must shine so that the world can see your good works and glorify your Heavenly Father. We are to be light bearers. *You* are a light bearer. Think about that for a minute. It's an illuminating thought...

Our light-bearing is "manifested" by our works – our deeds toward one another – such as showing kindness, mercy and just simple civility to our fellow man. What we "do" versus what we "say" goes a long way. It's always going to be about our actions – toward others and God Himself – and He's been showing us that all year long in this resource.

Darkness is the absence of light. We want to avoid anything that would cause that light not to shine in the darkness around us, whether we are at work, school, or just at the supermarket. In the same way, we want to avoid the things that would stop that same light from shining within us: fear, doubt, bitterness, unforgiveness and unbelief. How much easier it is to manifest the Light of Messiah to those around us when it permeates from within!

> *The night is far gone; the day is at hand. So then let us cast off the works of darkness and put on the armor of light.*
> *Romans 13:12*

I love that imagery: "armor of light." Especially since everything is spiritual, and there's that constant of spiritual warfare with darkness. Having on our armor of light to combat the darkness makes for a great visual and an absolute to our reality.

In the same way that our light-bearing is a manifestation of our works, the brightness of the moon is a manifestation – a reflection – of the sun. The brightness of *our* light is a direct manifestation, a *reflection*, of our own proximity to the Son. Jesus tells us to *believe* in the light so that we may *become* "Sons of Light" (Jn. 12:36). This is another aspect of our identity and the process of obtaining that identity: "believe to become."

> *For you were once darkness, but now you are light in the Lord. Live as children of light (for the fruit of the light consists in all goodness, righteousness and truth) and find out what pleases the Lord. Have nothing to do with the fruitless deeds of darkness, but rather expose them.*
>
> *It is shameful even to mention what the disobedient do in secret. But everything exposed by the light becomes visible— and everything that is illuminated becomes a light. This is why it is said: "Wake up, sleeper [Is. 51:17; 52:1; 60:1], rise from the dead [Is. 26:19], and Christ will shine on you. [Lk. 1:78-79]"*
> *Ephesians 5:8-14 (NIV)*

Jesus is teaching on the top of a mountain. What He's teaching is considered by many to be the definitive Gospel – the definitive Gospel of the Kingdom, the "Ethics of the Kingdom" – or the rules of engagement.

Scholars believe that this sermon, known as the Sermon on the Mount – or as I like to call it, "Torah on the Top" – is the only sermon the human race will ever need since it contains the basic tenets of Christendom. In all actuality, Jesus is simply paraphrasing much of the Scriptures, the Old Testament. Imagine that.

> *"You are the light of the world. A city set on a hill cannot be hidden. Nor do people light a lamp and put it under a basket, but on a stand, and it gives light to all in the house. In the same way,*

let your light shine before others, so that they may see your good works and give glory to your Father who is in heaven.
Matthew 5:14-16

Jesus says we are the light of the world, a description He used to define *Himself* in John 8:12 and 9:5. Remember when Paul tells us to put on the armor of light in Romans 13:12? He's fundamentally telling us to put on Jesus, to imitate Him. Look at verse 14:

But put on the Lord Jesus Christ, and make no provision for the flesh, to gratify its desires.

Remember, we are light bearers in that we are image bearers; being transformed daily into the image of God's Son, Jesus. As "Sons of Light," putting on the armor of light, *Messiah*, we can readily shine our light before men as the light of the world, illuminating our good works for men to see – our holy lives – so that they too can glorify our Father in heaven. Hallelujah!

But if we walk in the light, as he is in the light, we have fellowship with one another, and the blood of Jesus his Son cleanses us from all sin.
1 John 1:7

And I saw no temple in the city (the New Jerusalem), for its temple is the Lord God the Almighty and the Lamb. And the city has no need of sun or moon to shine upon it, for the glory of God is its light, and its lamp is the Lamb.

By its light shall the nations walk; and the kings of the earth shall bring their glory into it, and its gates shall never be shut by day--and there shall be no night there;
Revelation 21:22-25

○ FIELD NOTES

DATE: / / TIME: : AM/PM PLACE:

○		A±
○		
○		
○		
○		
○		
○		
○		
○		
○		
○		
○		
○		
○		
○		
○		
○		
○		
○		
○		

ARMOR CHECK: Ephesians 6:10-18

Belt of Truth	S ☐	M ☐	T ☐	W ☐	T ☐	F ☐	S ☐
Breastplate of Righteousness	S ☐	M ☐	T ☐	W ☐	T ☐	F ☐	S ☐
Shoes / Gospel of Peace	S ☐	M ☐	T ☐	W ☐	T ☐	F ☐	S ☐
Shield of Faith	S ☐	M ☐	T ☐	W ☐	T ☐	F ☐	S ☐
Helmet of Salvation	S ☐	M ☐	T ☐	W ☐	T ☐	F ☐	S ☐
Sword of the Spirit / Word of God	S ☐	M ☐	T ☐	W ☐	T ☐	F ☐	S ☐

No weapon formed against you will prosper. This is the heritage of the servants of ADONAI.
Is. 54:17

○ WEEK 50
BEZAL'EL, SON OF LIGHT
(EXODUS 31:2-4A)

"See, I have called by name Bezalel the son of Uri, son of Hur, of the tribe of Judah, and I have filled him with the Spirit of God, with ability and intelligence, with knowledge and all craftsmanship, to devise artistic designs [...]

"In Exodus 25, God begins to download, to communicate, to Moses the specific and detailed instructions, blueprints and designs for the following:

- The Sanctuary
- The Ark of the Covenant
- The Table for Bread
- The Golden Lampstand
- The Tabernacle
- The Bronze Altar
- The Court of the Tabernacle
- Oil for the Lamp
- The Priests' Garments
- The Altar of Incense
- The Bronze Basin, and
- The Anointing Oil and Incense

"There are six chapters worth of detailed and specific instructions for the design, materials and creation of these items.

"God, being a methodical God, is very specific when giving out instructions, and in this case it was absolutely crucial that every detail was followed precisely as He had communicated it to Moses. So crucial, in fact, that the Priestly garments alone, prophetic clothing actually, were "holy garments for glory and beauty" (Ex. 28:2); clothing that would not only consecrate Moses' brother Aaron, the High Priest, and his sons for God's priesthood, *but also keep them alive* while ministering in the Holy Place before ADONAI! There was no room for error when it came to understanding and communicating these designs, let alone in the construction of these designs!!

"So then, how was Moses going to implement here on earth these downloads from God, these supernatural blueprints and fashion designs inspired by heaven, and have them built and created exactly as God instructed?

"Cue the artists...

BEZALEL

> *The LORD said to Moses, "See,* ***I have called by name*** *Bezalel the son of Uri, son of Hur, of the tribe of Judah, and* ***I have filled him with the Spirit of God, with ability and intelligence, with knowledge and all craftsman- ship, to devise artistic designs****, to work in gold, silver, and bronze, in cutting stones for setting, and in carving wood, to work in every craft."*
> *Exodus 31:1-5 [Emphasis mine]*

"There you have it: the purest form of communication: God's Holy Spirit.

"Imagine when I came across this account in Exodus and the understanding of its implication as a believing career artisan. It not only confirmed what I suspected and believed to be true about my craft, it also affirmed everything I had learned and done up to that point and what I would continue to learn and do in the area of creativity – music, praise and worship and the leading of people into the Throne Room through those creative processes. This revelation *empowered* my art!

"The following occurred to Bezalel in order for him to be able to hear and discern Moses' instructions, and in order for him to realize and accomplish the creative and artistic tasks of those instructions:

- Bezalel was called by name

God knew this man and called him by name. That calling, along with His gifts, are irrevocable (Ro. 11:29). This includes your artistic / creative gifts and this would also include your gift to worship. Being called of God is the first step of His orderly way.

- Bezalel was filled with the Spirit of God

Being filled with His Holy Spirit was how Bezalel would achieve the creative tasks set before him. Because everything being required of him in the earthly was spiritual, only Holy Spirit could quicken and align his mind and abilities to enter into that spiritual realm; the realm of where these artistic prototypes existed. Having the "Spirit of God" gives us access to the deep things of God:

> *But we impart a secret and hidden wisdom of God, which God decreed before the ages for our glory. But, as it is written, "What no eye has seen, nor ear heard, nor the heart of man imagined, what God has prepared for those who love him"-- these things God has revealed to us through the Spirit. For the Spirit searches everything, even the depths of God. So also no one comprehends the thoughts of God except the Spirit of God.*
>
> *Now we have received not the spirit of the world, but the Spirit who is from God, that we might understand the things freely given us by God. And we impart this in words not taught by human wisdom but taught by the Spirit, interpreting spiritual truths to those who are spiritual. The natural person does not accept the things of the Spirit of God, for they are folly to him, and he is not able to understand them because they are spiritually discerned.*
>
> *1 Corinthians 2:7, 9-10, 11b-14*

It is important to note that the word "impart" is used twice in this passage in regards to how the secret and hidden wisdom of God is obtained. It was imparted by apostolic leaders to their disciples as modeled by Jesus in the gospels; it wasn't "acquired" in solitude or seclusion.

The Spirit of God within the leadership comprehends the thoughts of God and, in turn, the Spirit of God facilitates the understanding and the impartation of those spiritual truths to those disciples that are spiritual. There is nothing natural or physical / "earthly" about this. It is an entirely spiritual process that requires spiritual discernment to accept and understand as explained in the passage above.

- Bezalel was filled by God with giftings and abilities

Another version states "endowed with a divine spirit of skill, ability and knowledge;" Intelligence, knowledge and craftmanship: *to devise artistic designs*. I love that! I have been known for championing excellence in Christian Art since entering the professional Christian music industry in the early 1980's. For some reason, that industry struggled with meeting and exceeding the quality of their secular counterparts until just recently. The attitude of it being "Christian" was "good enough." I aggressively opposed that mentality. We needed our artforms to *surpass* the world's, simply because of Who it allegedly represented! We need to be endowed by His Divine Spirit of skill, ability and knowledge!

You shall speak to all the skillful, whom I have filled with a spirit of skill...
Exodus 28:3

He has filled them with skill to do all kinds of work as engravers [artisans], designers, embroiderers in blue, purple and scarlet yarn and fine linen, and weavers— all of them skilled workers and designers.
Exodus 35:35 (NIV)

These scriptural proof texts are why I say that the role of a Believing Creative, an artisan, musician, worshiper; these godly gifts and abilities – spiritual functions – must be founded, rooted and established in the Holy Spirit. These skill sets work in partnership – in tandem – with wisdom and understanding according to these passages (think Proverbs). These are heavenly skill sets / "gift clusters," and as believers they must be birthed and honed by the same Spirit that filled Bezalel.

Now concerning spiritual gifts, brothers, I do not want you to be uninformed [ignorant, no misunderstanding]. Now there are varieties of gifts, but the same Spirit;

For to one is given through the Spirit the utterance of wisdom, and to another the utterance of knowledge accord- ing to the same Spirit, to another faith by the same Spirit, to another gifts of healing by the one Spirit, to another the working of miracles, to another prophecy, to another the abil- ity to distinguish between spirits, to another various kinds of tongues, to another the interpretation of tongues. All these are empowered by one and the same Spirit, who apportions to each one individually as he [the Spirit] wills. But earnestly desire the higher gifts.
1 Corinthians 12:1, 4, 8-11, 31a

By being called and filled with God's Spirit, God Himself was the source of Bezalel's artistic abilities and creative inspiration. It was never a matter of talent. We must be aligned, willing, obedient and at the ready for His calling... to ensure that He is also *our* source and inspiration.

Bezalel:

- Son of Uri, is a shadow born with the light of the creator
- Son of Hur, purified
- Son of Judah, called to emphasize the Glory of God

In the same way Moses went up Mt Sinai and saw the heavenly temple, only the artist who loves God and respects His commandments is able to fulfill the calling of "Make from Me."

Only he can do something creative before the face of the Lord, and only he can be filled with the Spirit of knowledge and understanding that comes from God Himself.

- Ephraim Kalish

(Taken from "Bezalel, Son of Light," In *This Thing Is Spiritual*, 62-66, 68. Park City, Utah: Planet Blue Media, 2019. http://planetbluemedia.com)

○ FIELD NOTES

DATE: / / TIME: : AM/PM PLACE:

○		A±
○		
○		
○		
○		
○		
○		
○		
○		
○		
○		
○		
○		
○		
○		
○		
○		
○		
○		
○		

ARMOR CHECK: Ephesians 6:10-18

Belt of Truth	S ☐	M ☐	T ☐	W ☐	T ☐	F ☐	S ☐
Breastplate of Righteousness	S ☐	M ☐	T ☐	W ☐	T ☐	F ☐	S ☐
Shoes / Gospel of Peace	S ☐	M ☐	T ☐	W ☐	T ☐	F ☐	S ☐
Shield of Faith	S ☐	M ☐	T ☐	W ☐	T ☐	F ☐	S ☐
Helmet of Salvation	S ☐	M ☐	T ☐	W ☐	T ☐	F ☐	S ☐
Sword of the Spirit / Word of God	S ☐	M ☐	T ☐	W ☐	T ☐	F ☐	S ☐

No weapon formed against you will prosper. This is the heritage of the servants of ADONAI.
Is. 54:17

○ WEEK 51
SHREWD ISN'T RUDE
(LUKE 16:8B)

For the sons of this world are more shrewd in dealing with their own generation than the sons of light.

We're back to "aggressive Jesus" once again. I say that, because we have been taught to believe that Jesus was strictly a pacifist and that He wouldn't, then or now, do or say anything to ruffle our feathers, except maybe if you were a Pharisee. But then again, why have we been made to believe that it's ok to be aggressive only with those with whom we don't agree? Judge Judy says that if it doesn't make sense, it's probably a lie.

Jesus is an equal-opportunity aggressor. His aggressions are not limited to only those with a religious spirit or the simpleton, they're aimed at anyone, anytime. Think of Him as someone that has information you're not privy to, and that information can save your life. There's nothing passive about that.

On a side note, one of my favorite Jesus moments is when He was basically watching – staring through, not at – people putting their money into the Temple money box (Mk 12:41). I absolutely understand that and will one day incorporate that prophetic looking-into and assessing into a writing or maybe a video. But I digress…

Luke 16:1-13 is about the shrewd manager, a subject I don't recall ever hearing a pastor teach on in a church the last 40 years, and I think I know why. Go ahead and read it for yourself while I get a cup of coffee, and we'll circle back here in, say, 3 minutes?

Alrighty then. Let me say that I don't think I can unpack this thoroughly in this medium, so I most definitely want to discuss this the week of March 07, 2021 over at Facebook/E2iSeries, and we'll have an even more granular, interactive breakdown with the Exodus Expedition (http://patreon.com/E2iS) as well.

I want to focus on the four verses that really seem to challenge people in this passage – verses eight, nine, eleven and twelve. We're also going to look at various translations for each verse, like an old-school Bible study. Trust me, it'll all make sense contextually.

VERSE EIGHT

> *The master commended the dishonest manager for his shrewdness. For the sons of this world are more shrewd in dealing with their own generation than the sons of light.*

The God's Word Translation says, "Worldly people are more clever than spiritually-minded people when it comes to dealing with others." "More astute," states Holman Christian Standard Bible.

"Yes, worldly people are smarter with their own kind than spiritual people are," writes the New Century Version, and the New Living Translation puts it this way: "And it is true that the children of this world are more shrewd in dealing with the world around them than are the children of the light."

Ouch. This is Jesus telling us that we're basically stupid and clueless when it comes to the world around us / the world we live in in comparison to "worldly people," non-believers, the majority – and this wasn't a compliment. It's a rebuke – an "aggressive" rebuke – and it's true.

Yet, being clueless has become the standard – the hallmark trait by which God's people are defined. Not because we don't warrant it, but because we emulate this. It's offensive and close to my biggest pet peeve about Christianity and Christians since getting saved at the age of 15. It's unacceptable, and bringing it up triggers, well, just about everyone.

"Stupidity" and "cluelessness" are how you get yourself killed in the battlefields of this world and in the battles of the spiritual realm. Just ask Israel in the desert. You also see this warning against stupidity and cluelessness and how there's no room for it in the Kingdom in Jesus' other parables, in His interactions with His disciples and in the Proverbs.

I came from a very esoteric musical background. I was a punk rocker in Los Angeles by 1978, easily seven+ years before a slim "majority" would even consider it, and way before The Ramones became a soundtrack staple in family-fun films. This "early adaptor" quality fuels and motivates my pursuit of excellence, artistically and in my Christian walk.

I am credited for starting the first Christian punk rock band in the United States, and my disdain for Christian music and its lack of influence, standards, relevancy, etc. only made me seem more arrogant than I actually was. I was/am deeply passionate about the things of God and, like Moses, I hate it when we misrepresent God to the "Egyptians," to the "Canaanites," to the secular world around us – especially when it's by my own hand – and that's a volatile and difficult thing for the church at large.

When you have been taught consistently and dogmatically from the pulpit that you and your "worldly" life have no consequence or importance *in* or *to* "God's scheme of things" – when you have religiously been taught that mediocrity or even *less* than mediocrity is "godliness / holiness" – when you have been "discipled" to live in fear and ignorance toward the things and people of the world around you – when your Christianity is an insular ghetto – no wonder pastors don't preach on this! How could they?

It's no wonder that charismatica or the Seven Mountains are labeled "demonic." *Of course, they are!* That's the practical conclusion from that mindset – from One Talent / One Mina people! What other conclusion could they come to? Well, the same conclusions Israel came up with in the desert, of course!

Jesus is telling you that the world is smarter, more clever and more fruitful *in* and *with* the world around them than "spiritually-minded / spiritual people," than "the children of the light" themselves – *you and me.* That is highly offensive to me – *because it's true!* – and I will do *everything* in my power not to meet that definition. And so must you.

But why? Why is this our prevalent characteristic?

Fear, doubt, unbelief and an identity crisis. We're just like Israel, remember? And, we've even created theologies and doctrines to excuse this abhorrent behavior to accommodate our less-than-godly – less-than-spiritual – self-inflicted human constructs, just like they did. It's demonic. Stop it.

How, you might ask? Well, we'll have to unpack that over at Facebook/ E2iSeries and the Exodus Expedition. Running out of room here. My apologies…

VERSE NINE (AKA "TRIGGER #2")

> *And I tell you, make friends for yourselves by means of unrighteous wealth, so that when it fails they may receive you into the eternal dwellings.*

"…make friends for yourselves by means of the unrighteous money…" Holman Christian Standard Bible.

"…use worldly wealth to make friends for yourselves…" The Complete Jewish Bible. And, the New International Reader's Version states: "…use the riches of this world to help others."

"*Mammon*" in Greek is a Semitic word for money or possessions – "unrighteous / worldly mammon / wealth." Basically, mammon is the paycheck you get from your job. What's suggested in this verse is "wealth" above and beyond your weekly paycheck. This verse cross references, again, with the parable regarding stewardship and wealth, the Parable of the Talents and Minas. We haven't really touched on "stewardship" directly in this resource, even though everything we're discussing is about stewardship. Remember Deuteronomy 8:18 and how God gives us the power to make wealth? Jesus would know about that Chameleon-like ability.

Bill Johnson says that money is the lowest form of spiritual authority. Yikes. We don't like being told that the number of zeros in our bank account directly correlates with our spirituality. It's easier to cry "Foul! Prosperity Gospel!" than to correct our spiritual state and receive the blessings that both the Old and New Testaments state come with obedience and God's favor. Yeah, I said that. I also didn't write it. I'm just repeating it.

From 2009 to 2011, we toured in a tour bus we owned, which we named Judah. A young band said to me, "I wish we had a tour bus," to which I replied, "Are you willing to pay the cost for it?" "How much did it cost you," he asked. "Oh," I said soberly, "I'm not talking about money…"

Silly rabbit… not all godly wealth is factored by dollar signs. Much of it is, but if you think that's all I'm talking about, you haven't been listening.

In this part of the lesson, Jesus *is* talking about using money, worldly wealth, to make friends and influence people, *in and of the world*. Sinners. That way, when you and that money fail, when it "gives out," you'll be received into or have "eternal" habitations / tents / dwellings / homes. Funny, the Greek word for habitation is a derivative for the Greek word for "tabernacle(s)," Hebrew "*sukkah*," otherwise known as "ingathering."

VERSE ELEVEN

> *If then you have not been faithful in the unrighteous wealth, who will entrust to you the true riches?*

This verse begins with a warning rebuke. If we're not faithful to do verse nine: "making friends for ourselves / helping others with worldly wealth / money." *If* we have not been faithful in doing that:

"…who is going to trust you with the real thing?" says the Complete Jewish Bible. That's harsh…

"If, then, you have not been true in your use of the wealth of this life, who will give into your care the true wealth?" says The Bible in Basic English. "...the true wealth / riches" sounds ominous to me. Are you seeing where Jesus is going with this?

"...who will commit to your trust the true?" Jubilee Bible 2000. Man, that smarts. "...with the wealth that is real" is another.

In John 3, Jesus is rebuking the Pharisee Nicodemus who came to Him under cover of night:

> *"You are Israel's teacher," said Jesus, "and do you not understand these things? I have spoken to you of earthly things and you do not believe; how then will you believe if I speak of heavenly things?*
> *John 3:10, 12 (NIV)*

A very similar thing is happening here. Jesus is talking to His disciples, and some Pharisees can hear him, as we'll see in a moment.

VERSE TWELVE

> *And if you have not been faithful in that which is another's, who will give you that which is your own?*

"And if you have not been true in your care of the property of other people, who will give you that which is yours?" The Bible in Basic English. There's that pesky stewardship thing again.

"And if you haven't been trustworthy with what belongs to someone else, who will give you what ought to belong to you?" The Complete Jewish Bible. And, the New Living Translation: "And if you are not faithful with other people's things, why should you be trusted with things of your own?" Can't argue with that.

Want to know why we haven't seen an "end-time revival" to challenge the Jesus Movement of the late 1960s / early 1970s? We've been really bad stewards of that revival. Why squander more crops? Many Christians from that time that are still alive are no longer professing Christianity or, worse yet, they believe in a very twisted, unsound "Christianity." I say this because I've known many of them, including my own original spiritual father.

Luke 16:14-17 tells us that the Pharisees, "lovers of money" (the love of money is what?), heard this entire discourse and ridiculed Jesus, who in turn gives them a stern rebuke regarding

- Self-justification before men,
- God knowing the heart,
- How man's exaltation is an abomination in God's sight,
- The Law and the Prophets,
- John the Baptist and
- The Gospel of the Kingdom.

It also shouldn't surprise us, contextually, that Jesus also repeats Matthew 5:18 by bringing up how easy it will be for "heaven and earth to pass away than for one dot of the Law to become void." In Matthew 24:35, instead of "law" or "Torah," Jesus says, "my words will never pass away," simply because His words *are* the Torah.

Interesting – that's the second time He's said that in this resource, isn't it? He says it again in Luke 16:17, and in Luke 21:33, He replaces "Torah," again, with "my words."

It must be painfully, truthfully important, right? Yet, 99% of Christian churches on Sunday preached the exact opposite message.

Shrewd isn't rude, especially when it has to do with the power of Holy Spirit – the transformative revelation power of Holy Spirit – and how to use that power in tandem with the worldly resources necessary for our success in relevantly accomplishing God's will "on earth as it is in heaven."

○ FIELD NOTES

DATE: / / **TIME:** : AM/PM **PLACE:**

		A±
○		
○		
○		
○		
○		
○		
○		
○		
○		
○		
○		
○		
○		
○		
○		
○		
○		
○		
○		
○		

ARMOR CHECK: Ephesians 6:10-18

Belt of Truth	S ☐	M ☐	T ☐	W ☐	T ☐	F ☐	S ☐
Breastplate of Righteousness	S ☐	M ☐	T ☐	W ☐	T ☐	F ☐	S ☐
Shoes / Gospel of Peace	S ☐	M ☐	T ☐	W ☐	T ☐	F ☐	S ☐
Shield of Faith	S ☐	M ☐	T ☐	W ☐	T ☐	F ☐	S ☐
Helmet of Salvation	S ☐	M ☐	T ☐	W ☐	T ☐	F ☐	S ☐
Sword of the Spirit / Word of God	S ☐	M ☐	T ☐	W ☐	T ☐	F ☐	S ☐

No weapon formed against you will prosper. This is the heritage of the servants of ADONAI.
Is. 54:17

○ WEEK 52
JESHURUN
(ISAIAH 44:2)

"Jeshurun whom I have chosen."

A poetical name for the people of Israel, used in token of affection, meaning, "the dear upright people"
Easton's Bible Dictionary

From the Song of Moses:

"But Jeshurun grew fat, and kicked; you grew fat, stout, and sleek; then he forsook God who made him and scoffed at the Rock of his salvation.
Deuteronomy 32:15

Thus the LORD became king in Jeshurun, when the heads of the people were gathered, all the tribes of Israel together. There is none like God, O Jeshurun, who rides through the heavens to your help, through the skies in his majesty.
Deuteronomy 33:5, 26

Most moderns take it as a poetical or ideal title of Israel, derived from yashar, "upright"; it is held to contain a tacit reference to the word Israel (yisra'el), of which the first three consonants are almost the same as those of "Jeshurun"; in Numbers 23:10 the term "the righteous ones" (yesharim) is supposed to contain a similar reference. Most commentators compare also "the Book of Jashar," and it has been held that "Jashar" is similarly a name by which Israel is called.
International Standard Bible Encyclopedia

Jeshurun: an honorable and esteemed name for Israel meaning "Upright One." This is how Father God sees her, and that is why He calls her that.

In the Song of Moses, Israel is referred to as Jeshurun, the Upright One, in contrast to how they actually think, act, speak and behave. Moses, yet again, is "provoking" Israel into how the Father sees them, into being what they have been called to – how they have been called to be and what they really should be.

PURPOSE AND VISION

One of the first books I read as a new believer was written in 1978 by the apostle of the ministry, Gospel Outreach. The book was called *Purpose and Vision* by Jim Durkin, and by 1981, it had been retitled *Life with a Purpose.* Here's the basic premise of the book from their website:

"Life with a Purpose" shows that one of the more startling discoveries of the new Christian life is that simply accepting Jesus as Savior does not answer every human longing and need. After we come to Christ there are still questions to be answered and problems to be solved.

What is God's purpose for my life? What does God want me to do? What is his will for me? Where am I going? Such questions make us reach for something more. Leading a good life is not enough. Merely attending church does not satisfy us.

(Source: http://www.jim-durkin.tlchrist.info/books/jd_books.htm)

Concepts like "conformed to Christ" and "training your soul" created a foundation within me for these biblical concepts to build on, germinate, take root and mature. "Faith pictures" was another concept that made sense to me.

Following are a few examples of "faith pictures", which the author describes in Chapters 7-8 of Book Two: "Living the Word". A faith picture is not a magic wand, a form of wishful thinking or a way to mentally control reality or bend God to selfish wishes. It is merely a word picture that God has "painted" in his Word to help us grasp his truth.

1 Peter 2:9: But you are a chosen people, a royal priesthood, a holy nation, a people belonging to God, that you may declare the praises of him who called you out of darkness into his wonderful light.

What a marvelous 'faith picture" we are given here of who we are as the people of God. We are depicted as a royal priesthood, a holy nation and a people who belong to God. Not only that, as this nation of priests we are offering praises to God, bringing light into a dark world. This "picture" is not just a fanciful way that Peter was trying to encourage Christians. It is the truth about who we are in God!

(Source: Durkin, Jim. Life with a Purpose, Ann Arbor, Michigan: Servant Books, 1981)

You see, this is what Moses was doing in his song: speaking, *singing,* a "faith picture" of Israel into the atmosphere, into our paradigm, into our realm. Moses was proclaiming into our physical reality a reality of the spiritual realm regarding Israel.

I think one of the reasons why the concept and subject matter of identity resonates with me so deeply is because of my pre-salvation life. Many of us don't know and haven't been taught that the majority of what we were involved with before coming to Jesus was because God put those dreams, desires, likes and interests in us. That's how He made us – that's how He wired us. It's only after coming into church, a system that doesn't understand these things, that those dreams, desires and aspirations are squelched and starved to death.

There's that story of the band U2 – young Christian men with an obvious God-given gift and talent that was supported by their church leadership until after they were signed to a secular label and had success with their first two albums. They were basically told that they couldn't be Christians and rock stars at the same time and that they would have to choose one or the other.

They disagreed, as do I, and chose to continue in their careers, which alienated them from their church and the leadership, which only caused more damage. Their church leadership (once again, you can't teach or model a biblical principle that you don't know about), opted to go with the easier "religious spirit" route than the "determine what God is actually saying and doing here" route.

NOTE: I am not saying, in any way, that *every* desire to do music or entertainment professionally is from God.

I know a young man who was convinced that he was supposed to go to a middle eastern, Muslim country and start a house of prayer. Instead of asking the Father what it was He desired for this young man, His church leadership advised against it based on their own fear and ignorance. Last I heard, he was working a menial job in Texas. Le sigh...

The church doesn't have an infrastructure to accommodate God's purpose and vision for our lives. The majority of what identified us before Christ – B.C. – was placed there by God Himself. God put those dreams, desires, likes and interests in us, because that's how He made us – that's how He wired us. It's the majority of the church system that doesn't understand these things, and because they fear what they don't understand, they do what they can to stop it.

My experience was similar to U2's, and it occurred around the same time. I was a punk rock kid, a Bowie-phile, and getting saved in January of 1980 made me one of the first from that reality. In the same way the church couldn't / wouldn't manage the hippies from ten years prior – and failed to learn from it – they were now going to have to deal with spiked red and blue hair... or worse.

But, because of my "forerunner" wiring, I did something that had never happened before in Christian music, and I did it multiple times. I introduced and set the bar for at least two genres in Contemporary / Alternative Christian Music because of who I was in my pre-salvation life.

Each of you should remain in the place in life that the Lord has given you. Stay as you were when God chose you.
1 Corinthians 7:17 (NIRV) [See also verses 20 and 24]

Paul uses marriage, circumcision, uncircumcision and slavery as examples for the passage above. In the same context, if you were a painter, an accountant, a schoolteacher, a law enforcement officer, etc., Paul is saying to continue doing that in your newfound life in Jesus. The church has traditionally had a very difficult time with that, especially when it comes to politics and the entertainment industry.

I'm saying that the reason you have that interest in the arts, politics, teaching, the military, government, business or media is *because* of God. As spiritual leaders, we are to discern and mentor – *disciple* – these things, not discourage them and choke them to death.

As I was saying, I think one of the main reasons why the subject matter of identity resonates with me so deeply is because of my pre-salvation life. Coming from a Bowie / punk rock scene background meant that I came from a highly-identifiable past whose identity was defined by:

- Hair
- Clothing
- Makeup and
- A distinct musical style

It literally was "tomorrow's music today," and because it was defined by hair and clothing styles, it completely and unmistakably "set you apart" from literally everybody else. Well, when you read your Bible correctly, so does our faith:

- Hair (if you're a Nazarite)
- Clothing (not mixing fibers)
- Diet (eating biblically "clean")
- Worship (in spirit and in truth)

Everything about our faith is designed to set us apart from other faiths and the pagans / "non-believers" around us as described and mandated by God – just like we've been studying all year long with God prepping Israel to enter into her Promised Land.

GIDEON

Starting in Judges 6, we find that Israel has done evil in the sight of God and is now under the hand of Midian, their enemy and a local inhabitant of Canaan (the exact opposite of *everything* God taught Israel and forewarned them about in the desert).

It is approximately 130 years after Joshua entered the land of Canaan, and the Angel of the Lord appears to a man who is the least of his family and from the lowest clan of his tribe, Manasseh. Yet the Angel addresses this man, "O mighty man of valor." Identity.

That night, the man – Gideon – is instructed by God to pull down the altar of Baal and to cut down the Asherah that his father has beside it.

> *So Gideon took ten men of his servants and did as the LORD had told him. But because he was too afraid of his family and the men of the town to do it by day, he did it by night.*
> *Judges 6:27*

In the morning, the townsmen found the altar of Baal broken down and the Asherah cut down beside it, prompting a search and inquiry for the culprit. Gideon was named, and when the men of the town went to his father, demanding Gideon be turned over so that they could kill him, his father basically said that if Baal was a real god, let Baal take care of Gideon.

That's how we're introduced to Gideon – through an act of scriptural obedience that God had established with Israel almost 200 years before that – the destruction of foreign gods and their altars, even though the majority believed, by their actions, that their new life in Canaan "did away with that," and destroying pagan altars and gods "wasn't for today."

Here's why I bring up Gideon: The Midianites and Amalekites (remember them? Israel's nemeses?) came against Israel, and Gideon led the charge against them (read it in Judges 6-8). Gideon is chasing down two of the four pagan kings of Midian, Zebah and Zalmunna.

When Gideon catches them, he asks them, "What were the men like that you killed on Mount Tabor?" They answered, "They looked like you, like sons of a king."

This is the same Gideon that believed in his own identity as the least of his family and from the lowest clan of his tribe, Manasseh, but the Angel of the Lord saw him as a mighty man of valor. The pagan kings saw a son of a king.

The physical expressions that are a manifestation of the spiritual (like the mundane act of the eating of matzah being an act of covenant with God or the mundane acts of obedience like clothing, not wearing mixed fibers of wool and cotton and eating biblically what the Bible deems as "food for humans") will literally change your appearance, in addition to being an obedient act of worshipping the One True God in Spirit and Truth. It's called the countenance of the Lord, and Gideon had it.

When you position yourself through obedience to God's commandments, when you live a lifestyle of obedience to God's Word, when you offer yourself as a living sacrifice, these things change you and position you like what happened to Gideon before he went out to battle:

> *But the Spirit of the LORD clothed Gideon [...]*
> *Judges 6:34a*

JESHURUN

An honorable and esteemed name for Israel meaning "Upright One."

This is how Father God sees Israel.
This is how Father God saw Gideon.
This is how our Father God sees *us*.
That is why He calls us Upright One.

○ FIELD NOTES

DATE: / / **TIME:** : AM/PM **PLACE:**

○		A±
○		
○		
○		
○		
○		
○		
○		
○		
○		
○		
○		
○		
○		
○		
○		
○		
○		
○		
○		

ARMOR CHECK: Ephesians 6:10-18

Belt of Truth	S ☐	M ☐	T ☐	W ☐	T ☐	F ☐	S ☐
Breastplate of Righteousness	S ☐	M ☐	T ☐	W ☐	T ☐	F ☐	S ☐
Shoes / Gospel of Peace	S ☐	M ☐	T ☐	W ☐	T ☐	F ☐	S ☐
Shield of Faith	S ☐	M ☐	T ☐	W ☐	T ☐	F ☐	S ☐
Helmet of Salvation	S ☐	M ☐	T ☐	W ☐	T ☐	F ☐	S ☐
Sword of the Spirit / Word of God	S ☐	M ☐	T ☐	W ☐	T ☐	F ☐	S ☐

No weapon formed against you will prosper. This is the heritage of the ser-
vants of ADONAI.
Is. 54:17

ALSO FROM ALLAN R. AGUIRRE

Available at: planetBlueMedia.com

THE FEASTS UNLOCKED
A PRACTICAL UNDERSTANDING OF GOD'S HOLY DAYS

310 PAGES

ISBN 978-0-9991300-0-1

The Feasts Unlocked takes a practical approach to the apologetics, historicity and scriptural significance of Leviticus 23, their understanding, observance, and role in Modern Christianity. This version contains the exhaustive spiritual significance of these instructions and how to observe them.

Also available:

THE FEASTS UNLOCKED - "HOW TO" - ABRIDGED

160 pgs

If you're interested in simply the significance of the Feasts and the practical "how to" of their observance, get the "How To" version.

THE FEASTS UNLOCKED - WORKBOOK

A great companion piece to either version, this Workbook will also assist pastors, home church leaders, bible study groups, etc., in teaching others the yearly cycle of the Biblical Feasts. Bible study groups, large and small, will appreciate coupling the Workbook with the "How To" version for students while utilizing the "Practical Understanding" version as a teaching guide for group leaders.

○ ALSO FROM ALLAN R. AGUIRRE

Available at: planetBlueMedia.com

THIS THING IS SPIRITUAL

202 pages - ISBN 978-0-9991300-3-2

This Thing Is Spiritual looks at the spirituality of music, the arts in general and the respective responsibilities of both worshiper and artisan based on that scriptural premise. It explores how art evokes the demonstrative gifts of the Holy Spirit and the roles that spirituality / the supernatural and art play in Modern Christianity.

THE AMAZING JOURNEY FROM EXODUS TO INGATHERING

A 52-Week Devotional • Journal • Calendar - ISBN 978-0-9991300-4-9

The Apostle Paul in 1 Corinthians 10 tells us that what happened to Israel on their desert journey from Egypt to the Promised Land was written down as a warning example for us. Encouraging spiritual growth by deciphering and applying the instructions Paul mentioned "in our history books" is the purpose for this resource; a devotional, journal, calendar that will assist in guiding that spiritual growth, practically and weekly.

THE EXODUS EXPEDITION

Private Facebook Group: $7.00 / Mth

The Exodus Expedition is a private / monthly subscription Facebook group that serves as the digital basecamp for this expedition, this amazing journey. A safe place for you to gather with your fellow online travelers after being out in the field.

Signup at: patreon.com/E2iS